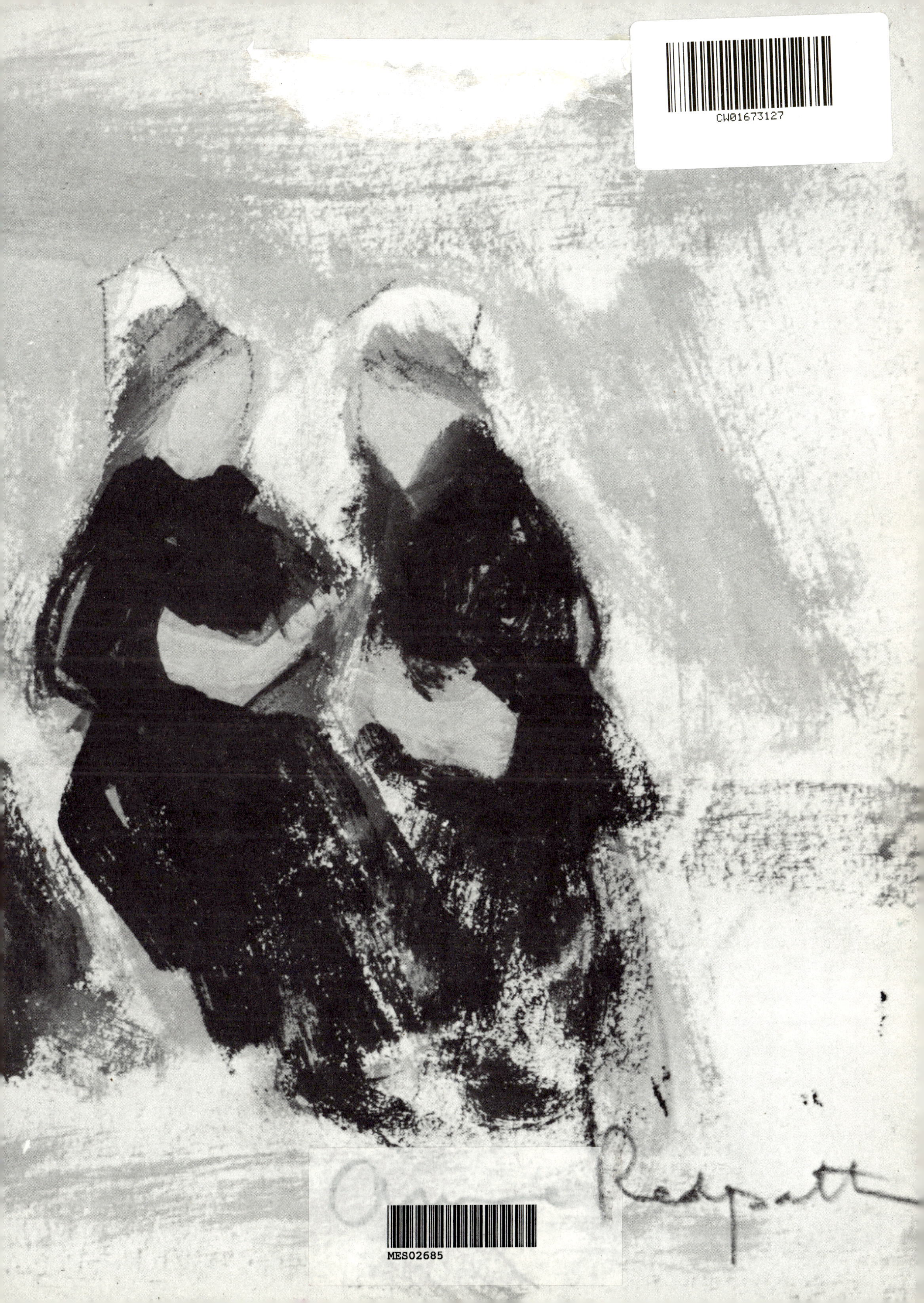

ANNE REDPATH
1895 – 1965

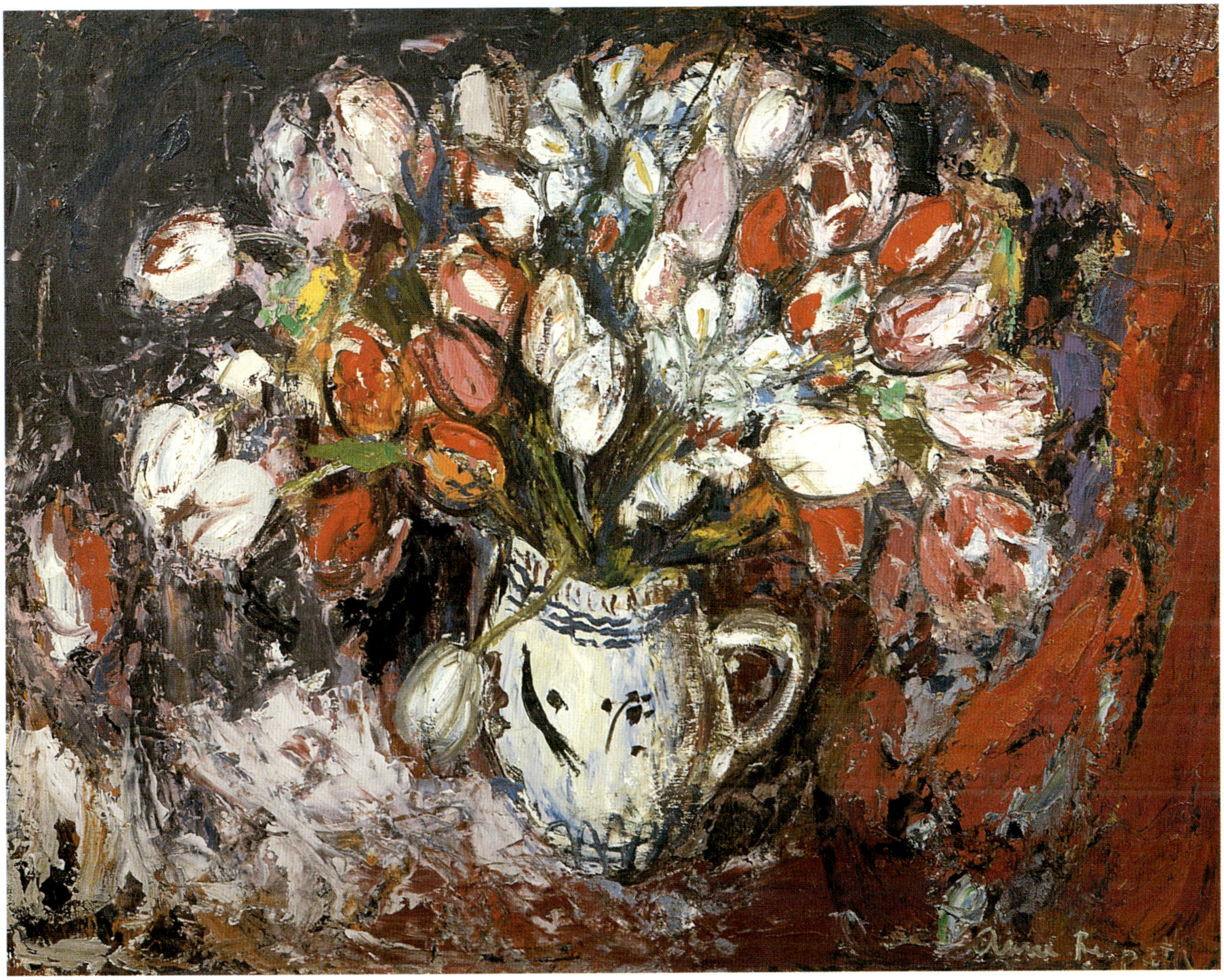

1 A Jug of Tulips c1958 oil

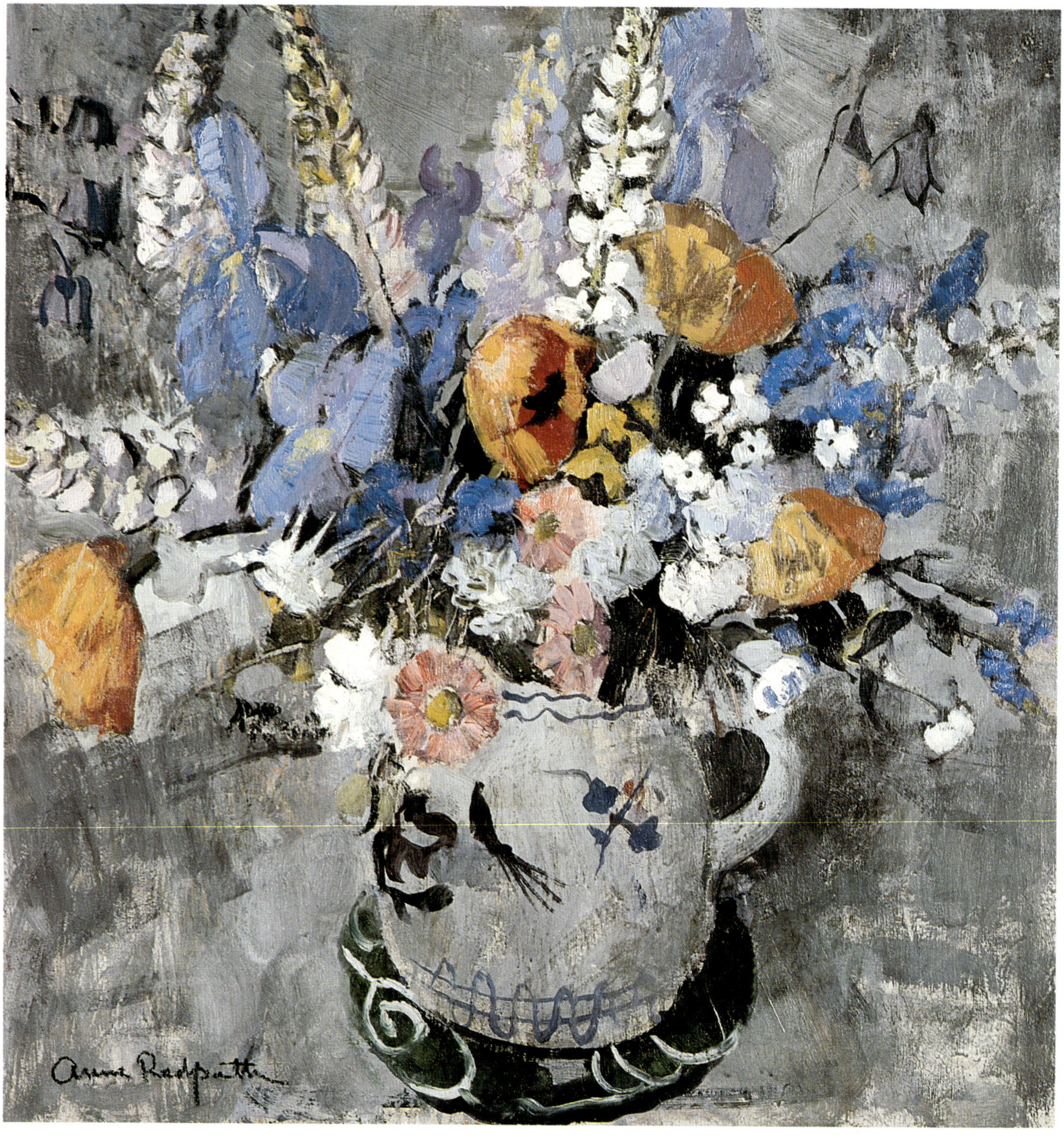

2 Summer Flowers c1950 oil

ANNE REDPATH
1895 – 1965

Her life and work

PATRICK BOURNE

BOURNE FINE ART
Edinburgh and London

in association with
The Portland Gallery
London

First published 1989 by
Bourne Fine Art
4 Dundas Street
Edinburgh
031 557 4050

in association with
The Portland Gallery
2 Holland Park Terrace
Portland Road
London

Editorial and production consultant Paul Harris
Printed in Yugoslavia by Gorenjski Tisk, Kranj

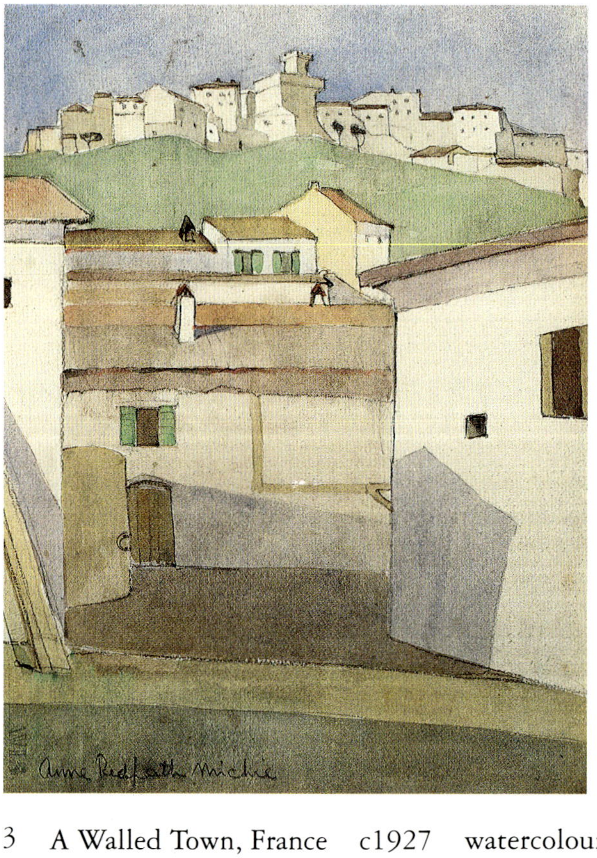

3 A Walled Town, France c1927 watercolour

Contents

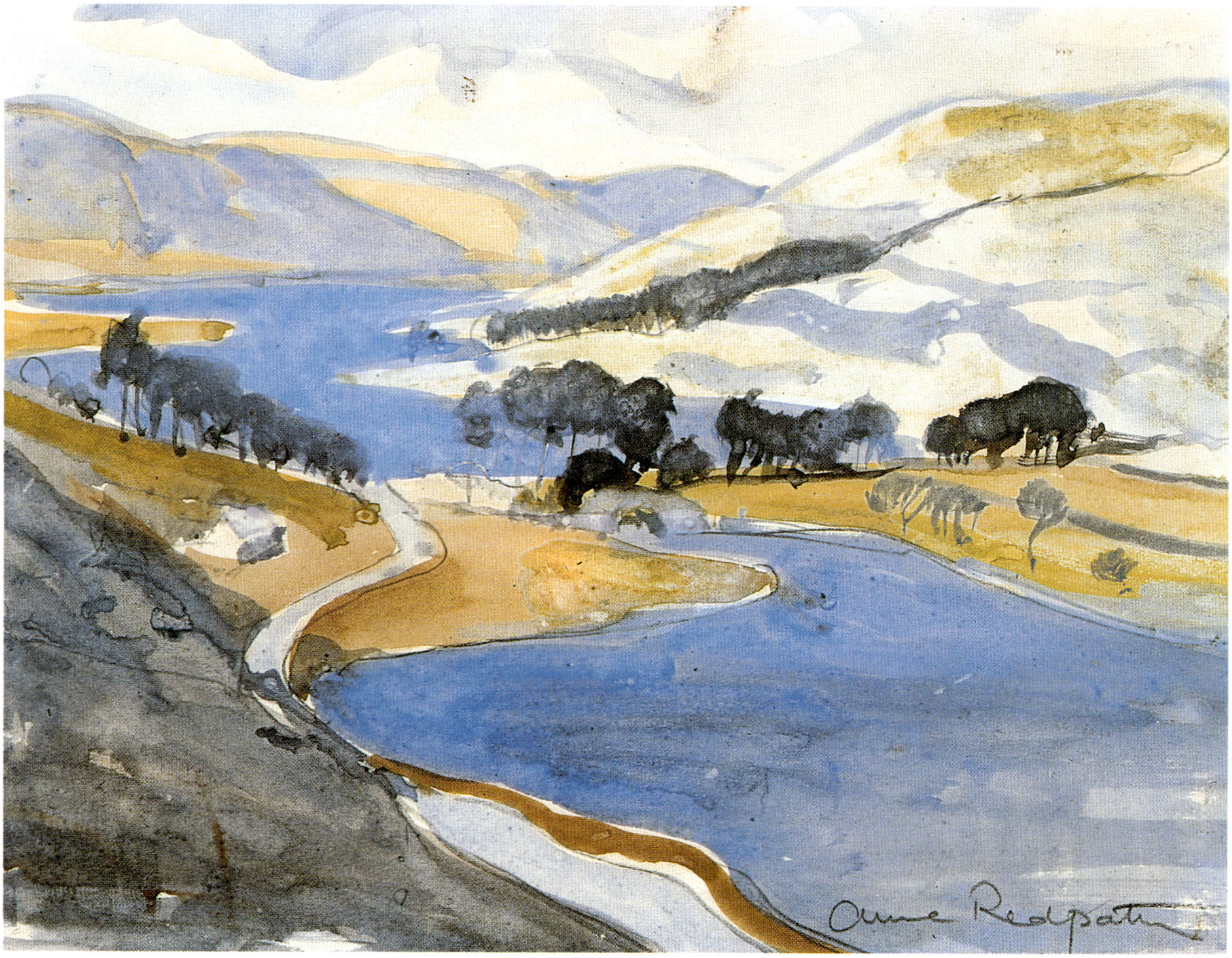

4 St Mary's Loch c1936 gouache

Acknowledgements

I would like to thank especially the members of Anne Redpath's family for their unstinting help. This book would not have been possible without the advice and encouragement of David and Eileen Michie, Alastair Michie, Lindsay Michie and Kim Redpath. I have also benefitted from the recollections of many of Anne's friends and am grateful to Katie Horsman, Derek Clarke, David McClure, John Houston, Elizabeth Blackadder, Bill Garrad, Sir Michael Weir, George Bruce, Jim Ritchie, Gordon Small, Maurice Kidd, Yonty Solomon, Lady Scotter, Dr Ralph Kauntze, Isabella Finlay, Vivien Chapman, Mr and Mrs Scotland and Mr Marshall of the Stone Gallery.

The help with editing and indexing from Bill Smith has been invaluable and I would like to thank Simon Donald and Genista Morgan for similar assistance. My gratitude is due also to Nicola Woodhead, Tom Hewlett, Susan Bourne, Paul Harris, Gilly Kinloch, Guy Peploe, Neil McIndoe, Joanne Cox, Bill Jackson, Bill and Di Bruce, Rachel Moss, Peter Haworth and John Dewar, as well as Margaret Kenyon of Withington Girls' School, Manchester, Richard Gray of Manchester City Art Gallery, Clara Young of Dundee Art Gallery, Joanna Soden of the Royal Scottish Academy, Philip Aikman of BBC Recorded Programmes Library, Anne Simpson of the Scottish National Gallery of Modern Art and Jean McKinney of the Royal West of England Academy. Finally, I would like to thank Stephanie Donaldson for her help and for running the gallery during my many absences.

I am grateful to the following for permission to include photographs of paintings owned by them:

Dundee City Museums & Art Gallery	pl 54
Robert Fleming Holdings Limited	pl 22, 24, 28, 48, 66, 68, 83
James Gulliver, Esq.	pl 2
Manchester City Art Galleries	pl 67
Royal Scottish Academy	pl 59
Royal West of England Academy	pl 63
Scottish National Gallery of Modern Art	pl 34, 74
Withington Girls' School, Manchester	pl 26

My thanks are due also to the large number of private owners who wish to remain anonymous.

Patrick Bourne
Edinburgh, September 1989

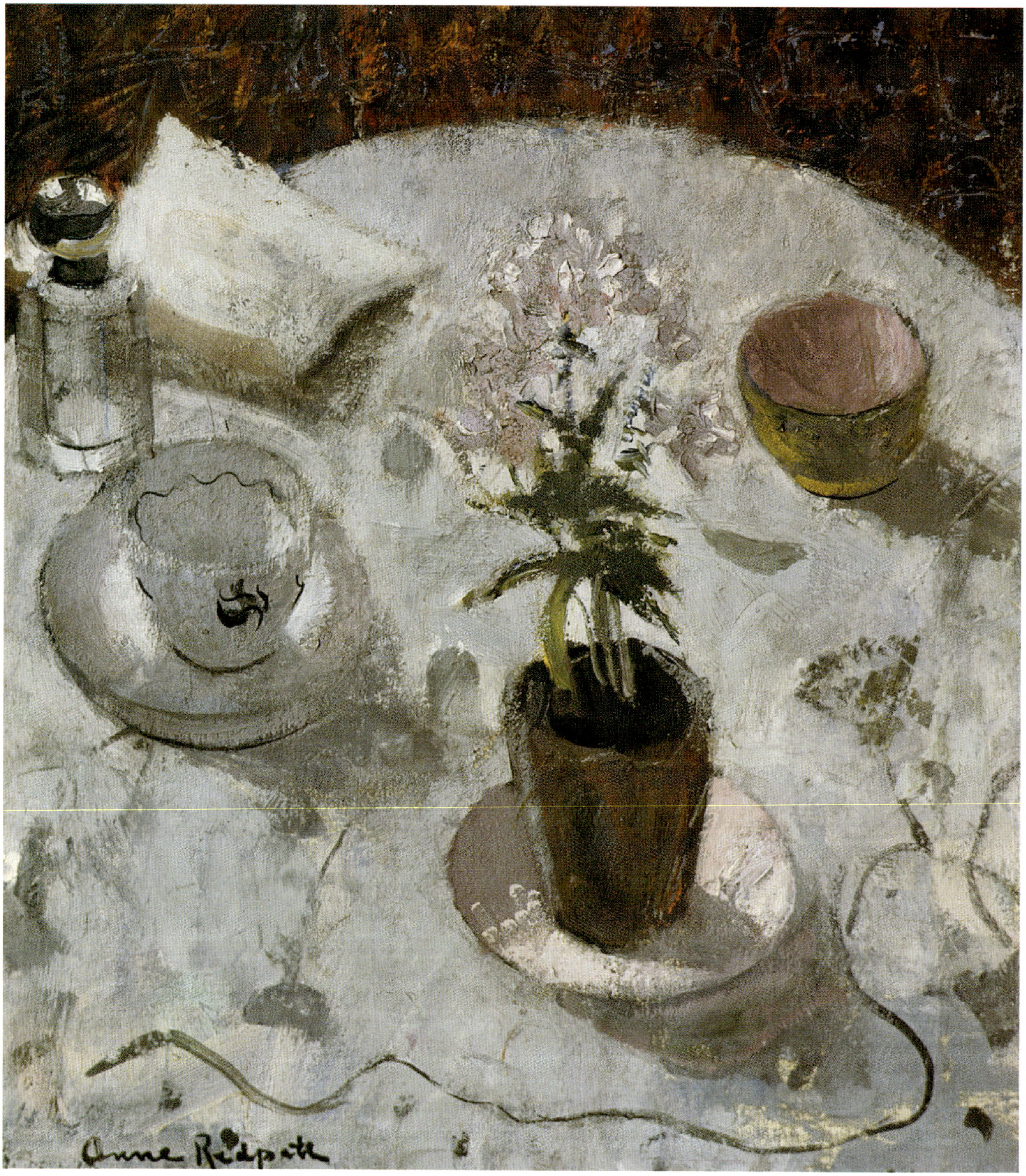

5 Contre Jour 1948 oil

PREFACE

Shortly after her death in 1965, Sir William MacTaggart described Anne Redpath as "something of a legend", and in this he was referring to her personality as much as her standing as a painter. To this day the clarity with which she is remembered as a person to some extent throws her reputation as a painter out of focus. It is well known that for fifteen years she abandoned her career for the sake of her family and that she came to be renowed as 'the social centre of Edinburgh's art world', and perhaps these things cloud our perception of her. First and foremost she was a tremendously committed and serious artist.

She was an exceptionally vital woman with a rare capacity for friendship. A quarter of a century after her death many people still remember her with an accompanying sense of loss. They recall her kindness and her courage, her sense of humour, acerbic and mischievous, that somehow never gave offence. She was extrovert and sensitive, and this balance between strength and subtlety is the key to her achievement as a painter.

Individual, adventurous, colourful and independent – her art was an extension of her personality and the same descriptions apply to both. When she died, at the age of 69, her painting was as fresh and inventive as ever. In some respects Anne Redpath's life has overshadowed her work, yet when the two are seen side by side it is to the benefit and better understanding of them both.

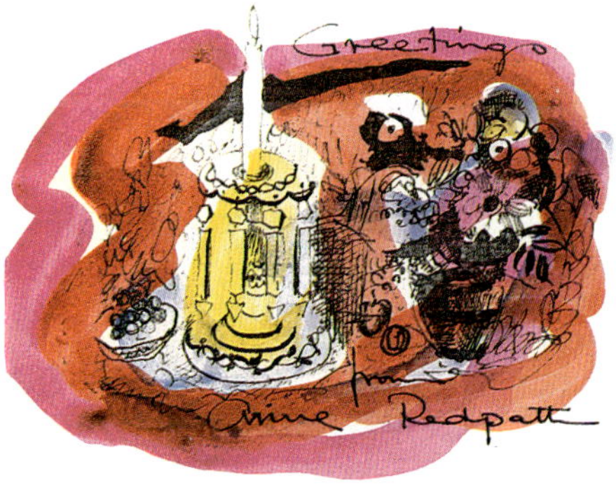

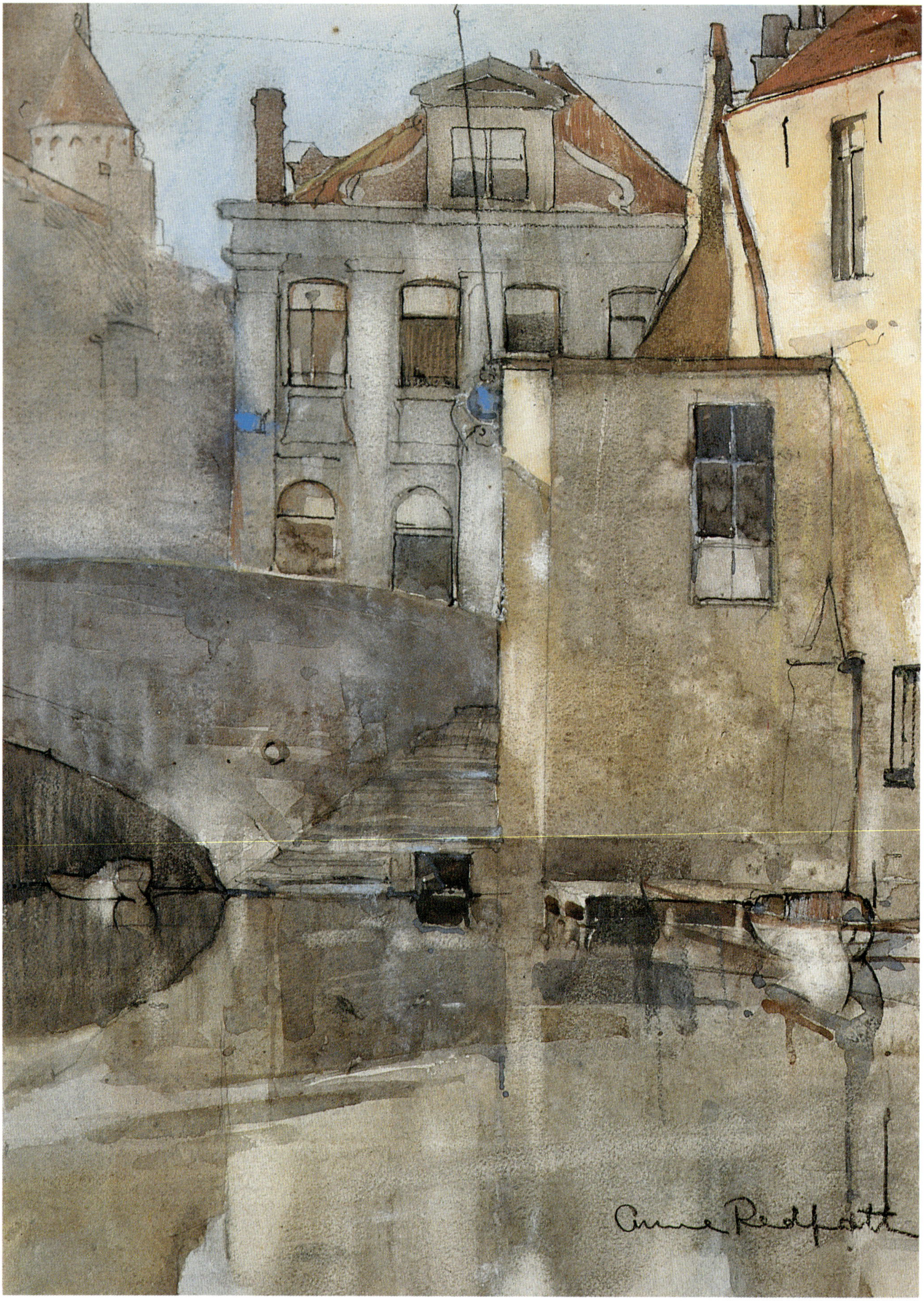

6 Quai Vert, Bruges c1922 watercolour

Chapter One

Anne Redpath was born on March 29th, 1895 in Galashiels, a Border mill-town in the old county of Selkirkshire at the heart of the Scottish tweed industry. Anne was the second of four children, two sons and two daughters, and her parents, Thomas Brown Redpath and Agnes Milne, both came from old Border families.

Redpaths can be traced back to the fifteenth century but it was in the sixteenth that they featured most prominently in the history of the region when members of the family were caught up in the fierce local rivalries that plagued the Borders, an account of which can be found in George Macdonald Fraser's grim history, "The Steel Bonnets".

The family name of Redpath most probably derives from a village of the same name in the neighbouring county of Berwickshire. We may choose between two possible sources for the name of the village itself. On the one hand, and in keeping with the violent history of the Borders, "Rid-peth" would be a bloody ravine, "The Peths" being the name for several ravines crossing the coastal route from Scotland to England near Cockburnspath. It is likely however that the name reflects a more civilised outcome to a local dispute and comes from the late fourteenth century "Thrid", meaning a third division, and "Pairt", a portion of land.

By the eighteenth century a powerful religious strand had developed in the Redpath family; two notable examples were the Reverend George Ridpath of Stichell in Roxburghshire, author of "Border History" first published in 1776 and still the standard work on the subject, and his brother the Reverend Philip Ridpath of Hutton in Berwickshire.

Around 1901 Robert Noble and Company, tweed manufacturers in Hawick, offered Anne's father promotion from his job as a pattern weaver at a mill in Galashiels to head of design in the Glebe Mills. Thomas decided to accept the promotion and make the move with his young family to the town of Hawick, twenty miles from Galashiels. He remained with Nobles for the rest of his working life.

Thomas was an ardent teetotaller and a member of the Hawick Congregational Church, where he and his family worshipped with unfailing regularity. In the Redpath household such frivolities as the playing of card games were absolutely forbidden.

Kim Redpath, the artist's nephew, relates a well known Hawick story of Thomas Redpath's speech as guest of honour at a Burns' Supper in the town. What would have been expected to be a traditionally convivial address on this, the most inebriate of Scottish celebrations, instead revealed itself to be a spirited diatribe on the evils of the demon drink and its calamitous influence on the bard's literary powers. The lecture was received in silence by a surly and resentful audience. While Anne certainly inherited her courage and sense of conviction from her father, her sense of fun was apparently from a different source.

Thomas became a town councillor, standing as a Liberal, and subsequently a bailie – a town magistrate next in line to the provost. He was regarded as a man of some standing in Hawick and he merited a substantial obituary notice in the local newspaper "The Hawick Express" on his death in 1935. Rather tellingly, his obituary records that "logic was more native to him than feeling". The reverse of this judgement would more aptly describe the character of his daughter.

As a pattern weaver in Galashiels Thomas Redpath had achieved advancement by hard work and the acquisition of great technical skill. As a designer of tweed he gained a reputation both as an innovator and as an inspired colourist. His designs were for sober tweeds with a thread of strong colour such as scarlet running through them. Many years later Anne said "I do with a spot of red or yellow in a harmony of grey what my father did in his tweeds." Colour harmonies and an unerring eye for singing contrasts were to become the hallmark of Anne's painting style and she was well aware that she had inherited this sensibility from her father. There was another aspect of her father's work which had a lasting and positive influence on Anne's artistic life – the designing of tweed involves a complete understanding of the complex weaving process and Anne inherited from her father a professionalism and seriousness of purpose which included great respect for creative craft and technique.

There were few indications of Anne's awakening interest in art as a child although she did paint watercolours of flowers and portraits of her family – all done with a brush made from a lock of her mother's hair, a custom which appears to have been something of a family tradition.

The four Redpath children attended Hawick High School and by the time Anne was in her senior year she was showing sufficient aptitude and ambition for the art master John Gray to take an interest in her. Anne was lucky that although Hawick could boast only one art teacher at that time, John Gray was a painter and teacher of some skill – indeed many years later he was to become President of the Royal Scottish Society of Painters in Watercolours.

A story survives from Anne's schooldays of John Gray bending over a drawing she was making, then, taking the pencil from her, saying "Look, this is how it's done." Anne took the pencil back and said defiantly "But I don't see it like that."

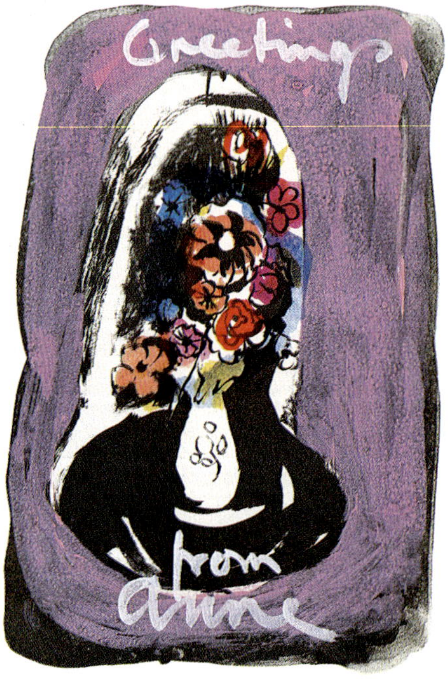

Chapter Two

While the Scottish Borders have a rich literary tradition, they have not produced many well known painters and, at that time, if Anne had confided to anyone that she wanted to be a painter, the response would have been "Oh, you mean like Tom Scott."

Scott was the most renowned local painter of his day but, although he had a rare gift for handling watercolour and was a full member of the Royal Scottish Academy, he had squandered his talent and was known to spend a large proportion both of his time and of his income from selling his watercolours in the local public houses. Little wonder then that Thomas Redpath was not completely enamoured of his daughter's announced desire to go to art college and follow the same profession as the intemperate Scott. Her father did have enlightened views on the subject of education – he was a member of the county education authority – but his ambition for Anne was that she should go to university. He finally agreed to a compromise. Anne would be allowed to study at Edinburgh College of Art if she simultaneously attended a course in teacher training at Moray House. While this plan of action satisfied Anne's father she knew that it would be unacceptable to either of the colleges. Anne had a friend, Carol Tennant – later to marry Anne's elder brother William – who had also been forced to double up on courses. The pair of them evolved a plan of regularly feigning illness and were thus able to satisfy the attendance requirements of both colleges and complete each course in parallel.

Edinburgh College of Art had only been at its present location in Lauriston Place for five years when Anne arrived in 1913. Through most of the previous century its teaching role had been filled by the RSA schools, with classes given by members of the Academy. This practice continued throughout Anne's time at college. The Department of Drawing and Painting was run by Robert Burns who, although he was an Associate of the RSA, had an uneasy relationship with the Academy and later resigned.

Burns was an artist of many accomplishments. He was a watercolourist of original and sometimes inspired style, an excellent book illustrator in a similar vein to Dulac, as well as a furniture designer and a commercial artist for Crawford's Biscuits. Burns' most direct influence on Anne's early style can be seen in her watercolour "Children in the Canongate" (pl 7). The sense of structure and emphasis of strong sunlight are so close to Burns' Moroccan work that it seems likely that this watercolour was painted in the summer of 1920, soon after Burns returned with a series of market scenes of Fez and Marrakesh. During the 1920's he designed and executed an ambitious decorative scheme for Crawford's Tearooms in Princes Street, which Anne visited and admired. However as an easel painter she thought him rather backward looking. Titian and the Venetian painters of the early 16th century were the major influences on his work, influences shared by his English contemporaries, Charles Ricketts and Charles Shannon. Whilst Anne acknowledged the inspiration she drew from the tireless energy of Burns the artist, she reacted against the emphasis on academic painting which Burns brought to his teaching.

David Alison, who succeeded Burns as Departmental Head in 1918, was an adept painter of portraits and interiors in an essentially Edwardian manner – another style not to Anne's taste. He was, however, a good teacher of drawing and it was largely due to him that the

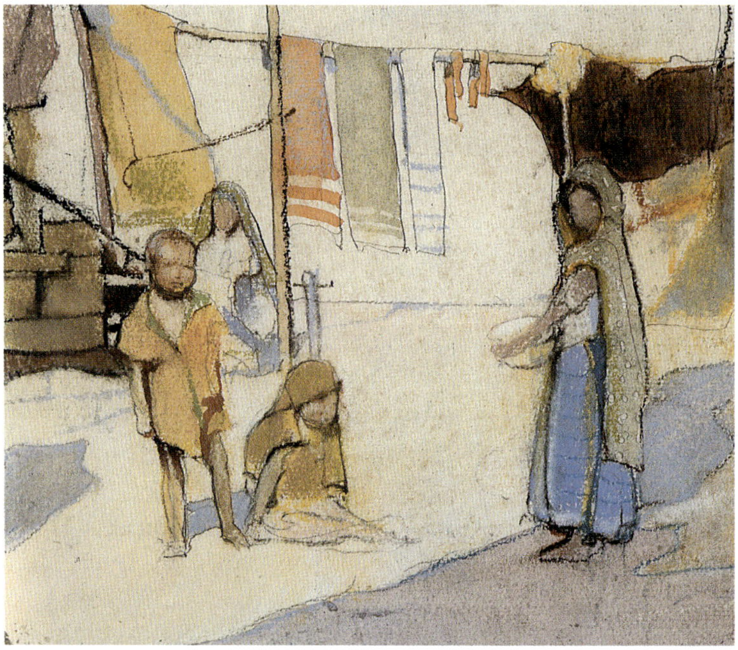

7 Children in the Canongate c1919 watercolour

College first developed its strong reputation in this discipline. He passed on to Anne his admiration of Degas and if in later years she felt that drawing was the weakest of her artistic accomplishments this was probably a reflection of the very high standards Alison had always demanded of his students. Anne liked to recall Alison's ruthless attitude towards models. If a girl fainted from lack of rest, he would say "Give her a drink and stick her up again!"

The younger members of staff had a more direct influence on Anne's painting style and three in particular, D. M. Sutherland, Adam Bruce Thomson and Henry Lintott, the only Englishman on the staff, became lifelong friends. Sutherland and "Adam B." were both called up to the Western Front in 1916 but Lintott remained, to be later acknowledged by Anne as her "most constructive" teacher. She appreciated the soft tonalities of Lintott's painting and developed a similar palette in her own early landscapes, although she had little fondness for the ethereal figures which populated his paintings – figures which Lintott himself referred to as "floaters".

From the outset Anne flourished at art college and was consistently mentioned in college reports. In the 1916/17 session she was awarded one of only two travelling bursaries in the drawing and painting section. The report for that session states that:

"The Head of Section (Robert Burns) reports that the work of Anne Redpath, while less in quantity than that of Violet Banks (the other bursar), was of a very high standard, probably the highest yet achieved by any minor travelling bursar."

The lack of volume might be accounted for in part by her absences at Moray House and partly by her pronounced distaste for the anatomy classes, which she skipped whenever possible. Yet she wrote of her general appetite for work in an undated letter to Nancy Gass, a girlfriend who was also studying at Moray House:

"I am working most terrifically hard this term. I can't believe that I am quite myself 'cos I've never worked in my life before but it does give me a lovely glow to do it occasionally."

In 1917 Anne was awarded a maintenance bursary of £50 and gained her diploma. Two years later her reputation as the most promising student of her year was confirmed when she became the sole recipient of a travelling scholarship worth £150. The adjudicators of this award were a distinguished panel of painters including Phillip Connard, Walter Grieve, E. A. Walton and Robert Burns. Interestingly, when Anne spoke about the work she did at college in an interview with George Bruce in 1962, she said that her paintings were "more impressionistic than I have ever done since".

In 1919 the Edinburgh Group held an exhibition in Shandwick Place in Edinburgh and invited Anne to show some of her paintings. The Group had held two exhibitions before the war but "The Scotsman" still characterised them as having "a youthfulness and ardour". Most of the artists were about ten years older than Anne, so it was a tribute to her new professional standing that she was invited to join them. Members of the Edinburgh Group included Eric Robertson, Alick Sturrock, John R. Barclay, Dorothy Johnstone and D. M . Sutherland. In his generally complimentary review of this exhibition "The Scotsman" critic wrote:

"Miss Anne Redpath sends a number of admirable impressionistic still lifes, fine in colour and in their decorative quality . . . marked by a pleasing purity of strength and colour."

Influences on her style from painters outside the College may be attributed to Peploe and Cadell, both of whom were exhibiting regularly in Edinburgh at that time. Cadell in particular has been mentioned as an influence on her landscape style, but she did not acknowledge this in later years.

Anne spent six weeks as an art teacher at Dumfries Academy before setting off on her travelling scholarship. This was the only period of teaching that she ever undertook. William Gillies, John Maxwell and most of her contemporaries from the Edinburgh School spent long periods of their careers teaching, but Anne's refusal to follow suit was the result of an independence that was central to her character.

The career of Dorothy Johnstone is an interesting contrast. She had been a brilliant and precocious student and was taken on to the staff of Edinburgh College of Art immediately she graduated. She developed a decorative style of figure painting, usually on a large scale (40 x 60 inches was a favoured canvas size), which employed strong, sure drawing and flat areas of subtle colour and was much admired. She was described in "The Studio" of 1924 as: "a brilliant daughter of Scotland" and seemed to have an exceptional career ahead of her.

In 1924 she married D. M. Sutherland and under the College rules regarding married women she had to relinquish her teaching post. Although Anne Redpath was a most outgoing and extrovert personality, she relished painting as a personal and private occupation away from friends and other painters, whereas it appears that Dorothy Johnstone, even though she had developed a very individual painting style, was lost without the stimulating company of the College. While Anne stored experiences and insights in the largely fallow years ahead during which she brought up her young family, Dorothy Johnstone's well of inspiration appears to have drained away. The life and stimulus of the College had obviously been of paramount importance to her because, although she painted until her death in 1980, she never again painted with the same vigour and conviction.

Anne made full use of her travelling scholarship and visited Brussels, Bruges and Paris before moving on to Italy where she encountered her main influences. Although she did study the Old Masters in Paris, there is no record of her reaction to the contemporary school of Paris painters. It was common for students to return home declaring that they had found their greatest inspiration in the artists of the High Renaissance. Anne, like John Maxwell on his travelling scholarship five years later, was much more affected by the Early Renaissance artists and the Siennese Primitives. Her visit to Siena had been prompted by the enthusiasm of a Swedish doctor she had met while copying a Renaissance painting in Florence. In Siena she was impressed by the frescoes of the Lorenzetti brothers in the Palazzo Pubblico – frescoes which mark a high point in late medieval art and are technically the opposite of primitive. She was struck by their combination of sophisticated and exquisite technique allied to a simple, powerful vision. Their painting emphasises line rather than volume and their vision of the natural world is heraldic rather than literal.

There is a painting by Ambrogio Lorenzetti in the museum in Siena that bears a fascinating similarity to Anne's paintings of thirty and forty years later. It depicts a bird's eye view of a hill-top town by the sea. Human figures and activity are absent, as they are in Anne's later paintings of hill-top towns, but there is a boat on the sea, painted with heraldic simplicity. Two trees are shown, at eye level in contrast to the general viewpoint. The picture is a summary of the artist's knowledge of the scene rather than a direct observation of it – a distillation of experience recollected in the studio. The influence of this and similar paintings is evident in Anne's work over many years. It is there in the simplified and refined landscapes of the 1920's and 1930's (for example pl 22) and again at the end of her life with her love of gold in her altarpieces. Her ability to mentally file away visual experiences for indefinite periods was one of the strengths of her artistic sensibility. At the time of her exhibition at the Scottish Gallery in 1950, she said that she considered the Italian Primitives to be the greatest single influence on her painting. Anne was always willing to acknowledge the variety of people, places and moments in her life which she felt had been inspirational. She attributed her love of rich dark colour to her father and declared in a BBC film interview in 1961 that Italy had opened her eyes to the other extreme:

". . . when I was a student in Italy, I had a wall in the room in a pensione in Lungarno in Florence, and the walls were white, rough white plaster. There was a gay orange and red rug hung on a wall. There were cool, white tiles on the floor. I had never seen a rug on a wall and not on the floor, but for the heat it was a necessary thing to do, and coming in from the heat of Florence in the summer, to this cool room, and the lovely bit of colour which had far more intensity because it was against white, I think that was the beginning of my love of a white wall . . . and everywhere I have gone, in all the houses I have ever been in, I have had a pure white wall."

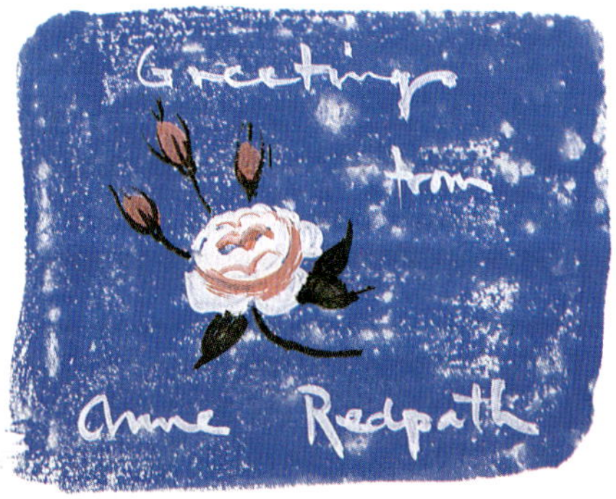

Chapter Three

On her return from Italy Anne became engaged to James Michie, a young architect she had known since childhood. They married in 1920 and moved almost immediately to St-Omer in the Pas de Calais region of France. Jim had accepted a job with the War Graves Commission to design cemeteries and memorials for sites on what had been the Western Front in Northern France. Despite being depressingly close to the battlegrounds of two or three years before, their new home was also near to Montreuil, a favourite painting ground of many British artists, and, perhaps more significantly, to Paris-Plage where Peploe and Fergusson had painted with so much inspiration fifteen years earlier.It was in St-Omer that the first two Michie sons were born: Alastair in 1921 and Lindsay three years later. For the first couple of years at least Anne was so thoroughly immersed in the responsibilities of setting up a home and looking after her new husband and small child that she found no time and perhaps little inclination for painting. "Windmill, Northern France" is one of the very few oil paintings which is known to date from this period. There are also two watercolour versions of the same subject (pl 8), with only minor variations of emphasis and accent. This consistency of subject, along with the uncompromising and careful composition of all three pictures, shows that she had begun to abandon the "accidental quality" and "impressionistic" style that she herself described in her student work.

Anne completed enough paintings to be able to hold an exhibition in St-Omer in 1921 for which, unfortunately, no catalogue has ever been traced. The exhibition probably consisted of watercolours and perhaps a few works she had completed before leaving Scotland. She never dated either her watercolours or her oil paintings at any stage of her life and consequently it is difficult to determine the exact chronology of her pictures. Stylistically though, and in terms of subject matter, "Boat on a Canal, French Village" (pl 8) seems to date from this period in the early 1920's. The tonal control is reminiscent of James Paterson's watercolours, which Anne knew from RSW exhibitions, and the atmosphere is similar to the English artist William Lee Hankey's watercolours which depict this same corner of France. The blue costume of the figure in the boat articulates the colour scheme particularly successfully. "Quai Vert, Bruges" (pl 6) shows a concern with tone rather than colour.

While the Michies lived in a large house in the St. Martin suburb of St-Omer, they had little money to spare for furniture and it was at this time that Anne began to decorate what were basically very humble tables and chairs, sometimes made from plywood, in a colourful manner, making use of folk art motifs such as birds and garlands of flowers in the same way as a bargee decorates his barge. She maintained this custom as a form of relaxation over the next three decades and many of the later pieces became presents for her grandchildren and featured in her paintings.

In 1925 Jim was offered a position as private architect to an American millionaire called Thompson, who had bought a villa at St. Jean, Cap Ferrat, an exclusive resort between Nice and Monte Carlo, famous for its grand villas. This resort could boast many splendid residents, including Somerset Maugham, The King of The Netherlands and the Singers, of sewing machine fame, who owned the villa next door. Thompson had made his fortune

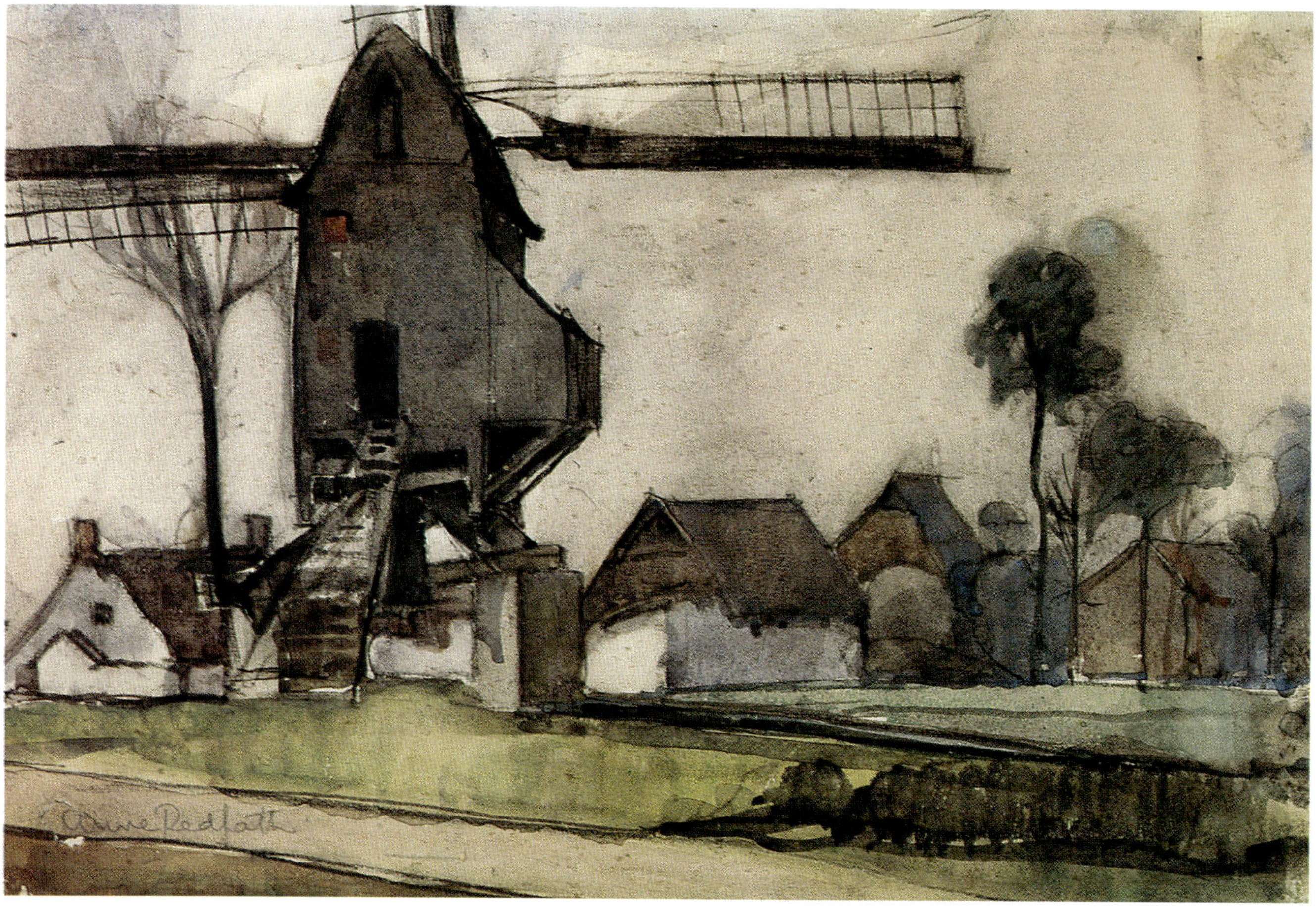

8 · Windmill, Northern France c1922 watercolour

manufacturing aeroplane carburettors. His ambition now was to create a palatial residence on a classical theme. Undeterred by the fact that the villa he had bought had been designed with a gothic facade like a Venetian palazzo, he renamed it "Chateau Gloria" after his wife and set about altering it in the style of his dreams.

The Michies moved into the boathouse, which they shared with Thompson's speedboat, another "Gloria". This boathouse, in its private harbour below the main house, must have made an idyllic home for the young family. A third son, David, was born in 1928. The elder two went to school locally and turned native to the extent that, according to Alastair, Lindsay was spotted one day chasing English tourists down the streets, shouting "Sales Anglais! sales Anglais!".

The grounds of Thompson's villa were a paradise for small boys. They could play with Mrs Thompson's pack of thirty Dalmatians which she kept in a large pen. When the Thompsons were away in America, the boys would creep into the garage at the Chateau and play in the Rolls Royce and Cadillac that were parked there awaiting the millionaire's return. Alastair remembers sitting on the quay one day when a very large, very black steamer appeared and unloaded tons of golden sand on to what had been a very rocky, private beach. There were weeks of excitement when, in 1933, the house and grounds were taken over by a film company who had arrived to film "That's a Good Girl", starring Elsie Randolph and the Scottish matinee idol Jack Buchanan, who was also the director.

Jim Michie's work at the Chateau involved designing four classical bathrooms with sunken baths in black marble and turquoise mosiac. A swimming pool with a Roman loggia was also built and he designed a massive pair of wrought iron gates for the top of the drive which are still there today. Much of his time during the nine years he was employed at the Chateau Gloria was taken up with painting a series of murals in the reception rooms of the house, featuring scenes from classical mythology. Not all of Thompson's "improvements" adhered strictly to the classical ideal – as part of the transformation of "Chateau Gloria" he had a forty foot bar from a Western saloon shipped over from America and installed beneath the tennis court.

Jim had studied Italian fresco painting and was still as interested in painting as he was in architecture. Anne does not appear to have been involved in the execution of the murals, but the scheme and all its technical problems must have been of interest to her as a result of her studies ten years earlier in Florence and Siena.

The architect Charles Gray obtained a commission for Jim to paint two murals in the Chapelle St. Rosaline, part of a Carthusian monastery and Anne was invited to assist her husband. The murals were to be done in the Quattrocento style and Anne painted the heads of the saints.

Anne's personal output at this time was hardly prolific, certainly by her later standards, but she did produce enough work to be able to hold an exhibition at the casino in St. Raphael in 1928. From the pictures that survive it would again seem that the majority of the works were watercolours. Melville Shepherd wrote of this exhibition thirty years later that some of the paintings "found their way into the homes of discerning French people".

9 Anne at St-Omer, 1921

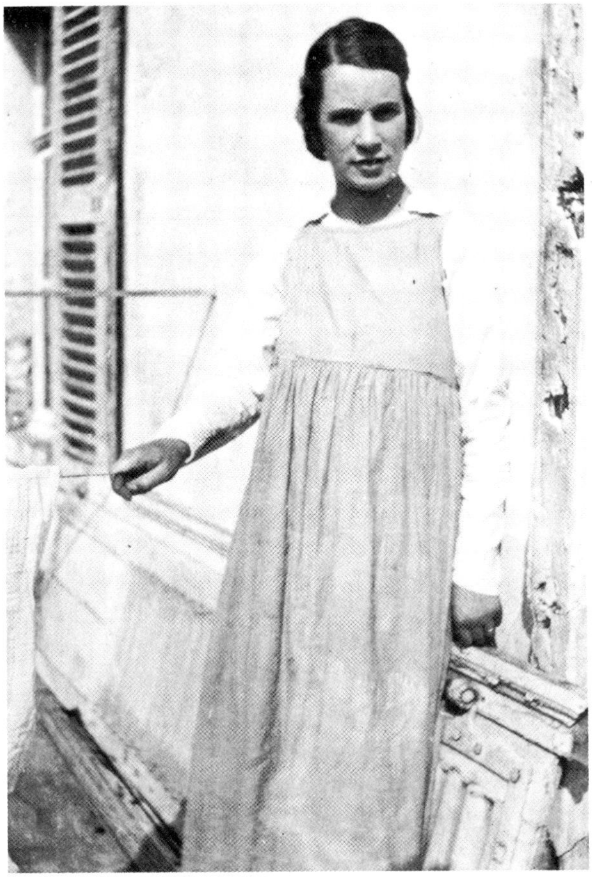

10 Jim at St-Omer, 1921

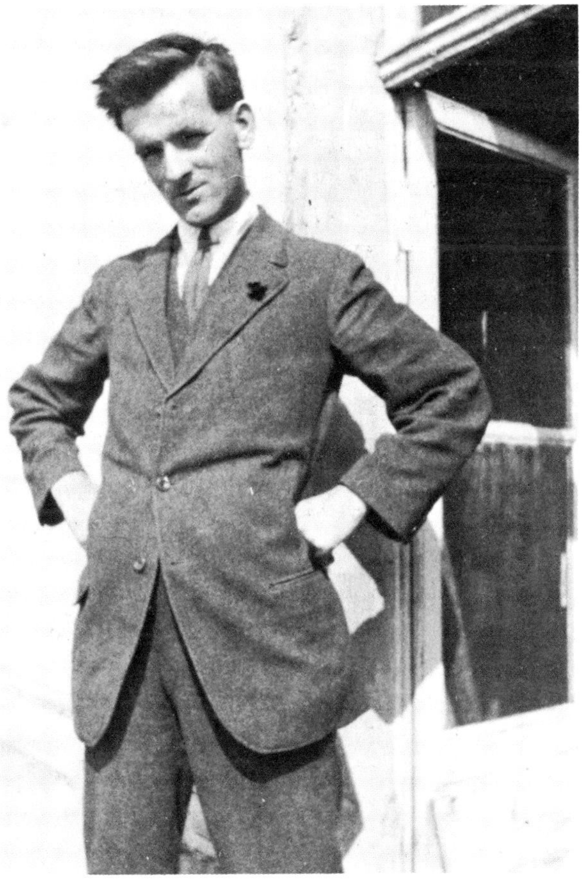

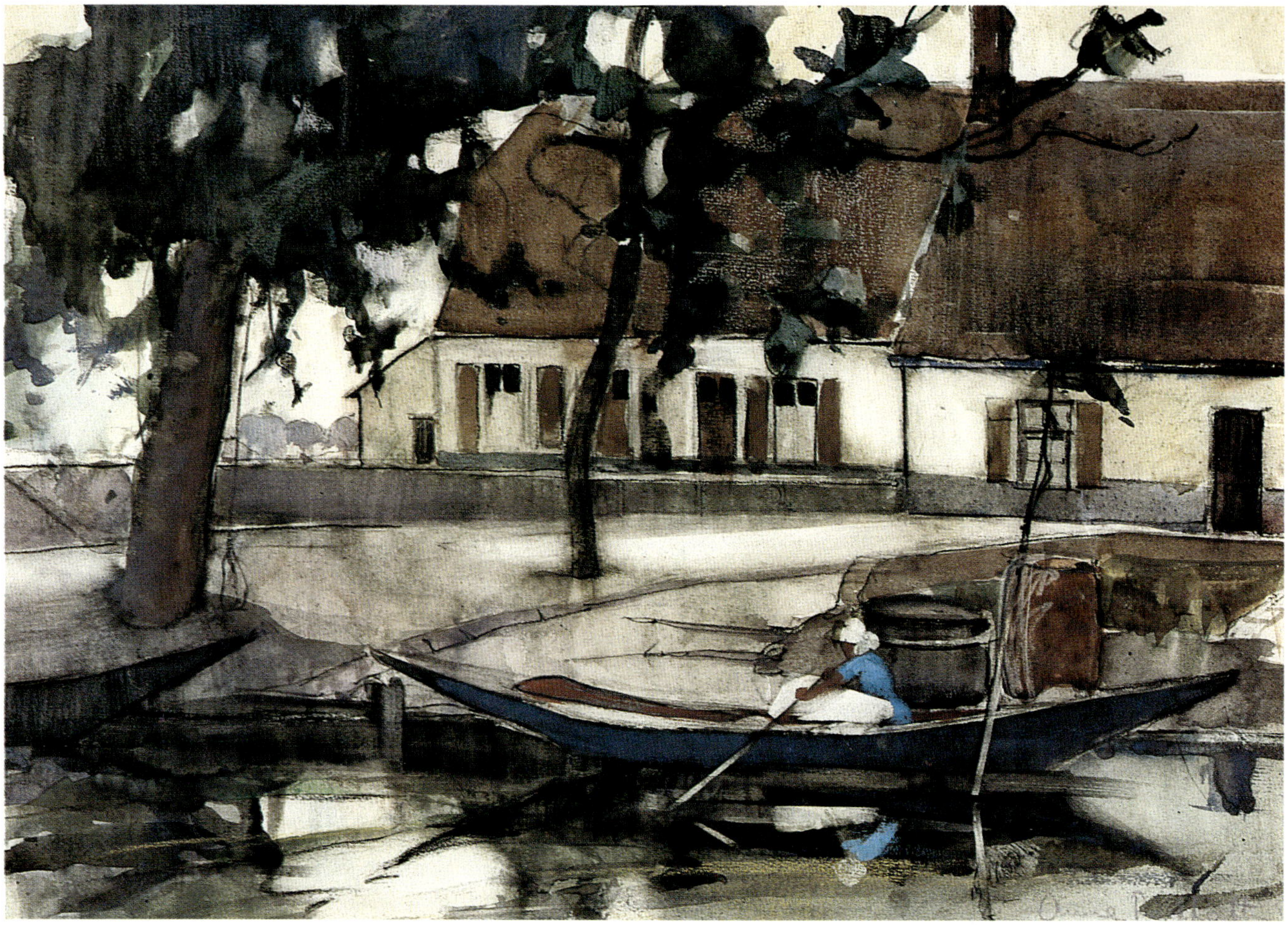

11 Boat on a Canal, French Village c1922 watercolour

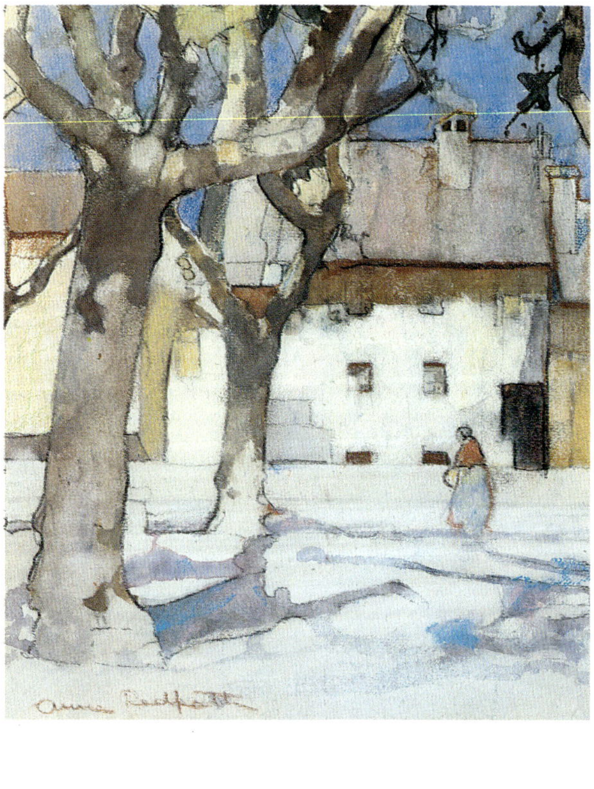

12 Chambery c1925 watercolour

13 Sea at Villefranche c1928 watercolour

"The Sea at Villefranche" (pl 13), which was painted at this time and exhibited at the Society of Scottish Artists in 1925, is simpler and more refined in style than those painted five years previously at St-Omer. In choosing to paint this view of buildings climbing up a hill she found an opportunity to flatten perspective in a picture that is a forerunner of scenes which would appeal to her throughout the rest of her career. Charles Rennie Mackintosh was at Port Vendres to the west of St. Raphael, painting very similar subjects but with different emphasis. Whereas Anne was aiming for texture and simplicity Mackintosh's watercolours are more intricate and linear. It is unlikely that Anne knew of the work Mackintosh was doing in watercolour in the late 1920's. The importance that architecture began to have in her work can be traced to the influence of her husband's architectural drawings which were always far more elaborate and imaginative than was strictly necessary.

The restraint of the watercolours Anne was painting in France at this time could occasionally be slightly listless in effect, but with notable exceptions. The watercolour of "Chambery" (pl 12) c. 1930 is a fine example of a carefully crafted composition that fully retains a sense of spontaneity. She creates a satisfying rhythm between the geometry of the background buildings and the organic lines and mass of the plane trees in the foreground, perfectly punctuated by the positioning of the figure. She captures splendidly the hot, languorous atmosphere of an afternoon in the South of France.

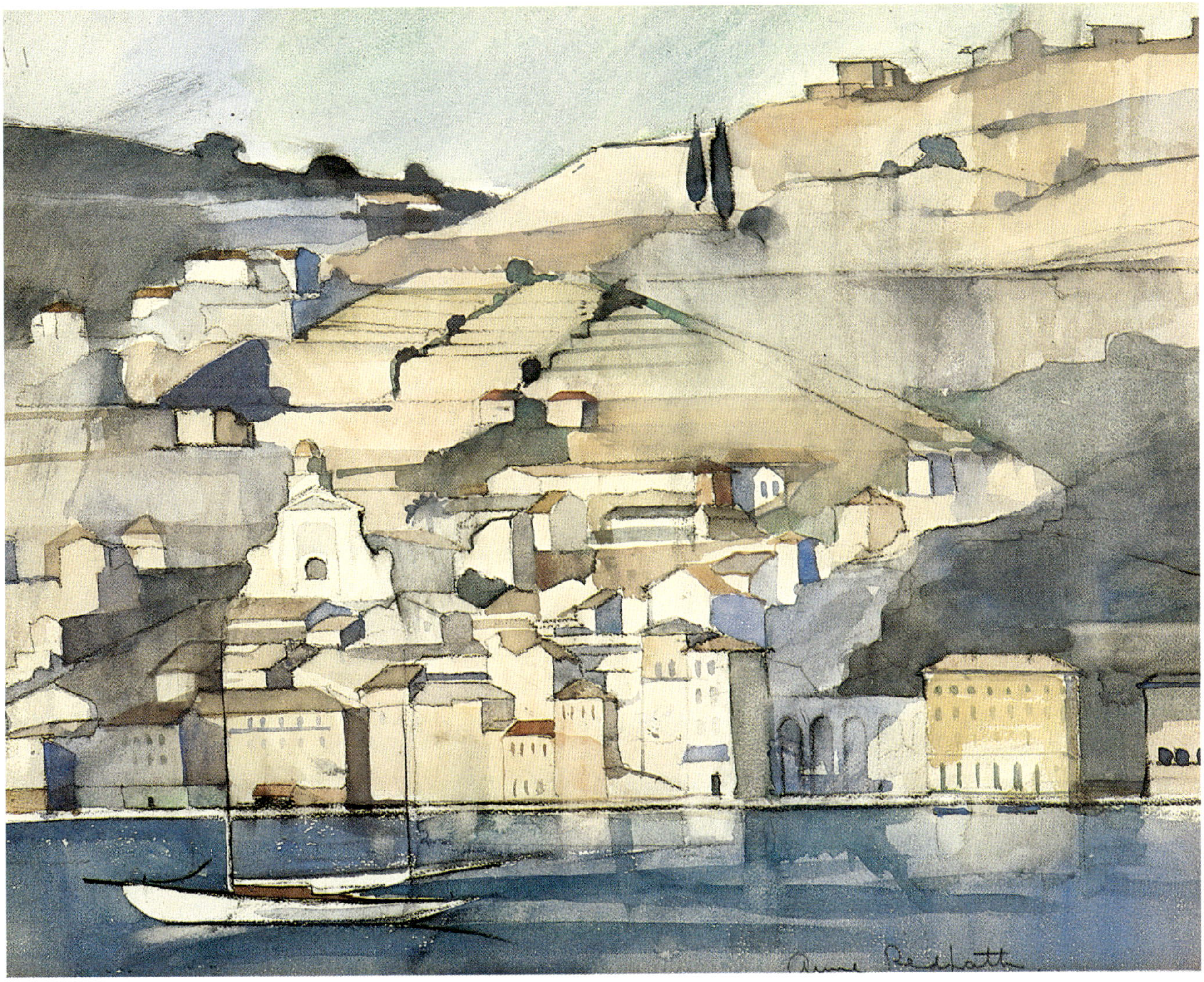

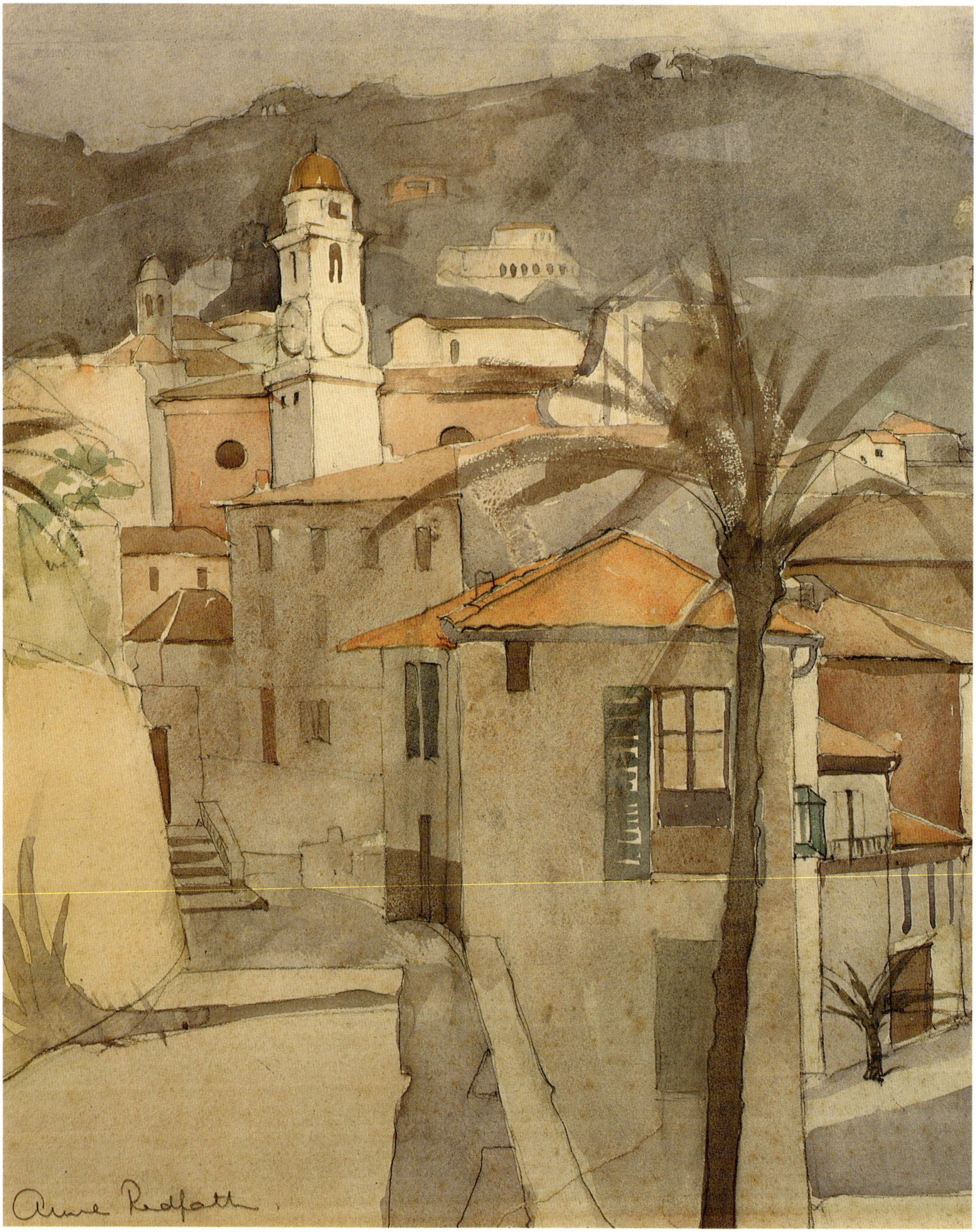

14 St Raphael c1930 watercolour

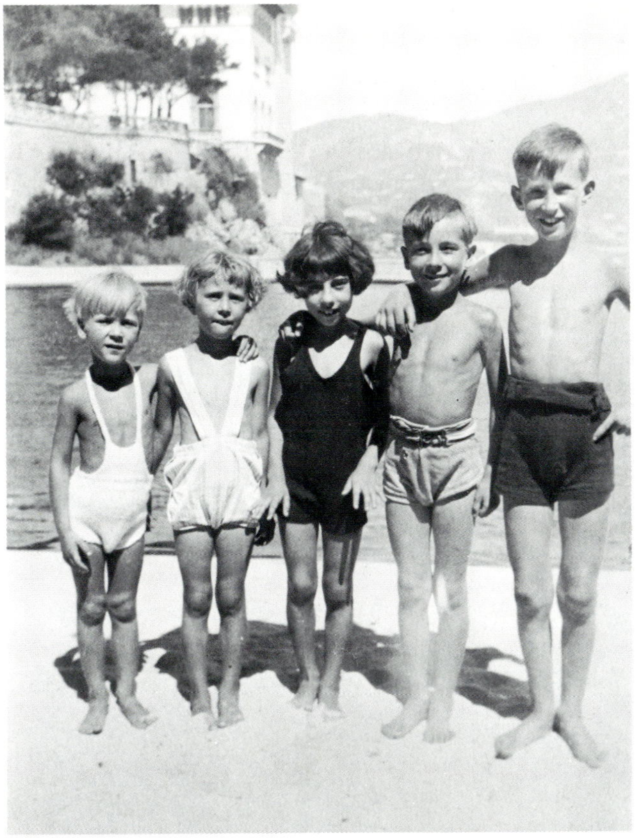

15 Alastair, Lindsay and David with friends at Cap Ferrat

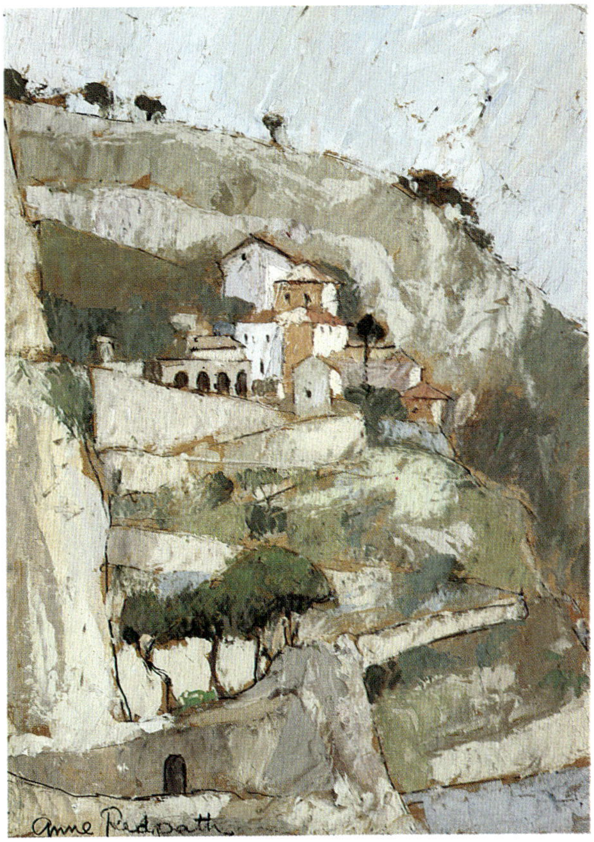

16 Cap d'Ail c1934 oil

"Cap d'Ail" (pl 16) c. 1934 is one of the few oil paintings known to have been made in the Cap Ferrat years. The flattened impasto applied with a palette knife, the revealed soft pencil underdrawing and the pale colouring all conspire to give the effect of a work done in pastel. In her choice of subject, the village against the hill, and in her obvious interest in the abstract pattern made by the road zig-zagging up to the village, the picture is again reminiscent of Mackintosh, but there is an abstract and arbitrary use of colour that looks forward to Anne's later work.

Anne Redpath and Charles Rennie Mackintosh were not alone in finding the South of France perfectly suited to their artistic preoccupations. It was a popular painting ground for many British, and especially Scottish, artists throughout the 1920's. J. D. Fergusson was nearby at Antibes and Sir William MacTaggart was a regular visitor to St. Raphael, sometimes accompanied by William Crozier. John Maclauchlan Milne lived with his French wife at St. Tropez and both Cadell and Peploe were at Cassis in 1923 and 1924.

MacTaggart was the Michies' most frequent visitor and he became, according to Alastair, like an uncle to the boys. Although both he and Anne were eventually to develop a heavy impasto technique, there were few similarities in their work and neither seems to have influenced the other to any great extent. William Crozier on the other hand was a significant influence on both of them. Crozier was the sort of intelligent, cosmopolitan character whose company she loved. He was a haemophiliac and died in 1923. Many of Anne's friends remember her speaking fondly and often of Crozier, even thirty years after his death. His approach to painting, intellectual and cubist-influenced, can be seen reflected in Anne's work until the late 1930's, but ultimately was too reserved to affect her robust, mature style. It may be that her affinity with his work through those years in France in some way accounts for producing a body of work that, whilst it was of a high standard technically, was ultimately a little unconvincing. There is a restraint and lack of passion, so alien to her mature style, as to suggest that she was painting without the commitment for which she later became renowned. Her responsibilities in bringing up a young family prevented her from participating fully in the exciting developments that were taking place both in France and in her native Scotland. To a certain extent this may explain the apparent stagnation which infected her stylistic development during those years she lived in France – in absolute contrast to the ever quickening evolution in her art which marked the rest of her career.

17 Jim with his Italian workforce at Chateau Gloria

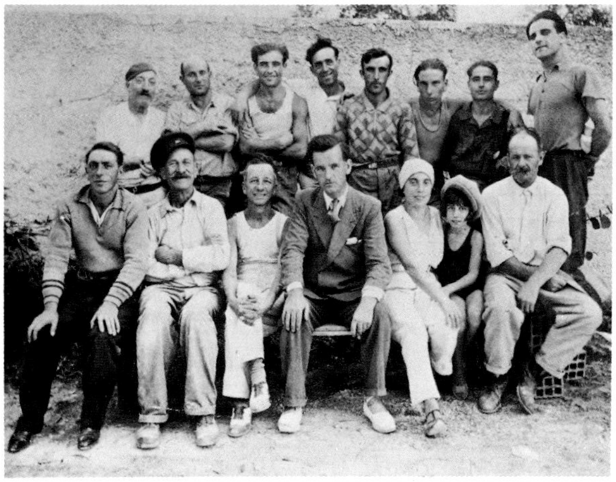

18 Chateau Gloria

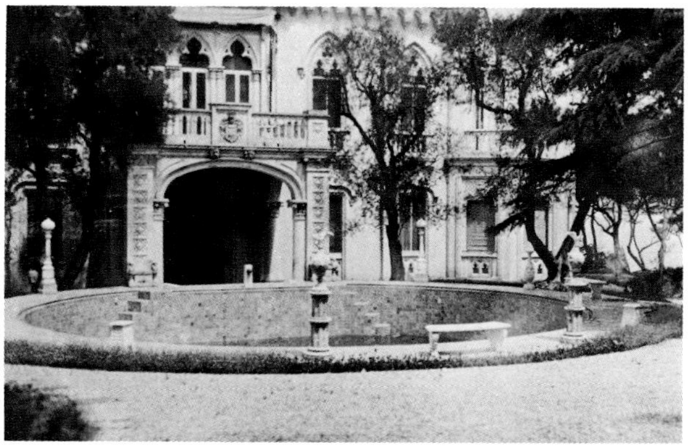

19 Anne's sister, Nancy, with David at Cap Ferrat. The private harbour is in the background

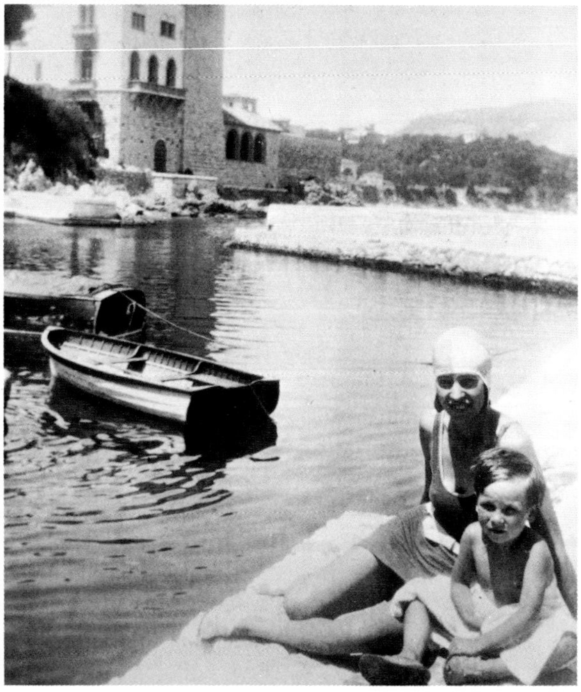

20 Chateau Gloria showing, in the background, the loggia that Jim designed next to the swimming pool

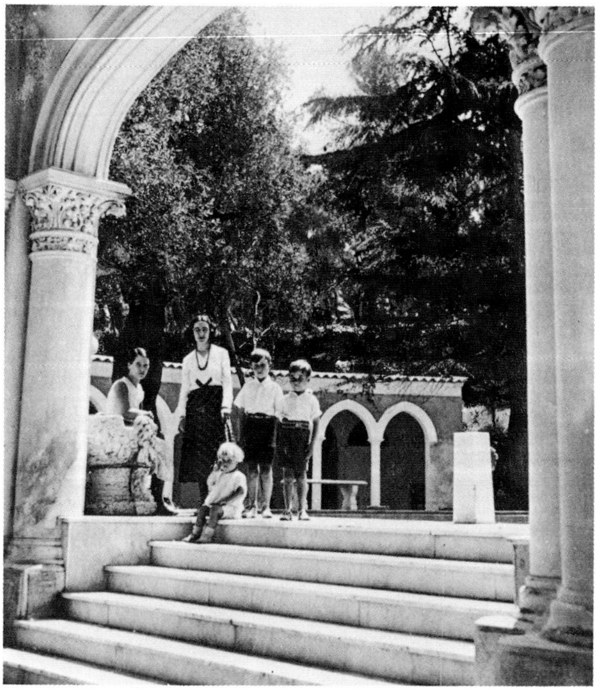

Chapter Four

During the fourteen years Anne spent in France she returned with the boys to Scotland for holidays on several occasions, staying at her parents' home at Orchard Terrace in Hawick. She used these trips to bring back paintings for exhibition at the Hawick Art Club, of which she was made an honorary member, and to show at the Royal Glasgow Institute and the Society of Scottish Artists. The fact that she showed only five paintings – four of them watercolours of Riviera ports – during all her trips home may have contributed to the mistaken impression that she had all but given up painting in favour of bringing up her family.

The Memorial Exhibition catalogue of 1965 states that the Michies returned to Scotland in 1934 because of international tension between France and Italy, but this wasn't the main reason. Their idyllic way of life had ended abruptly when Thompson sold "Chateau Gloria" and dismissed all the staff. Thompson's fortune had been badly dented by the Wall Street Crash and continued to decline during the Depression. By 1934 he was bankrupt. The Michies were homeless and Jim was owed a substantial sum of money in unpaid wages. The family were left penniless. Anne took the boys back to Hawick, where they moved into Orchard Terrace with Anne's parents and her sister Nancy, who had never left home. Instead of joining the family in Hawick, Jim went to London and found a job with the firm of architects, Charles Holden and Company. Anne took some time to settle back into the way of life of a Borders town before she could begin to paint in earnest. The house was run by Anne's mother and sister, Alastair and Lindsay were at the High School, David at St. Mary's Primary School and at last Anne was free to paint without interruption. The family could not rely on money arriving from London regularly and so, for the first time, it became necessary for Anne to earn a living as a painter.

She took as her subjects still lifes and the landscapes of the farms around Hawick. In 1934,.as if to underline her new determination, she was elected a Professional Member of the Society of Scottish Artists. In 1935 she exhibited eight paintings in Edinburgh, including four watercolours of subjects from the South of France.

On her return to painting full time and professionally, her attitude was that:

". . . taking up art again is different from music. The actual technique doesn't matter quite so much as it would in music. But at first it is difficult to attain the same kind of abandon and bravura in your painting."

It was not until 1942 that her painting found the confidence and brio that her brilliant student days had promised. In fact the unproductive years may have secured for her an independence from received responses – a pitfall for many young painters. She had retained her technical skills and now had the maturity and individuality to create a personal vision.

In 1961, referring to her time in France, Anne said:

"Whatever I did for my home was creative but I never ceased to be a painter – I have a painter's mind. But even yet, were the choice to be made again, there would not be any division in my mind: my family would come first."

However, there was conflict, reflected by her admission that:

"I always had a rather guilty conscience. I always knew I would come back to painting."

"Frosty Morning, Trow Mill" (pl 22), which was exhibited at the SSA in 1936, is a large oil on plywood, her preferred support of the period. The application of the paint, leaving bare areas of board, and the tone and hue of this painting are very similar to "Cap d' Ail" (pl), painted in France two years before. There is a quiet dignity, but no passion. It is necessary to look at the still lifes of the period to find excitement and commitment. "Still Life with Painted Chest" (pl 28), painted in the late 1930's, has the same simplified planes and forms as the landscapes, but excitement is created by the choice of colours from opposite sides of the "colour wheel" – the blue of the painted box and the orange of the marigolds.

Anne found studio work, with the freedom to create such interactions, more stimulating than the surrounding countryside, and it was in the interiors that her style and individuality began to develop. The two still lifes "White Tulips in a White Vase." (pl 27) and "Red and White Tulips in a Vase" (pl 30) are examples of Anne's love of whites and cool harmonies. They also successfully convey an impression of mass and a feeling of sculptural quality. The objects seem to occupy their own definite space, an illusion in complete contrast to her later paintings, where objects appear to float and the space has been flattened. She said ". . . as far back as I can remember I have lcved painting white". This she shared with Christopher Wood, who had died in 1930 but whose work continued to be an influence throughout her life.

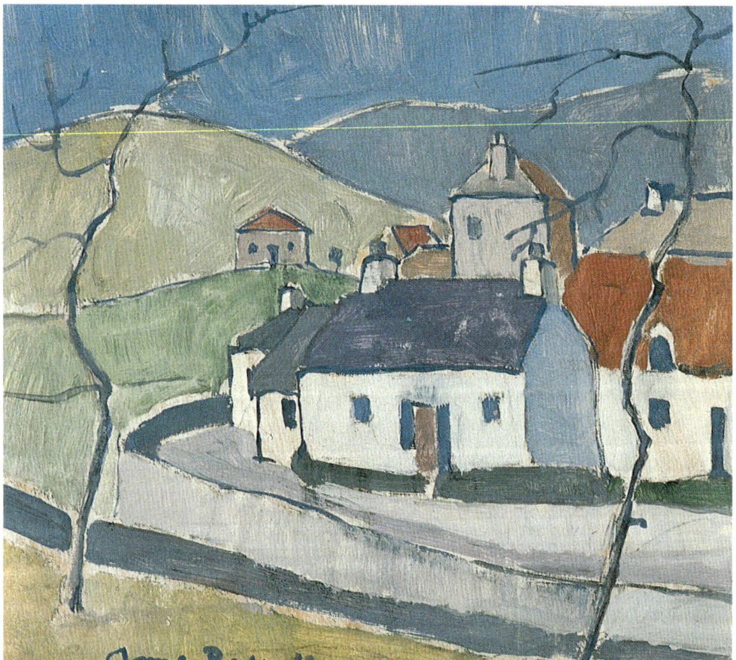

21 Farm at Ruberslaw 1940 oil

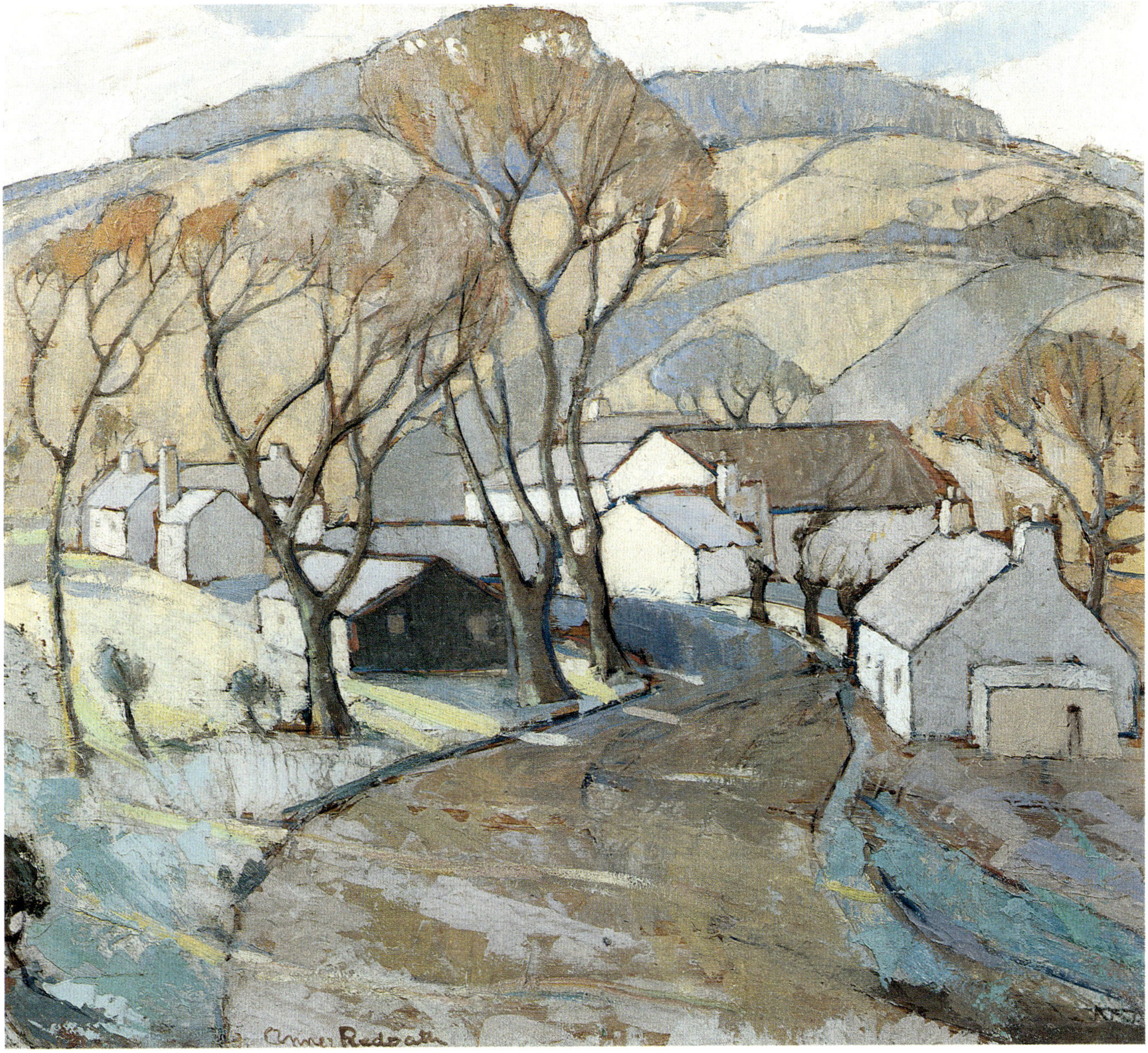

22 Frosty Morning, Trow Mill 1936 oil

When Anne's father died in 1939, he left his daughter a small sum of money with which she bought a house in Beaconsfield Terrace in Hawick. In this new home she began to paint a series of intimate interiors. "Still Life with African Sculpture" is similar in palette and subject to some of the still lifes Cadell had painted in the 1920's. Each painter arranged a harmony of cool colours, predominantly blue and white, in delicate contrast to the warmer hue of the flowers. The sculpture serves as a foil to the blue and white of the china; Cadell used his Burmese Buddha to similar effect.

"Red Slippers" (pl 34), probably the picture exhibited at the SSA in 1942, is indebted to Matisse for the Fauvist red of the chair and slippers and the flat patterns of the rug. But in the painterly enjoyment of pigment and impasto and the use of whites and greys as a contrast to the strong colours, the picture is distinctively Anne Redpath. This painting marks the re-emergence of an abundant talent that had been, if not dormant, certainly under-exercised since those college days when she had been ". . . working most terrifically hard".

In "Red Slippers", "The Chinese Rug" (pl 26) (exhibited at RGI and RSA 1944) and "Still Life with Orange Chair" (pl 24) Anne has taken material from her immediate surroundings – domestic objects, furniture, rugs and vases of flowers – then re-arranged and interpreted them, transforming them in the process. These paintings convey a sense of involvement that the Border landscapes of the same period conspicuously lack. Her landscapes were painted in the studio from colour notes and occasionally from watercolours, and often they do not survive the transition. It seems likely that the Border countryside failed to engage her in the way that the landscapes of the Mediterranean did in later years. Amongst Anne's friends and contemporaries this Border landscape provoked extremes of reaction. William Johnstone alluded to the motif of the Eildon Hills, even in his abstract works, almost to the point of obsession, but Anne declared that the landscape lacked contrast, and when Donald Moodie was asked why he had decamped early from a painting week in Kirkcudbrightshire, he muttered: ". . . too green, too green".

By the early 1940's Anne's work had become manifestly professional. From an early age she had accepted the necessity of unremitting hard work as a precondition of artistic achievement. Kim Redpath describes her attention to technique as "a loving process".

Her delight in the physical act of painting stands in stark contrast to the experience of less painterly artists. For example, her contemporary, Stanley Spencer, admitted to being thoroughly bored by the actual painting of a picture once he had conceived the image. Anne's freedom with paint was almost culinary – imbued with a sense of experiment and discovery and relishing the accident of invention. Each painting was a new experience, never merely the stale reiteration of a past success. However, whilst this meant that her work was distinguished by a compelling artistry, it left a significant number of only partly successful paintings, which she could not afford simply to scrap. This was particularly true of a proportion of her flower paintings. Some of these were the painterly equivalent of literary potboilers and, unlike her friend Johnny Maxwell, who had no need to sell to live, Anne was forced to part with them in order to make ends meet. The decision not to be an art teacher, a job for which she was fully qualified, had a high price. She sold less successful works to give her breathing space for the production of the series of masterpieces which were starting

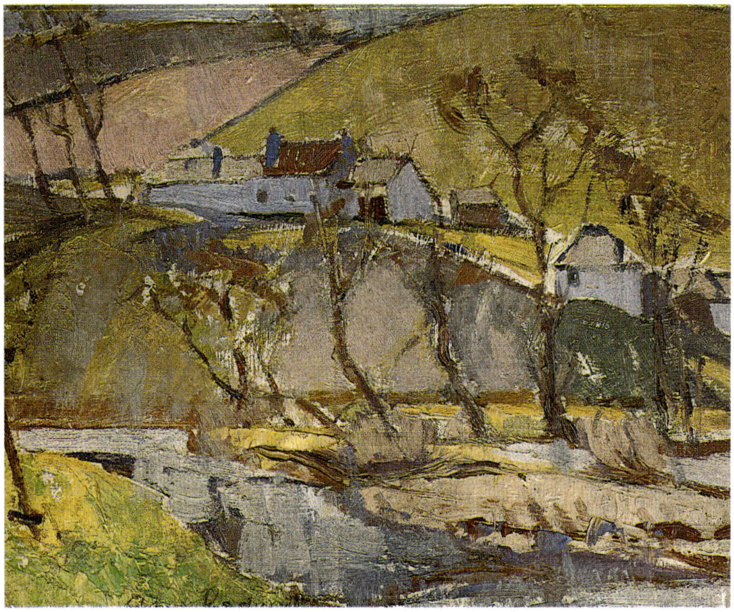

23 A Border Farm c1938 oil

24 Still Life with Orange Chair c1944 oil

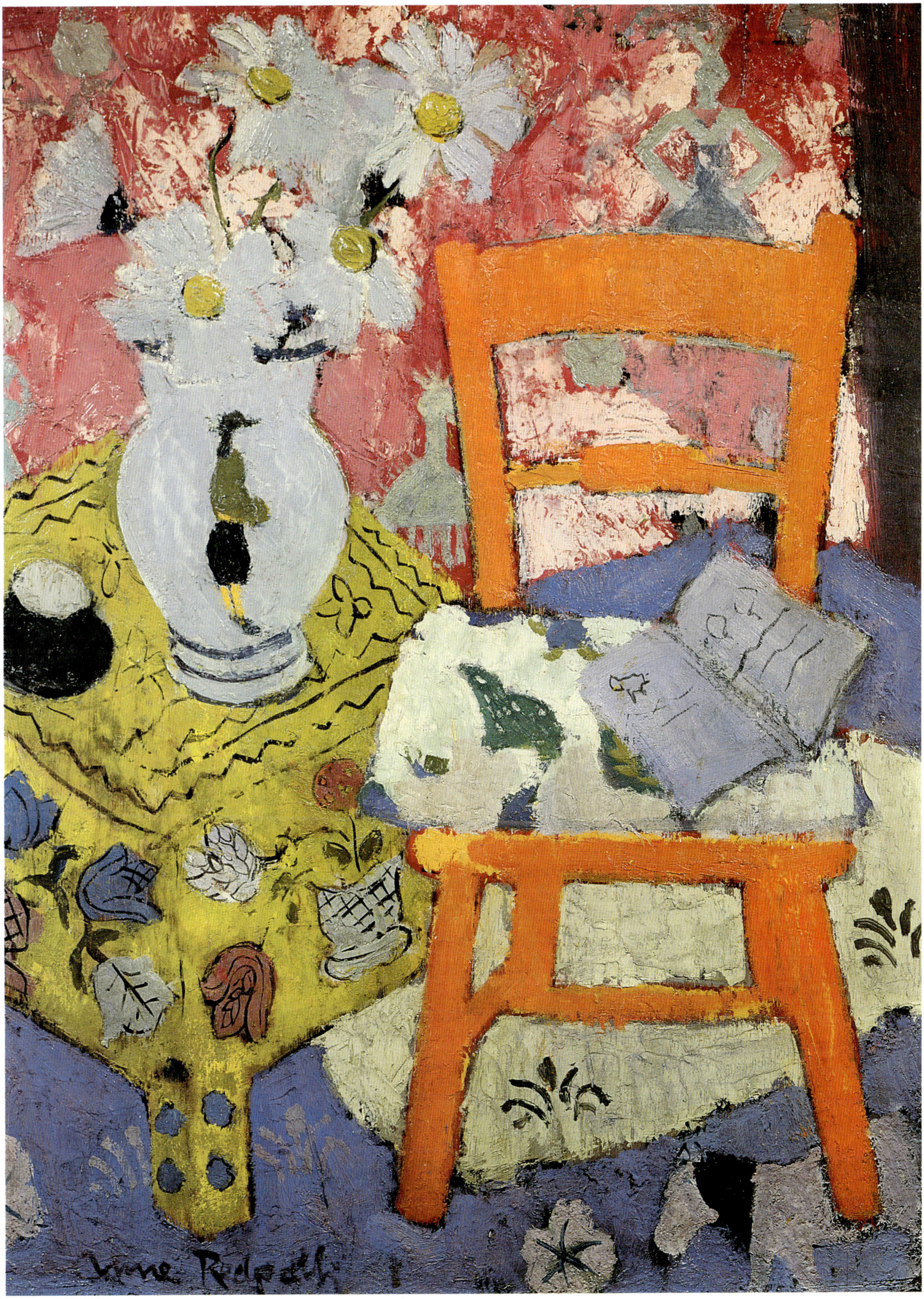

to flow from her brush by the early 1940's. Amongst her fellow artists this was an all too familiar compromise. Cadell painted and sold literally hundreds of Iona seascapes, identical in size and very similar in subject, in order to subsidise his more ambitious work.

Money was so short in the Michie household in the late 1930's that Mrs. Stiven a minister's wife, mother of seven and not herself well off, was so worried by the Michies' poverty that she tried to give Anne five pounds. Anne refused to accept the money as a gift but took it as payment for a watercolour, priced at ten pounds, that had recently been returned unsold from an exhibition. Alastair Michie, however, has no memory of ever being aware of the shortage of money. His mother was an excellent cook, with a great capacity for improvisation, and he remembers a happy, well-fed adolescence.

By the late 1930's Jim seldom visited Hawick. His search for the kind of work which would satisfy his ambition took him far away and he and Anne had grown apart. Nevertheless, he often sent presents back to the family from trips abroad. From Paris in 1938 he sent Anne a dramatic woodcut of figures in a yard, bearing an indecipherable signature. It was not until she visited the Edvard Munch exhibition in Glasgow in 1957 that she discovered, with a shock of recognition, "The Last Hour" – the self same woodcut.

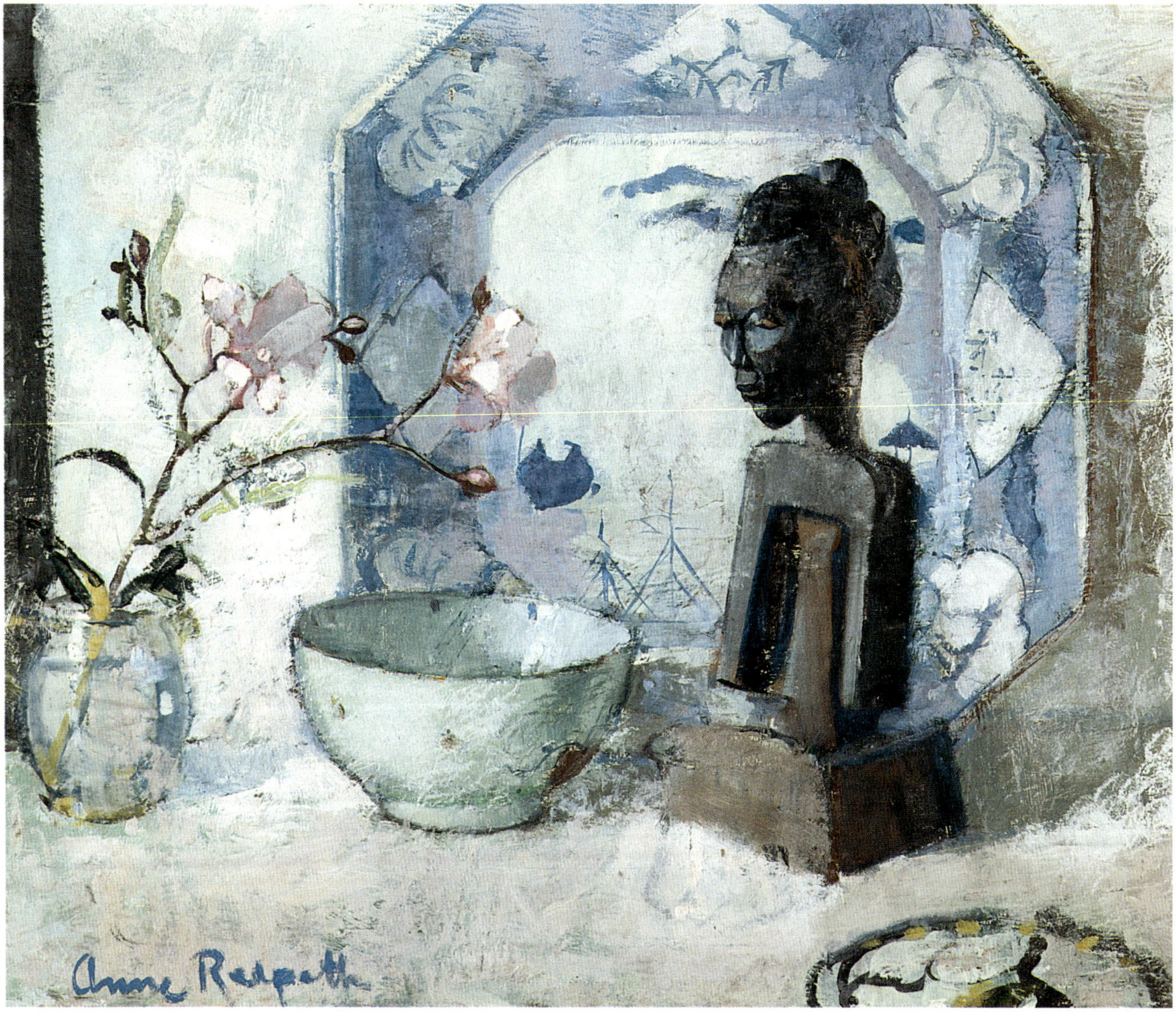

25 Still Life with African Sculpture c1942 oil

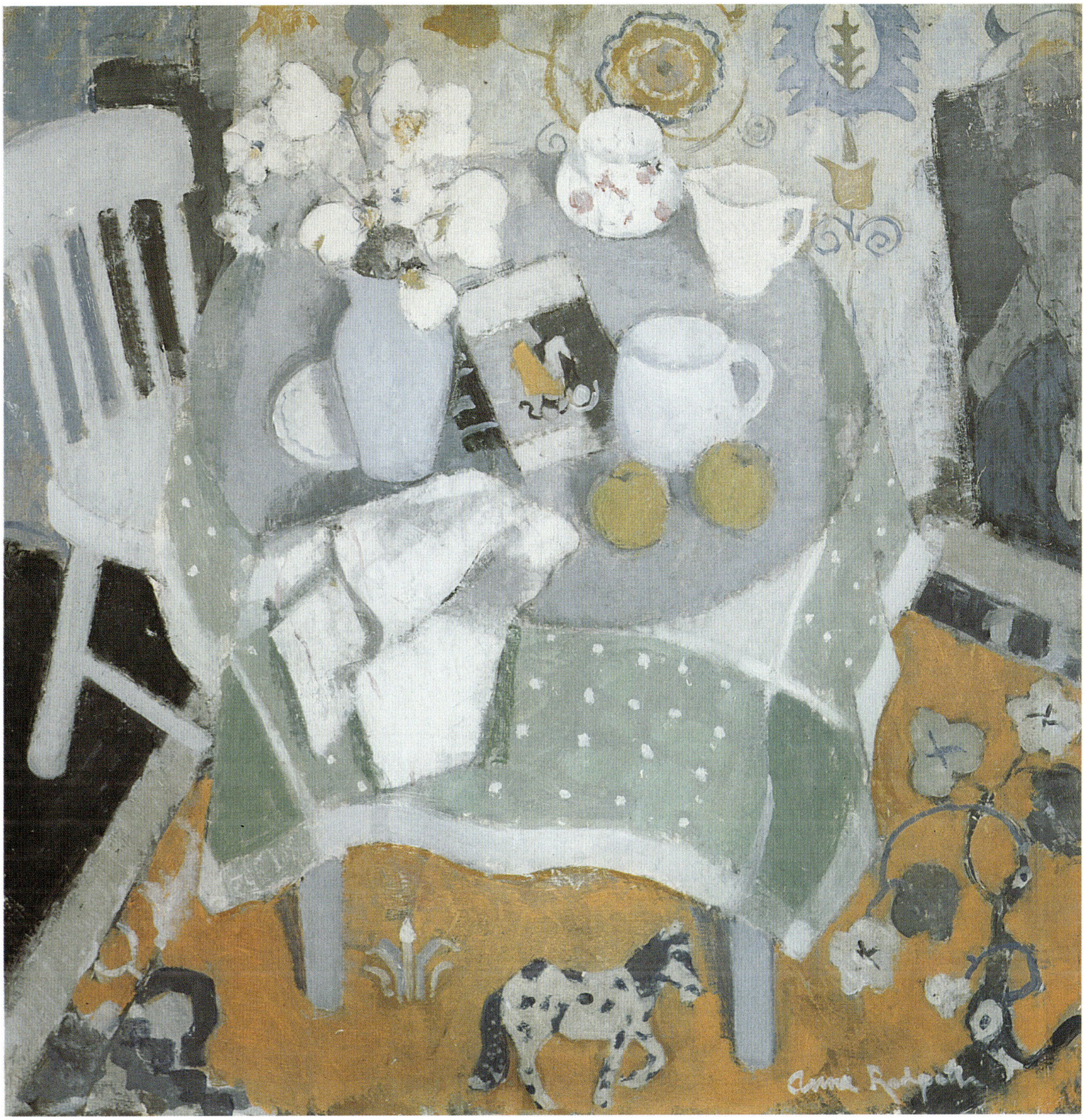

26 The Chinese Rug c1944 oil

Through this formerly anonymous print, Munch influenced her work – especially the figures in the Spanish paintings of 1951-53. Had she returned from France earlier and visited the 1931 Munch exhibition at the SSA, an exhibition which had "staggered" MacTaggart and been a "startling confrontation" for Gillies, then the sixteen large canvasses, infinitely more potent than any reproduction, would certainly have galvanised her restrained and formal style of the time. Anne's knowledge of the masters of the modern movement was gained mainly through reproductions. David remembers his mother having great admiration for Gauguin, Van Gogh, Matisse, and Indian and Persian painting. In her studio in Beaconsfield Terrace she had prints of all of these and also some Japanese woodcuts.

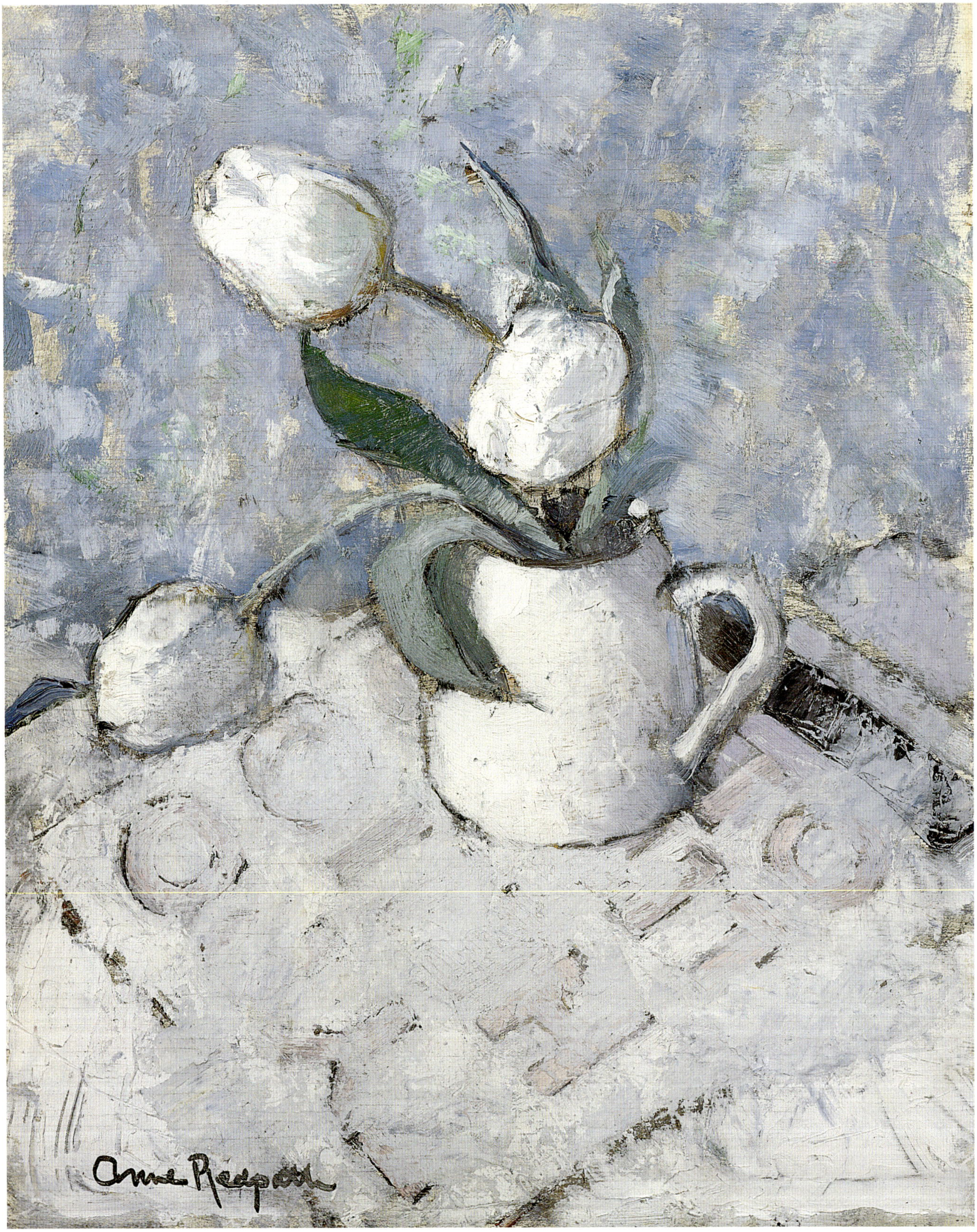

27__White Tulips in a White Vase c1938 oil

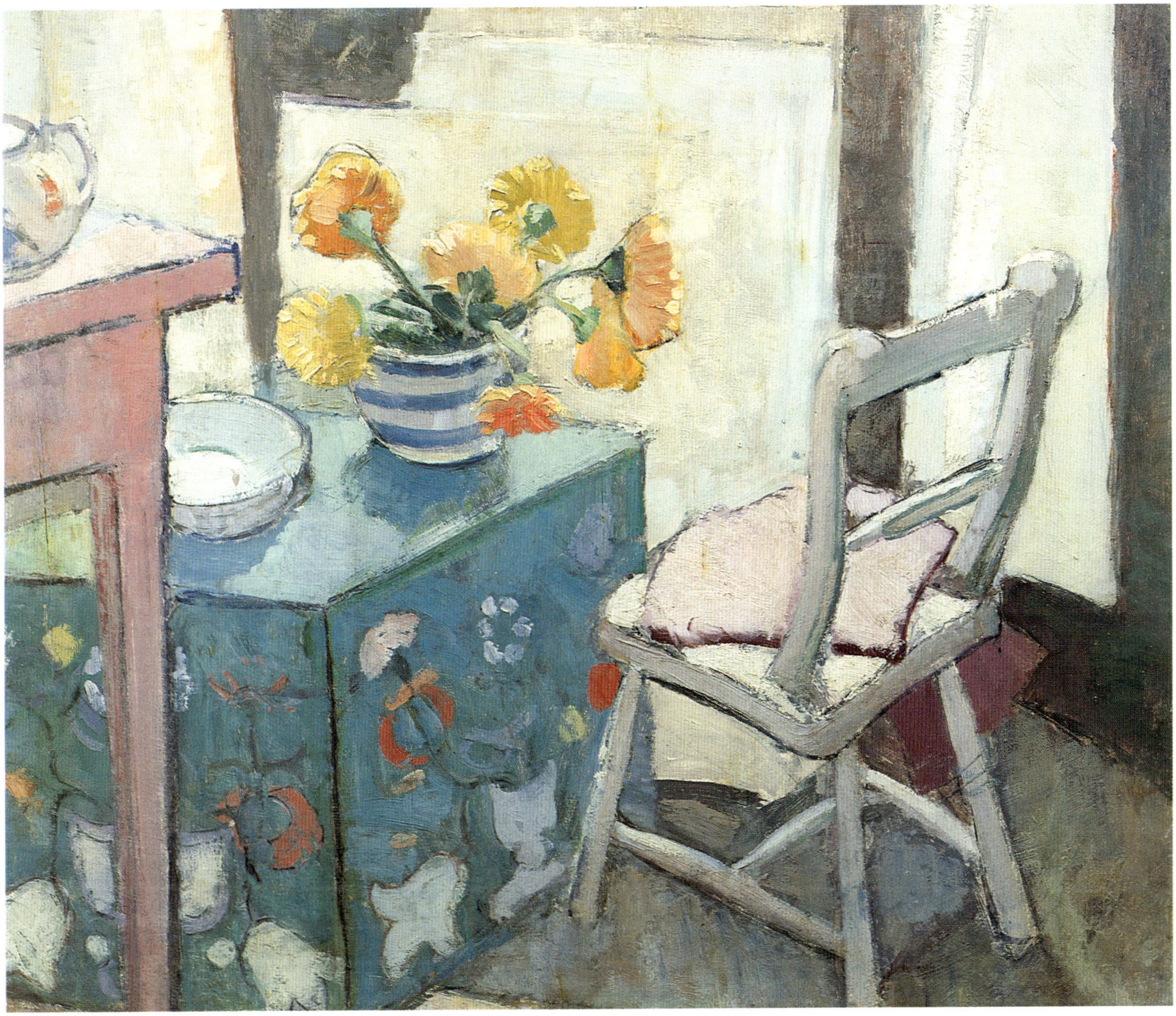

28 Still Life with Painted Chest c1948 oil

In common with many of her fellow artists, Anne's views were left wing. She had become involved in the life of the town and joined the Russia Today Society and the Left Book Club, where politics were discussed. Along with many of her contemporaries, she had been politicised by the Spanish Civil War. Mussolini's imperial ambitions for the French Riviera in the early 1930's convinced her of the dangers of fascism. Advocates of Russian Communism, however, found her a fierce critic. She would suggest they live in Russia ". . . instead of sowing discontent amongst those of us who are quite happy to be Scottish".

Throughout the war years, Anne's painting career continued without too much interruption. Jim had enlisted in 1939 – at the very earliest opportunity – becoming a Captain in the Gloucester Regiment. He had served in the First World War as a Royal Scot, attached to a Sikh regiment, so perhaps his choice of attachment to the Gloucester Regiment is best explained by the fact that it enabled him to become billeting officer for the Borders region. Anne was upset by her husband's rush to get into uniform – she felt he was trying to run away from his career before he had given it a chance to work out as he had planned.

Alastair joined the Royal Air Force in 1940 and in 1942 Lindsay joined the Royal Navy. Hawick was full of soldiers and through the Debating Society Anne become friends with many of them. Indirectly, her hospitality led to a brush with the authorities when she left her kitchen door open in contravention of the blackout regulations. During her court appearance she caused great hilarity by switching from an imitation of the bailie's anglicised Hawick accent into the local Hawick dialect and, finally, when she got excited, by speaking French! The result was a five shilling fine.

In 1944 Anne was elected President of the Society of Scottish Women Artists. The Society had been founded in Edinburgh in the 1920's to give women painters the showcase they felt they were being denied by the RSA and RGI. By the 1940's it had lost its way. Restrictions placed upon it by the war forced it to move its headquarters from the RSA to two separate venues; Moxon and Carfrae, an Edinburgh department store, and the premises of Doig, Wilson and Wheatley, art dealers in George Street. For some time the Society's selection process had not been strict enough and there was an element of amateurism about many of the craft and design exhibits. Annie Black, the outgoing President, was a painter of the old school and under her influence the Society had become distinctly old-fashioned. During Anne's presidency, however, younger painters were encouraged and standards improved. Members' paintings were no longer simply accepted automatically, but they were judged against the standards set by a nucleus of good painters, which included Lily McDougall, Mary Armour and Penelope Beaton. In later years Anne changed her opinion about the practice of women exhibiting collectively. She told Sydney Goodsir Smith that it was as silly ". . . as would be a special exhibition by men over six feet tall taking size fourteen shoes".

The reason for this volte face was that in the 1940's women still had difficulty getting work included in the male-dominated exhibitions, but by the 1960's this had changed, largely due to the reputations made by such women artists as Joan Eardley, Elizabeth Blackadder and Anne Redpath herself in Scotland, and Dame Barbara Hepworth, Dame Ethel Walker and Dame Laura Knight in England.

In the years after the War Anne regularly travelled to Edinburgh. There was a good train service from Hawick and she often went for the day. As well as her work at President of the SSWA, she had started giving lectures for the Arts Council, and was increasingly in demand all over Scotland. In Edinburgh she became close friends with many artists, including Alick

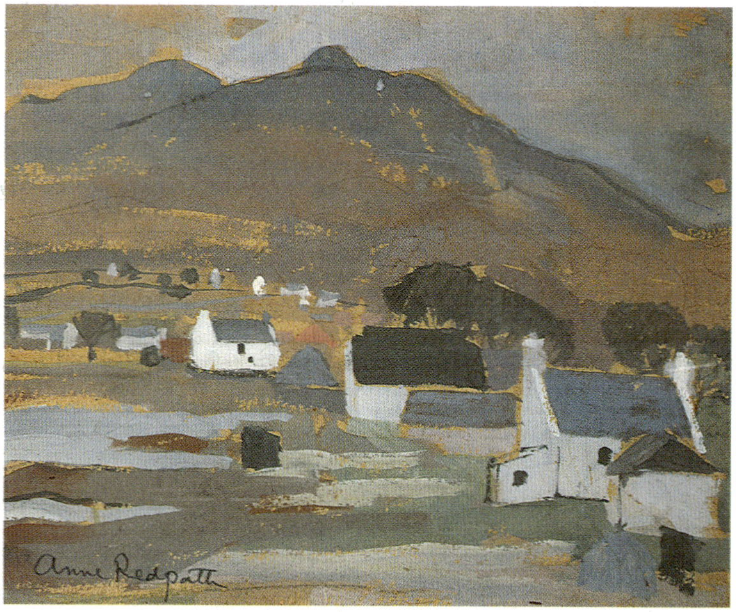

29
Crofts in Skye c1946 gouache

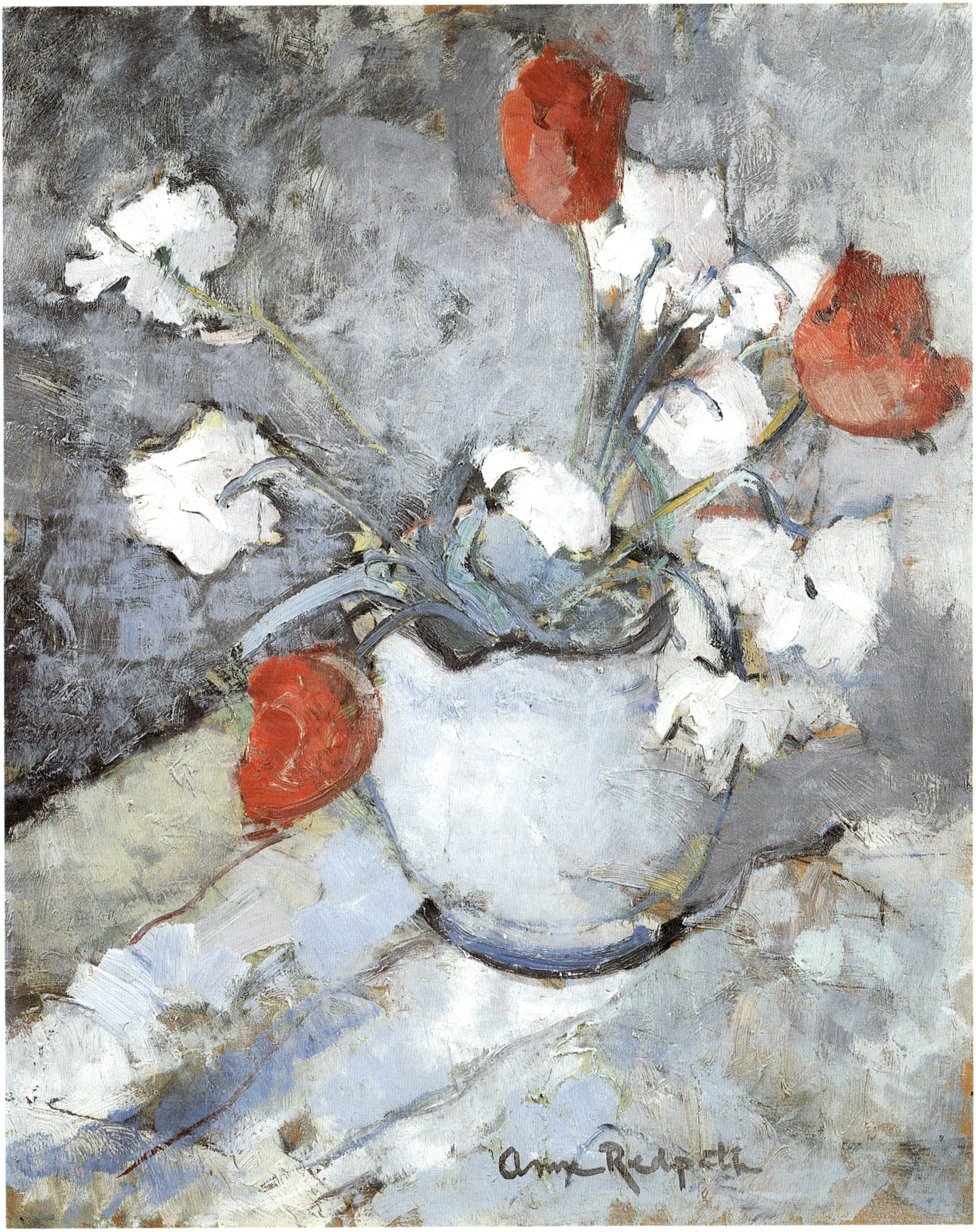

30 Red and White Tulips c1940 oil

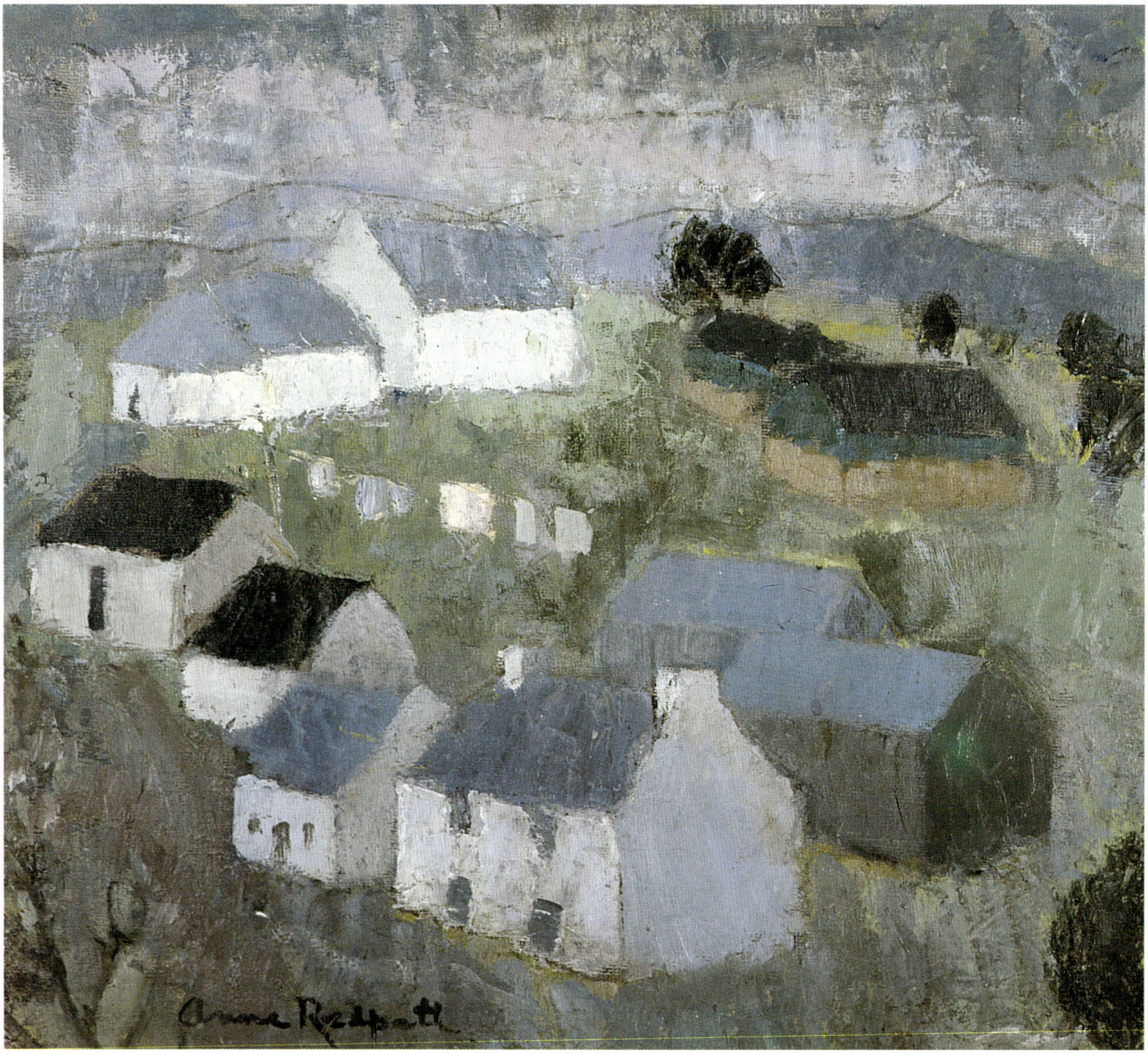

31 Farm at Spittal on Rule 1944 oil

and Mary Sturrock (with whom she had exhibited at the 1919 Edinburgh Group exhibition), the MacTaggarts, Katie Horsman (a fellow SSWA council member), Willie Wilson (the painter and stained glass designer) and the writers Compton Mackenzie and Sydney Goodsir Smith.

One of the reasons for Anne going to Edinburgh at this time was the weekly meetings of the Hanover Street Group. It was set up by the painter Derek Clarke in 1947, shortly after he had joined the staff at the College of Art. He was prompted by Anne remarking that she envied the other members of staff their opportunity to draw from life at the College whenever they wished. On discovering that other artists felt the same, he rented a studio above a printer's workshop in Hanover Street, hired a College model, and set up the Hanover Street Group. They met on Tuesday evenings, usually about fifteen of them, to draw and paint. Anne was amongst the regular members, who also included Leonard Rosoman and James Cowie, who was made honorary president. The Group lasted from 1947 until 1950 and provided Anne with a valuable opportunity to exchange ideas with fellow painters in a working environment. Although the sessions were mainly taken up with drawing, they would occasionally paint as well. One of the paintings produced there was "Girl in a White Chair", which was exhibited at the RSA in 1951. Derek Clarke, whose easel stood next to Anne's when she was painting this, noticed "her liveliness and concentration, walking back and forth, turning suddenly to spring a surprise on the image and catch it unawares, screwing up her eyes to diffuse the focus and generalise the image. She was at every stage concerned with the whole of the painting rather than concentrating on a small area. It was a lesson to younger painters."

In 1946 she visited Skye with her friend Katie Horsman, her son David and his girlfriend Eileen. Anne had been to Skye several times before; a gouache of Broadford is dated 1942. On this occasion they rented a cottage on the island and stayed for four weeks. While the others amused themselves with holiday pursuits, Anne worked steadily, producing a prodigious number of gouaches, which were the basis for some of the paintings exhibited throughout 1946. These subsequently formed the core of her first one-woman exhibition in Scotland, at the Gordon Small Gallery in Edinburgh's Princes Street in March, 1947.

32 Table Top with Teacup and Book c1940 oil

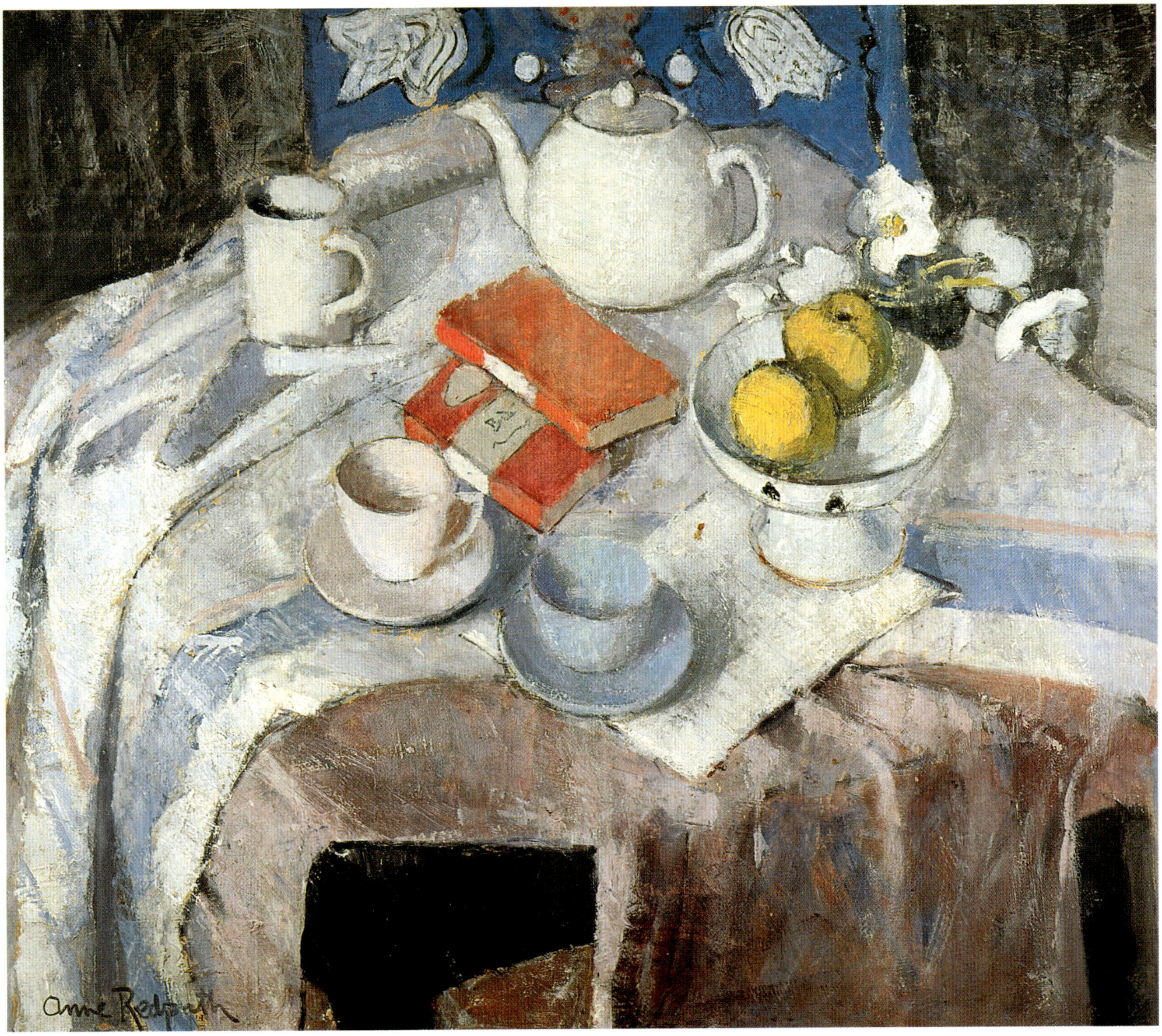

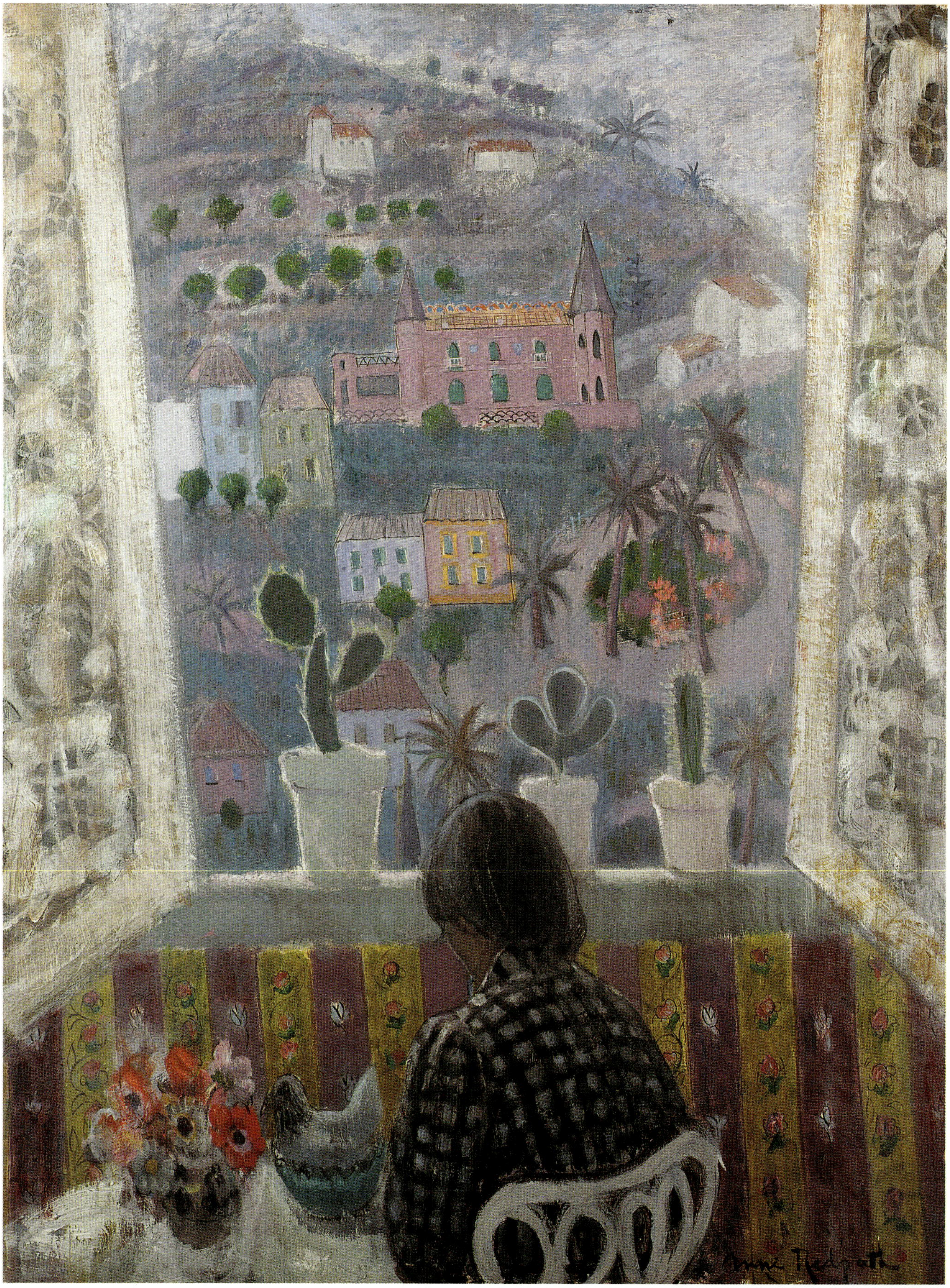

33 Window in Menton 1948 oil

The exhibition had been suggested by Alick Sturrock, the landscape painter and Treasurer of the RSA. He was a tireless champion of Anne and was always the first to tell her when her paintings had been accepted and favourably received at the RSA. The exhibition consisted of fifty oils and watercolours, of which all but a dozen sold. Gordon Small generously declined to take any commission on the sales. The exhibition was extremely well attended and the visitors' book shows that a great number of her fellow painters came – Gillies, Maxwell, D. M. Sutherland, Moodie, Penelope Beaton, the MacTaggarts and many others. It was an encouraging success. The watercolours and oils of Skye gained most attention since, prior to the exhibition, she had been known mostly for her still lifes. "The Glasgow Herald" critic described the pictures as having been painted ". . . with a technique as rounded and flowing as the artist's signature".

Although at this stage in her career she was frequently noticed by the critics, she often received mixed reviews and qualified praise. "The Glasgow Herald" also noted ". . . the slight flimsiness which has sometimes intruded even in her best examples" and "The Scotsman" in a review of the 1949 SSWA exhibition stated that ". . . "Old Port Menton" is not a success, her colour, here, having fallen for once, from the sweetness she manages so expertly, into the sugary". In 1946 the same newspaper had complained of "naivete, which at times is hardly adult". This last criticism would hardly have worried her because she had noted and admired the consciously naive element in Matisse's paintings. She was quite happy that this made her work more easily acceptable to the innocent child than to the man in the street.

From 1946 Anne exhibited regularly in London – at the Royal Academy and the Royal Society of British Artists – and soon came to the notice of the London critics. By the end of the 1940's she was receiving frequent and complimentary reviews in the London press. Indeed, by 1950 "The Observer" could state that her ". . . highly individual paintings attract at least as much attention in London as they do in Edinburgh". Eric Newton, the art critic of "The Sunday Times", compared the RSA favourably with the RA and made the further point that Anne's ". . . bright, feminine colour, which is so arresting in the London exhibition, is distinguished but by no means startling in Edinburgh". This was partly because the RSA attracted the best of Scottish painters whereas the RA was going through a reactionary period under the presidency of Sir Alfred Munnings and was avoided by many of the more progressive artists. In a "Sunday Times" review of an RA exhibition in 1948, Newton wrote that in comparison with the rest of the paintings ". . . Anne Redpath's still lifes stand out like patches of blue sky on a grey day".

In 1947 Anne was made an Associate Member of the RSA. She had first exhibited there in 1919 and since 1938 had consistently shown the maximum three paintings allowed to a non-member. From 1948 she exhibited between fifteen and twenty paintings each year at the major exhibitions in Edinburgh, Glasgow and London. However, she would sell an even greater number of paintings to friends and admirers directly from her studio. Many people have commented on how little she was prepared to ask for a painting from her studio. She liked to sell to friends, wanted to know where they were going to hang the painting and had mixed feelings in later years when her paintings sold for sums beyond the means of her early admirers.

The success of the exhibition at the Gordon Small Gallery enabled Anne to plan a trip abroad for the first time since her return from France in 1934. In June, 1948 she set off alone for Paris, from where she continued south to Menton on the Italian border, about

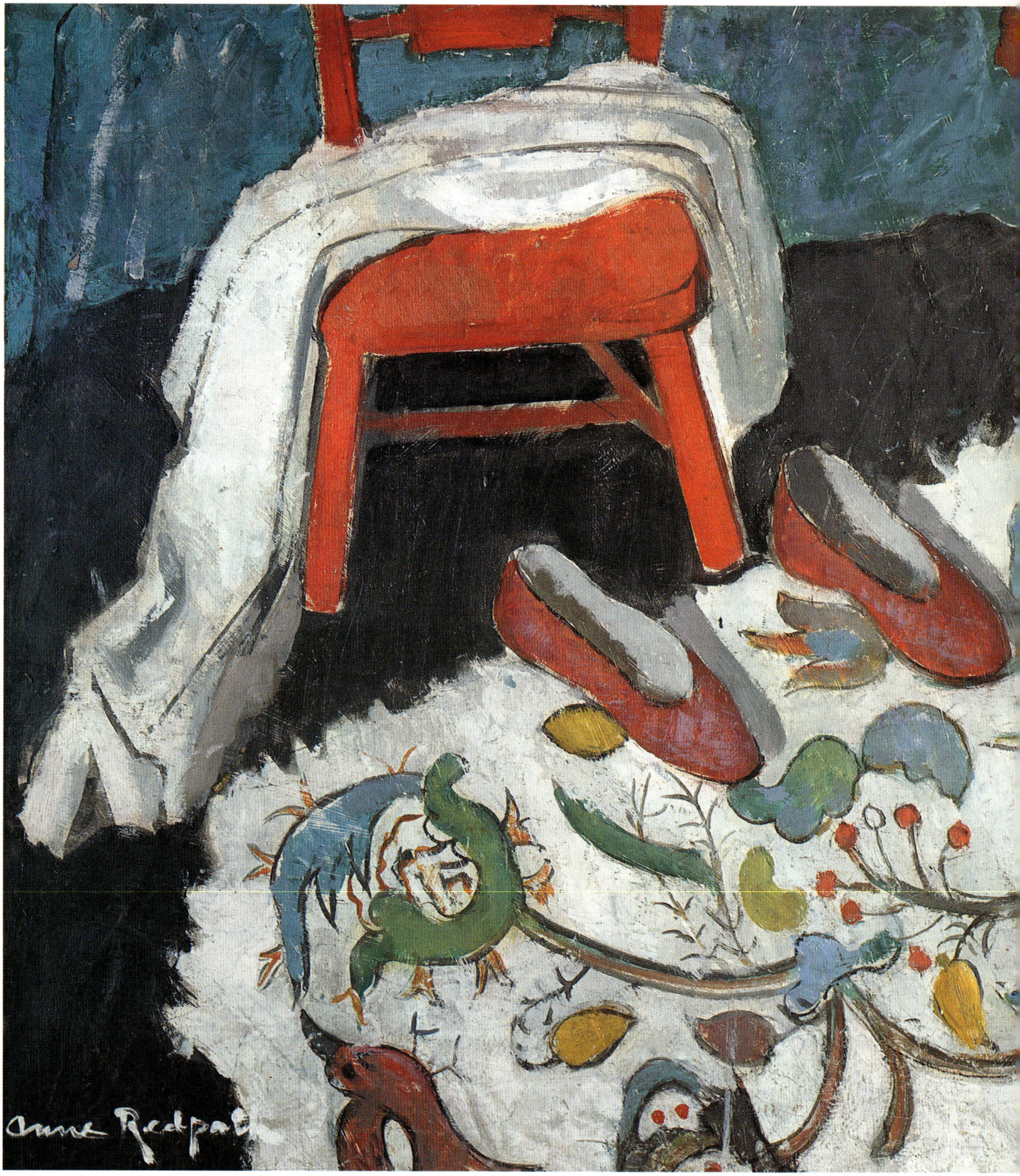

34 The Red Slippers c1942 oil

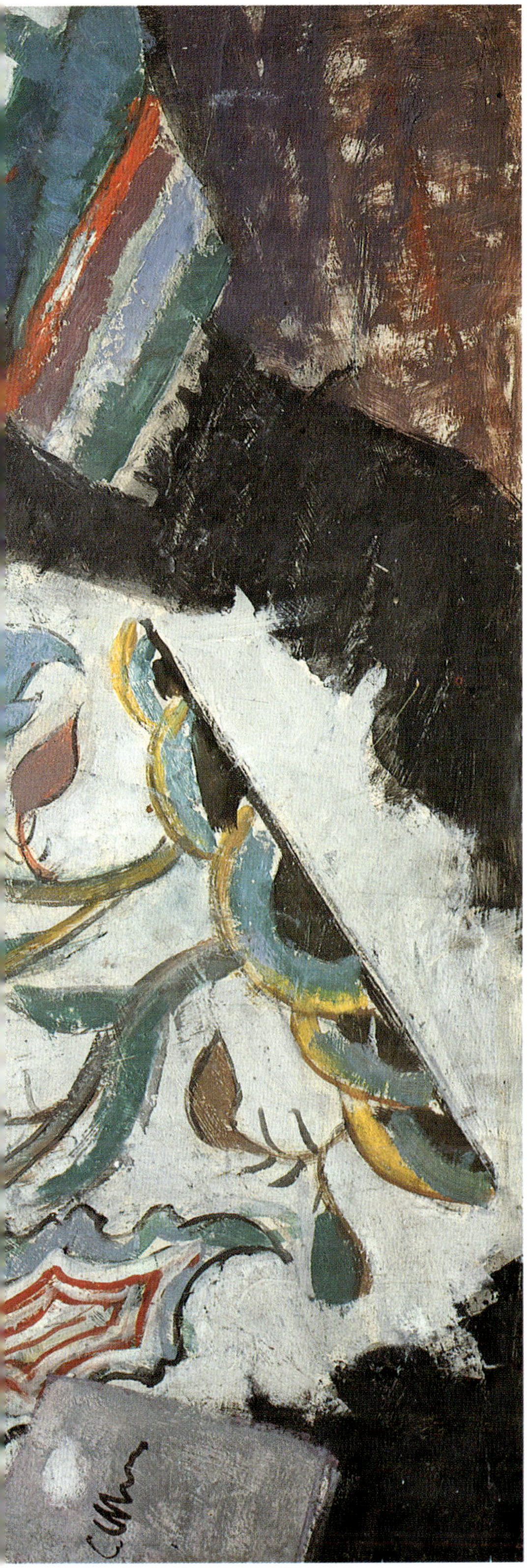

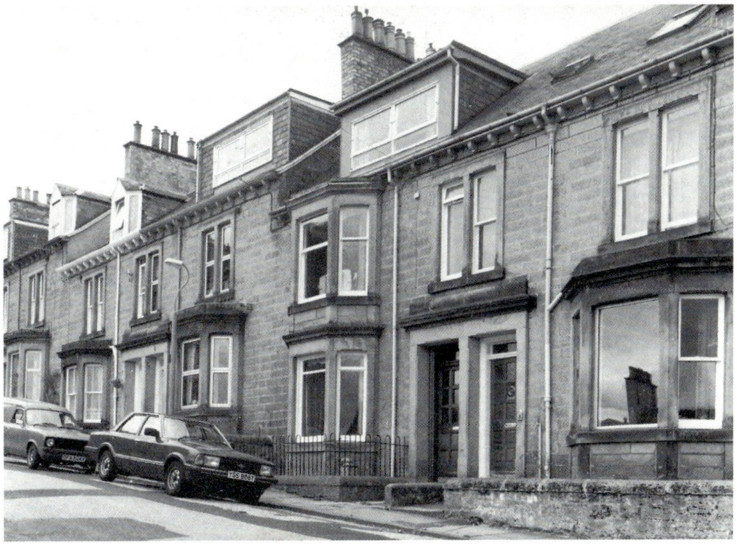

35 52 Orchard Terrace, Hawick

36 Beaconsfield Terrace, Hawick

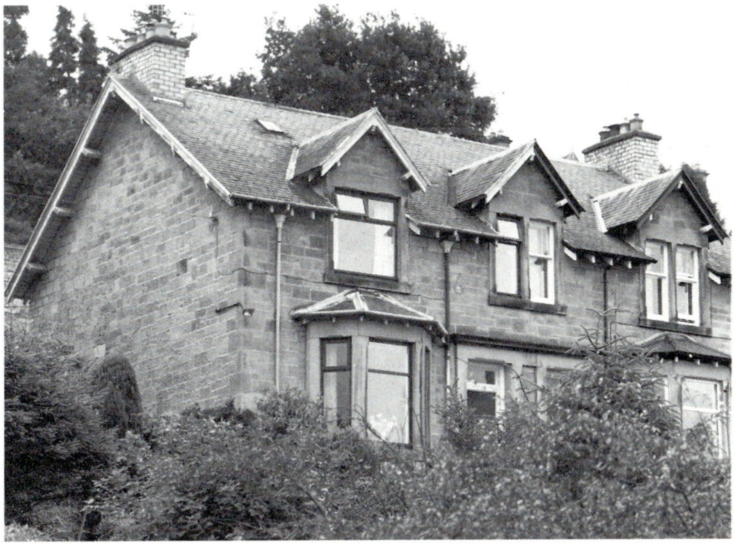

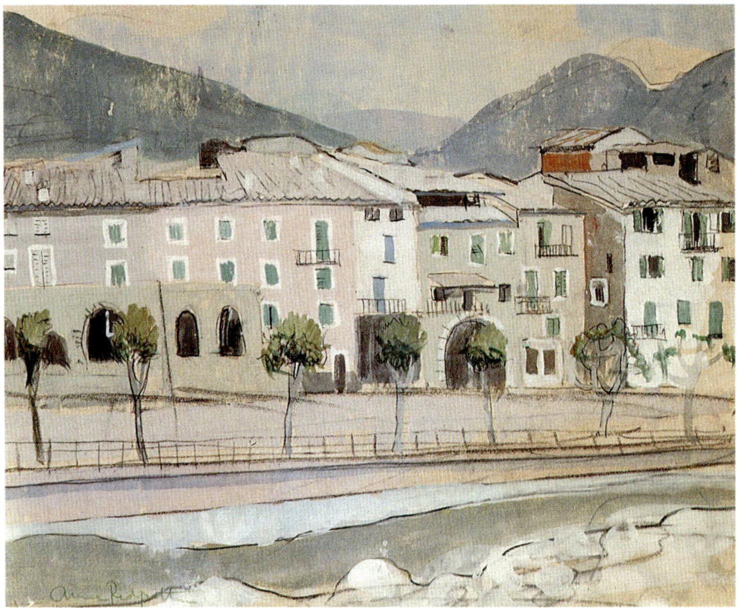

37 Sospel, Alpes-Maritimes 1948 gouache

38 Sospel, Alpes-Maritimes 1949 oil

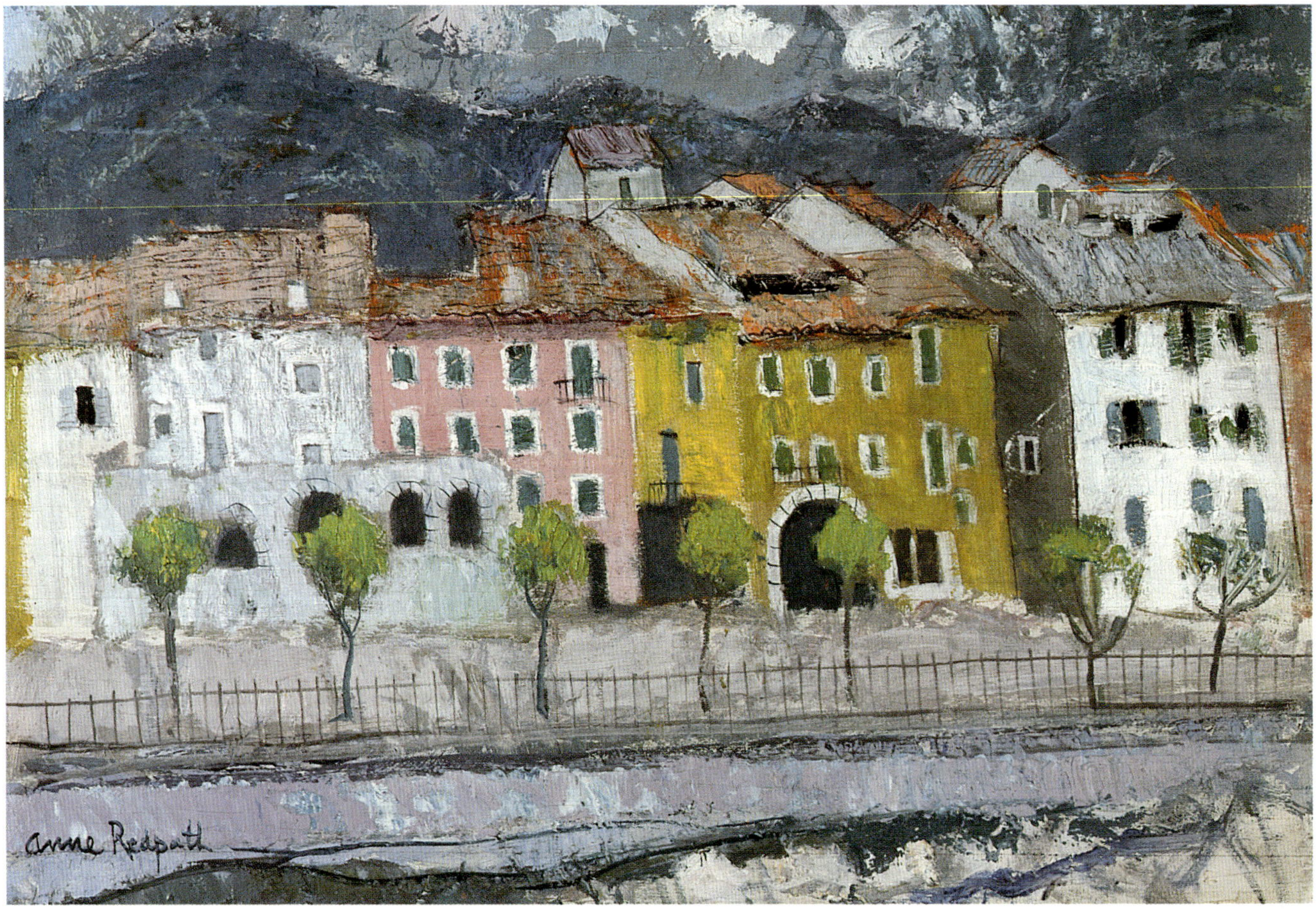

twenty miles from where she had once lived. This was the first of several trips abroad to places as varied as Corsica (1954) and the Canary Islands (1959). New and exotic surroundings became the source of her inspiration and a catalyst for the development of both technique and subject matter.

In Menton she stayed with the Viale family – old friends from the St. Jean days. The landscape was familiar to her and she produced a number of oil paintings that show the extent to which her style had changed since the 1930's. "Window in Menton" (pl 33) is one of her most ambitious compositions, encompassing still life, figure study, interior and landscape with buildings. The Viales had an apartment in a new block of flats which stood across the valley from the old quarter of the town. Anne painted a gouache of three cacti on the ledge of the open window, with a view beyond of the buildings on the other side of the valley. On her return to Scotland, this painting became the basis for a large oil into which she also introduced a back view of her future daughter-in-law, Eileen, seated beside a table on which stands a vase of anemones. Although on close inspection the picture comprises a wealth of broken colour, the effect is subtle and harmonious. This picture became the centrepiece of two solo exhibitions in the early 1950's, but Anne kept possession of it, hanging it in the London Street flat in Edinburgh which she bought in 1952. It is her chef-d'oeuvre of the late 1940's, as "The Red Slippers" is of the beginning of that decade.

Another product of her stay at Menton was a gouache of Sospel (pl 32) in the Alpes-Maritimes. Like the gouache of the cacti in the window, this also served as the basis for an oil painting executed on her return to Scotland. However, in this instance, the two versions are much closer in composition and effect. This piece has a robust charm, with bright and buoyant colour that is typical of her French paintings. They reflect her love of a country in which she felt completely at home.

39 A Fife Port c1944 oil

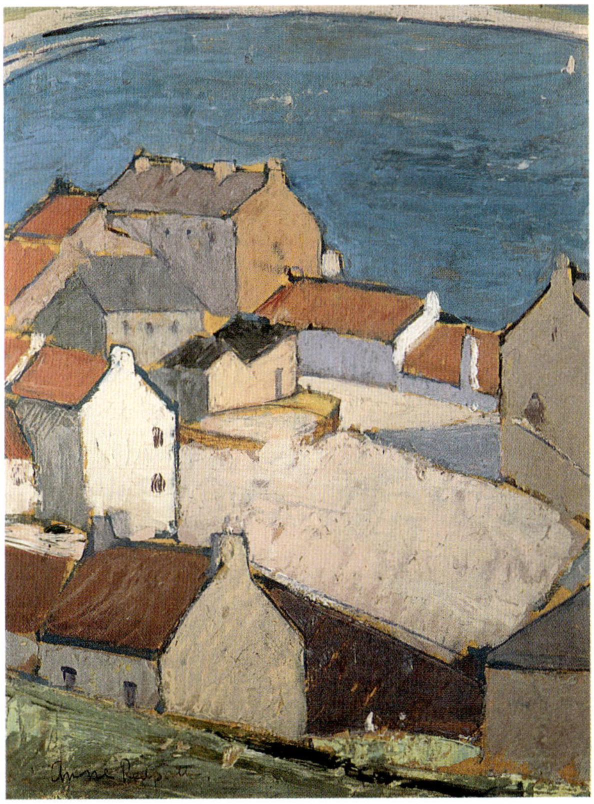

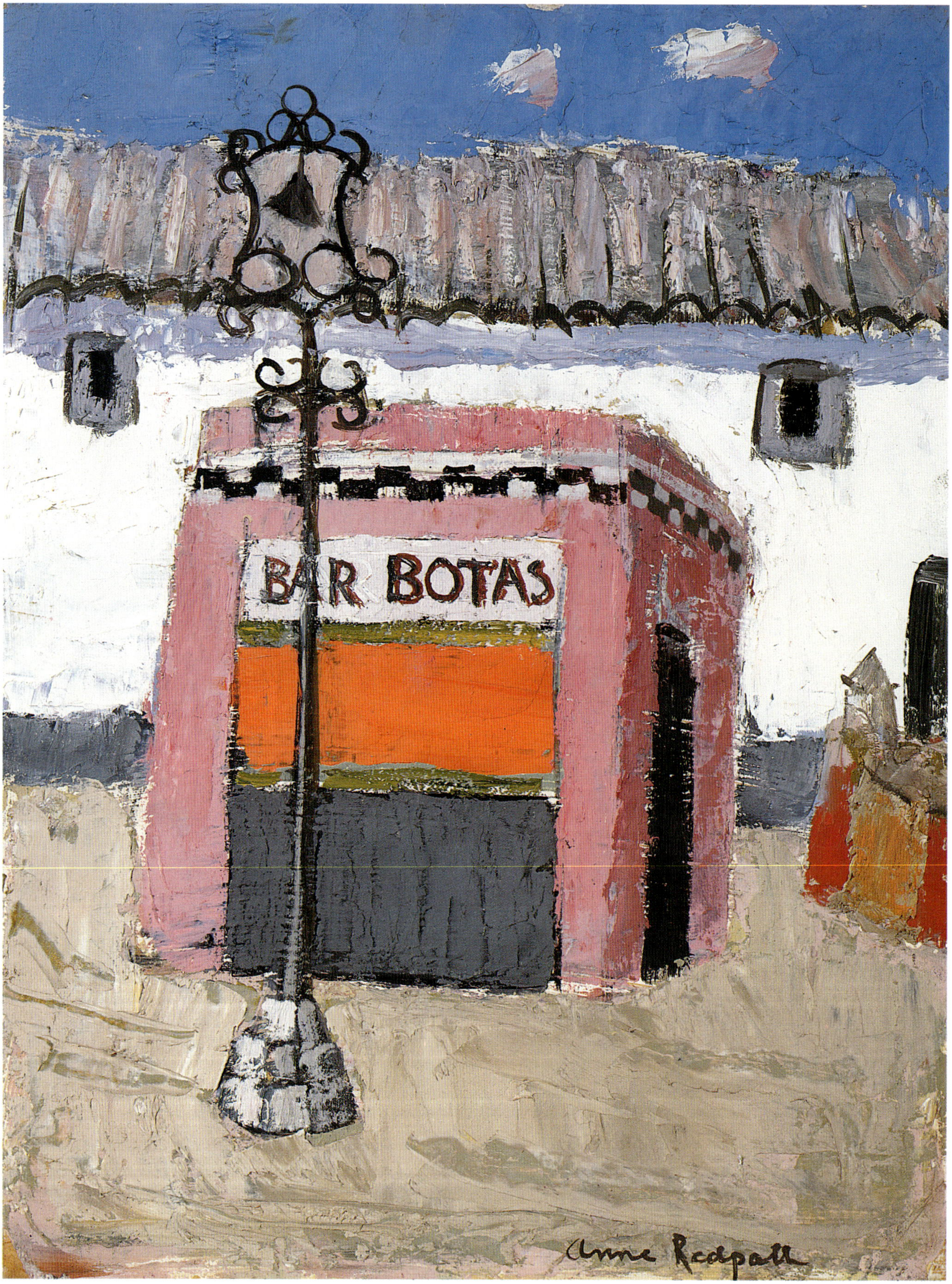

40 The Wayside Bar 1953 oil

Chapter Five

By the late 1940's Alastair, Lindsay and David had all moved away from Hawick, and in 1949 Alastair prevailed upon his mother to move as well. Jim Michie had accepted an appointment as a lecturer in architecture at the Royal West of England Academy in Bristol and was living there. Now there was nothing left to tie Anne to Hawick. She and Alastair bought a house in Mayfield Gardens on the south side of Edinburgh, and this became Anne's first Edinburgh home. David and she lived in the upper flat, while Alastair, his wife and baby daughter had the ground floor and basement.

Edinburgh was an exciting artistic centre – the Festival was in its infancy, with an atmosphere, according to Katie Horsman, "as heady as a Mardi Gras". It was a period of great civic and artistic activity and from the beginning, Anne was completely in her element – so much so that "Vogue" magazine, in its issue of May 1950, reported that "she acts as a social centre for Edinburgh's art world".

Through the Festival Anne got to know a number of composers and musicians, including Clifford Curzon, Benjamin Britten and Peter Pears, all of whom bought her paintings. Tertia Liebenthal, who organised the lunchtime concerts at the National Gallery in Edinburgh for over fifty years, referred to her Anne Redpath paintings as her "household gods". When Yonty Solomon, the South African-born pianist, visited the city for the first time in the early 1960's as a soloist in one of the Liebenthal concerts, he asked Clifford Curzon what he ought to do and who he ought to meet. Curzon instructed him to introduce himself to Anne Redpath and to make sure that he bought one of her paintings. Yonty Solomon said of Anne that although she herself was not musical, her paintings have a lyricism that is attractive to musicians.

These were happy times for Anne. Apart from her own burgeoning career, her family was doing well. After studying architecture in Edinburgh, Alastair had become a successful graphic artist, a leader in his field, producing fashion drawings for Jenners, the Edinburgh department store, and Braemar, the Hawick knitwear firm. Lindsay, the most independent of her sons, was abroad, working for GEC, and David, at Edinburgh College of Art, was starting to display the talent that was to make him a successful painter. In 1951 he married his second cousin Eileen, a favourite of Anne. Jim, in his lecturing job in Bristol, was more settled than he had been since returning from France fifteen years earlier.

Anne had a very close relationship with her sons and is remembered by other members of their generation as being an exhilarating companion. Michael Weir, the son of Anne's college friend Nancy Gass, often stayed at Mayfield Gardens when on holiday from Oxford University, and found her fascinating company, extremely well-read, with the ability to talk on a wide range of subjects. According to her son David, she was ". . . very intellectually active, curious, and would always seek out things that would be of interest to her".

She held strong, reasoned opinions on other painters, and could express her views in an articulate and unpretentious manner. As well as lecturing for the Arts Council, she spoke about Georges Braque on BBC Radio when he was made an honorary member of the RSA in 1957, following the major exhibition of his work at the previous year's Edinburgh Festival.

She also wrote articles for "The Scotsman", including one on Degas to mark the exhibition of his work in the 1952 Festival. In addition to her favourite English contemporaries, Matthew Smith and Christopher Wood, she also admired Gillies, envying him his easy and masterly draughtsmanship, an area in which she felt herself to be weak. She told George Bruce that "the artists I really envy are Eardley and Philipson".

Her admiration, however, was not uncritical. She was uneasy with Eardley's use of materials such as sand, newspaper and grasses; this offended her own belief in truth to materials and she doubted its long term value. The approach of Redpath, the intellectual, contemplative artist, who created a work of art to be treasured, is in marked contrast to Eardley, the highly-charged expressionist artist, who employed whatever materials were to hand, and painted for the here and now.

When Bill Garrad resigned as Director of Edinburgh International House in the spring of 1951, he came up with the notion of "an exploratory visit to Spain". He mentioned this to Anne and she suggested that they go together, sharing the costs. They set off in Garrad's 1935 Rover shooting brake, stopping in Paris to attend the wedding of the Director of the

41 Rain in Spain – Ubeda 1951 oil

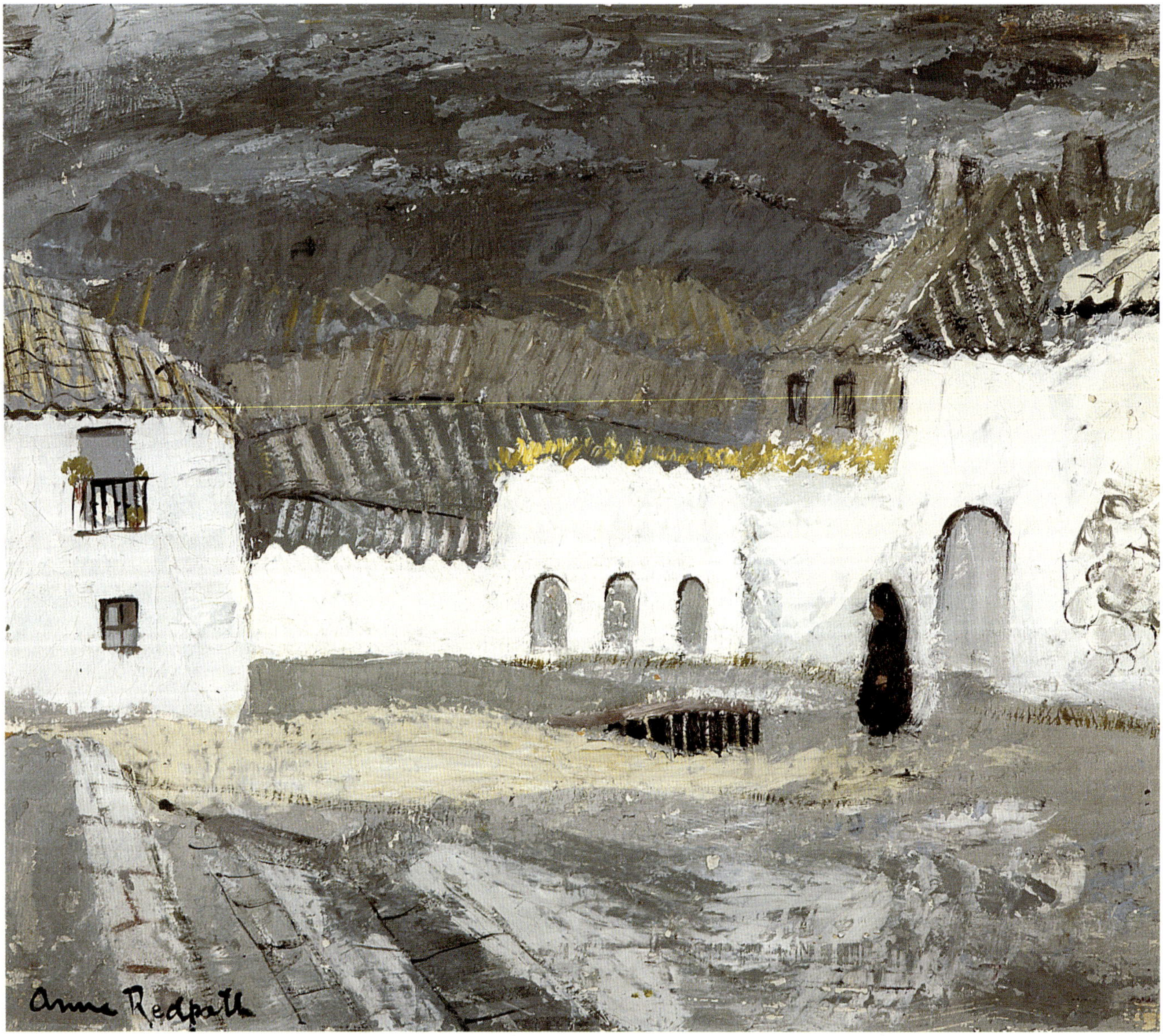

French Institute in Edinburgh. From Paris they continued on to Collioure, near Perpignan, where Anne made sketches for "Funeral at Collioure" (pl 43). Crossing the border into Spain, they travelled along the Costa Brava, then totally undeveloped. The weather was wild and stormy, and Garrad wrote:

"After a difficult drive and many diversions (bridges washed away etc) we settled for a few days at Requena, where she made a few paintings on canvas on a folding easel, very inconvenient in the wind, using white soup plates as palettes, which she threw away when dirty, squeezing her tubes of oil paint from the middle so that the paint came out of both ends – up her sleeves as likely as not, and wrestled in the wind, conversing with all the population that passed (mostly Catalan speakers) in French and Italian, before getting hopelessly involved and surrounded and needing aid to escape (paint on both sides of the canvas, and all over her!)."

Anne learned a valuable lesson from this experience; on subsequent trips abroad, when

42 The Last Hour, 1920, woodcut by Edvard Munch

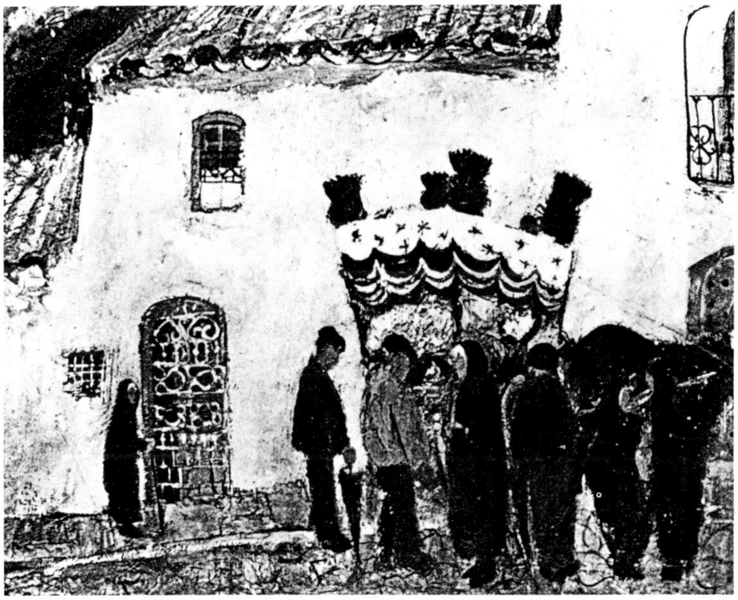

43 Funeral at Collioure 1951 oil

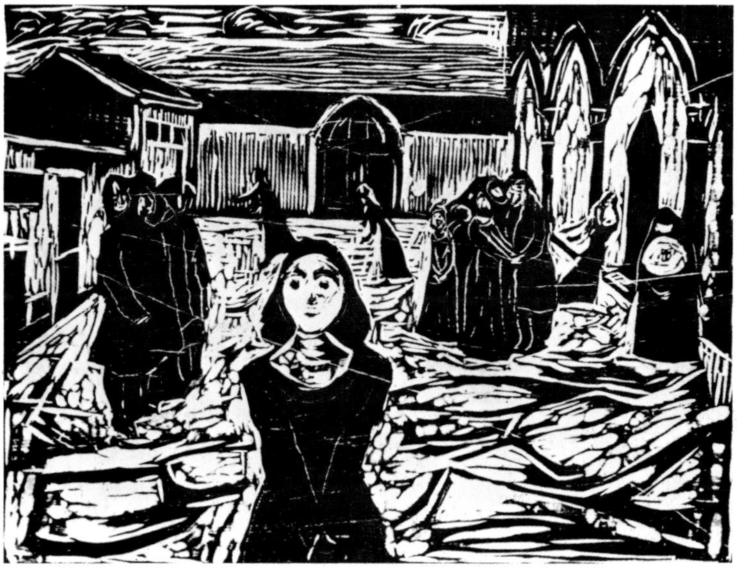

painting out of doors, she used only watercolour or gouache.

In Valencia they ventured into hill villages which were unapproachable by road, even during dry weather, and where the villagers had not seen any outsiders since before the Civil War. They were treated with kindness and great generosity by people who were extremely poor. They travelled further south, visiting many churches on the way. One of Anne's first paintings of the interior of a church was made at Cuenca. It was the start of a series that was to culminate in 1964 in the interiors of Venetian churches.

They visited Ubeda, Granada and Toledo, which they found to be still very poor and dilapidated. They studied the El Grecos and Murillos, drawing and painting on the spot. Crowds of curious onlookers gathered to watch them and, at one stage, they had to be rescued by the local police. Garrad recalls that:

"There were always social difficulties – Anne looked like Queen Victoria; black hair correctly parted in the centre and bun behind, but she wore *colours*! In the cafes on the pavements the waiters had to defend her with the soda-water siphon."

Lastly, they visited Madrid, where, rather than paint, they spent their time at the Prado, studying the work of Goya, Velasquez and Bosch. In a talk to the Spanish Circle, Edinburgh, in 1951, Anne said that the paintings by Velasquez, El Greco and Goya which interested her most were the ones in which there was little colour but an intense interplay of light and shadow.

Turning north, they passed quickly through the Basque country, before stopping in France for a few days' rest at Labastide-Murat in south western France, just north of Cahors, where "all was bland and blue and green, instead of scarlet or black". The trip had taken two months and according to Garrad:

"Anne Redpath's excursion into Mediterranean lands after several years of 'douce' residence in Scotland was a substantial shock to her, and the beginning of all the riches which occupied the last years of her life."

Ten years later, Anne herself said:

"I couldn't paint Spain the way I painted France. It was a much harsher, starker country . . . very bad weather when I was there, and therefore it wasn't the blue-skied Spain, it was a dark, grey sky, and the white buildings looked sinister, sometimes, in little villages with little black figures. Most of the paintings I did there were black and white and grey, and really quite sinister . . . They had to be painted with a kind of strength of manner which I didn't have before, when I was painting the gentleness of even the South of France, with its blue skies and palm trees, and therefore when I came back and painted still life . . . of course they showed the influence of this kind of painting."

Later in the 1950's, when Anne went on painting trips in Fife with David McClure, she used to curse the bright sunny days, declaring that strong sunlight destroyed form and local colour. She preferred dull weather with no shadows, when colour becomes a property of form and not of light.

It was after the Spanish adventure that Anne passed the stage of being merely an abundantly talented decorative artist. Although she continued to declare "I am not an intellectual!" she was developing an essentially intellectual approach to painting. David

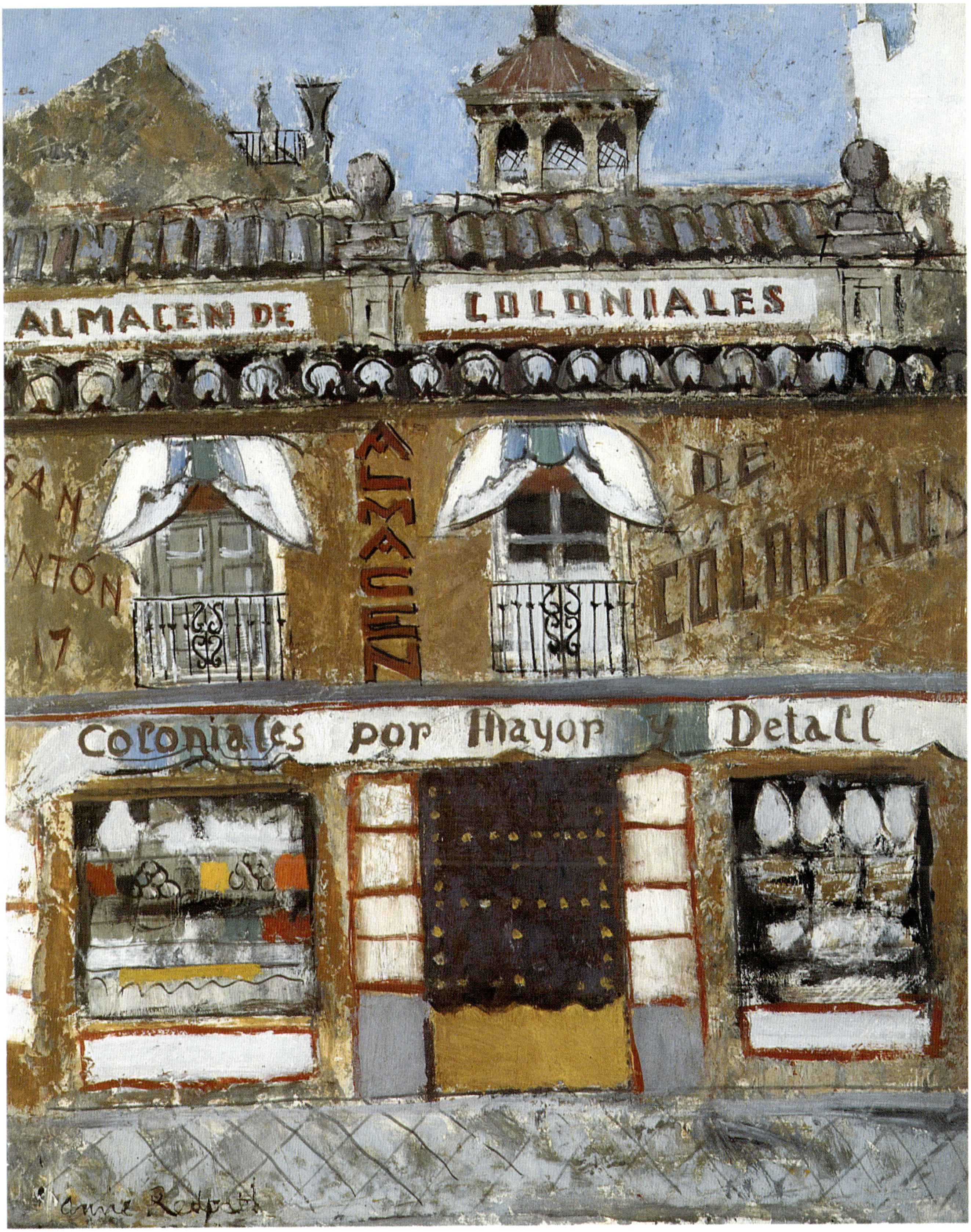

44 Shop Front, Granada c1953 oil

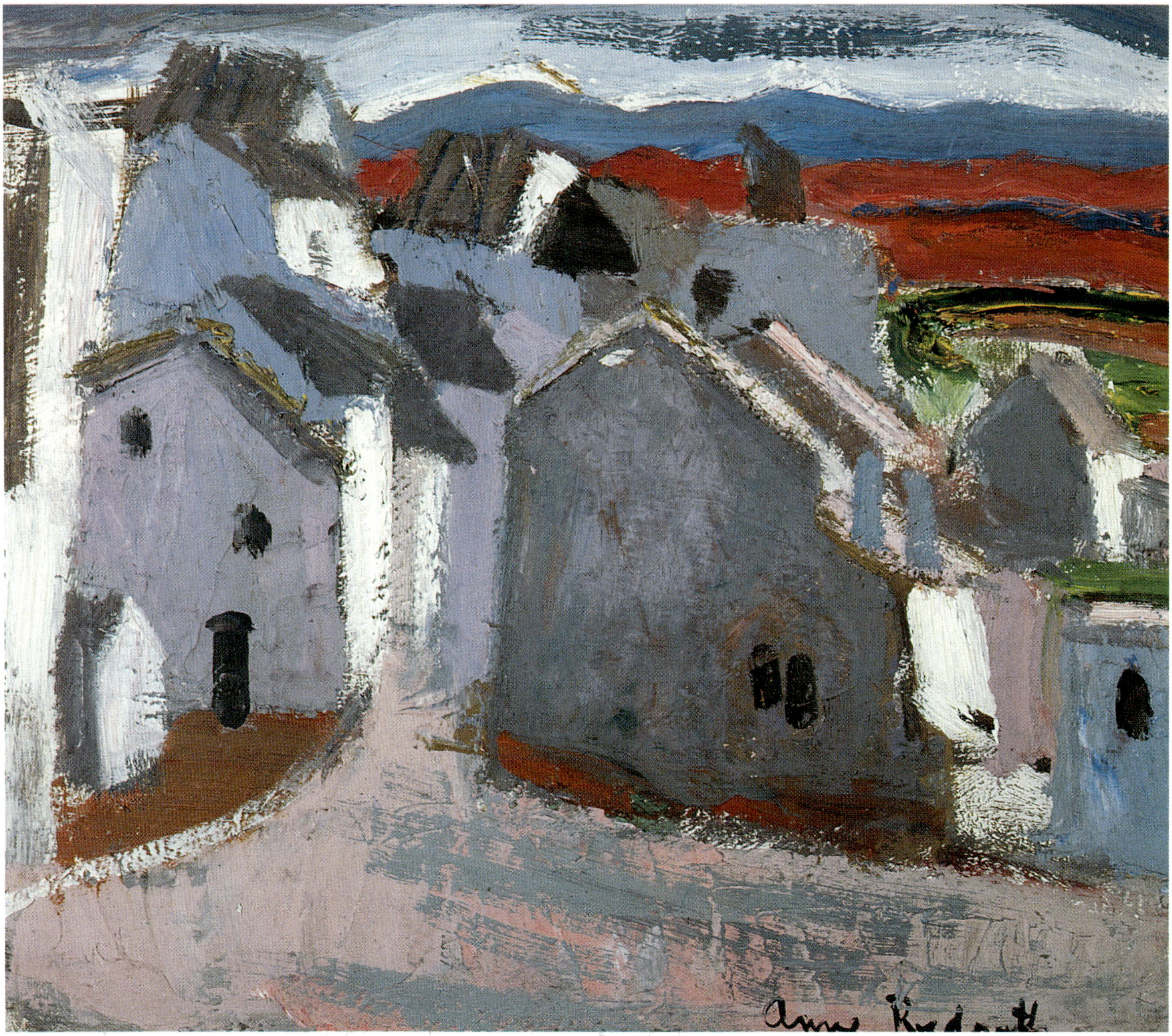

45 Requena, Spain 1952 oil

McClure remembers the occasion when he came into her drawing room to find her sitting in an armchair contemplating an unfinished canvas of a Parisian street scene, which she had loosely fitted into a suitable frame. He asked her what she was doing and she replied "Oh, I'm just doing tomorrow's painting". The amount of forethought implicit in this working method belies the impression the pictures themselves create of having been painted directly and quickly. What Matisse referred to as "the truth beneath the surface" cannot be captured in haste. Katie Horsman remembers a great deal more thought than actual activity going into Anne's oil paintings. The gouaches and colour notes would be executed quickly, on the spot, in order to capture the "essentials", but the painting of the oil itself reminds one of the description of Cezanne at work – fifteen minutes between each brushstroke, occupied by the painter staring at his subject.

Further confirmation of this contemplative approach is found in the BBC's short film of Anne in 1963:

". . . sometimes I just simply see the picture without having anything actual in front of me. I see it as a completed picture and that means that half the picture is done for me. I see it in colour and shape."

In her paintings, the subject, be it landscape or still life, was a point of departure – the raw material of her distillation.

On the 16th October, 1950, Anne's first exhibition at the Scottish Gallery in Edinburgh's Castle Street opened (both the Arts Council's Memorial Exhibition catalogue and the National Gallery of Modern Art's broadsheet erroneously state that her first exhibition at the Scottish Gallery was in 1951). The exhibition was a huge success, both financially and critically. "The Daily Record" urged its readers to go to the exhibition at "an unfashionable hour" because the artist was ". . . one of the most popular, to judge by the crowd found milling around her one man show, . . . and the rash of red spots betokening 'sold' that breaks out wherever her pictures appear".

There were sixty four paintings and watercolours of a wide range of subjects – landscapes of the South of France, the Hebrides, Ireland (which she had visited in 1947), the Borders and Fife, French street scenes, flower paintings and interiors. The most expensive painting in the exhibition was "Window in Menton" at £150. The majority of the paintings were priced at under £100 and they sold very well. Anne commented "I can remember, in the Academy, prices of £800 and £900, but it is no use the artist putting such prices on now". As the artist John Houston has pointed out, it was very difficult to sell contemporary paintings in the 1950's. Collectors with money were in short supply. Anne had good reason to be satisfied.

The Scottish Gallery (then known as Aitken Dott) was the most renowned commercial gallery in the country. Since 1842 it had shown the best of Scottish painting, including several one-man exhibitions for both Cadell and Peploe. In more recent years, Gillies and MacTaggart had shown there, and with this exhibition Anne Redpath had become an established name.

There were no Spanish works in that exhibition, but at the SSA in October and the SSWA in December all Anne's paintings were oils of Spain. Perhaps the Spanish pictures had been held back for separate display so as not to unbalance the Scottish Gallery exhibition, or perhaps Anne was not yet confident enough of their reception. In the following year, at the Lefevre Gallery in London, thirteen of the thirty four exhibits were of Spanish subjects. Anne preferred to show the products of her trips abroad in groups in order to establish a theme. In her 1953 one woman show at the Scottish Gallery all but two of the paintings were of Spain.

One of the first products of the Spanish trip was "Funeral at Collioure" (pl 43) , exhibited at the SSA in the autumn of 1951. It depicts a sad little group of figures, with heads lowered and shoulders hunched, that have an affinity with the figures in the Munch woodcut, which Anne had treasured for so long. The figures are faceless, but, nevertheless, extremely expressive. The painting possesses a sense of gravitas that is far removed from the whimsical, even jaunty, pictures that she had been painting in France. This study in melancholy had actually been conceived before Anne arrived in Spain, but it is suffused with the simplicity and poverty she found in that country, and galvanized by the drama of the weather that greeted her arrival there.

"Rain in Spain – Ubeda" (pl 41), also exhibited at the SSA in 1951, is an example of the grey/white colour scheme that Spain and the bad weather inspired. It relies on subtle tonal values and simple but sure design for its effectiveness. The Munch-inspired black figure appears again.

In contrast to "Funeral at Collioure" and "Rain in Spain – Ubeda", "Shopfront, Granada" (pl 44) recalls one of the few hot days. Anne painted it from her hotel bedroom window during siesta time, and it was the most colourful picture the trip produced. It shows a scene devoid of activity as the town rests in the afternoon sun. The artist explores her fascination with the decorative details of the place – the sign on the grocer's shop, the writing on the wall, the fine intricacies of the trellis work resembling notes on a musical score, all are counterpointed and orchestrated. Whereas many of the Spanish paintings are simple contrasts in tonal value, "Shopfront, Granada" is a work of high pitched colour and movement across a single plane, celebrating a fascination with surface pattern.

A similarly colourful painting, "The Wayside Bar" (pl 40), creates an atmosphere of heat and gaiety. The orchestration of such large areas of strident local colour in such a compressed area demands considerable technical virtuosity. The flat blocks of colour vibrate with life and, to quote Matisse, "sing together like a chord in music". Although Anne's work throughout the 1940's was characterised by a fluency and gathering facility, a criticism that could be levelled at it was that it had become 'cosy'. She had achieved that ambition, shared by Matisse, of creating an art "devoid of any troubling subject matter . . . as relaxing as a comfortable armchair". She painted the "intimacies of bourgeois life" and had arrived at a stage where the public knew what to expect.

Her journey to Spain in 1951 was the first of a series of exploratory visits to new countries which galvanised her outlook. Anne's worry over the reception these paintings would receive proved unfounded. "The Scotsman" critic wrote "Spain has done something to her and she passes it on. She has the mark of the artist – a real reaction to the theme."

46 Church by the Harbour, Spain 1951 gouache

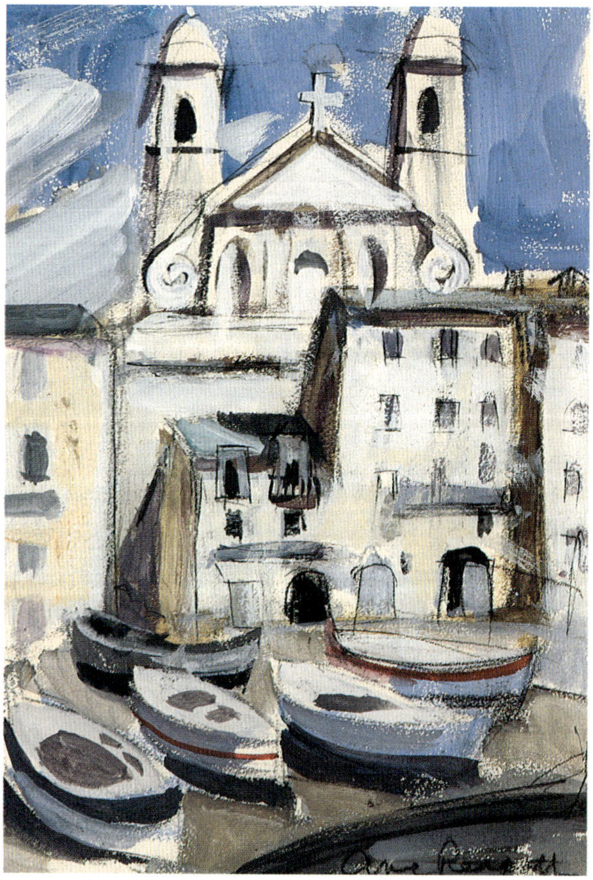

Chapter Six

In 1951 the household at Mayfield Gardens began to split up. Alastair's career took him south to Wareham in Dorset. Immediately before Anne's Spanish trip, David and Eileen had married and decided to buy a flat of their own. At Mayfield Gardens Anne's studio had doubled as her sitting room. Now she decided to look for a house that would give her the space she needed to paint in comfort.

In 1952 she found a first floor flat in London Street in Edinburgh's New Town, which perfectly suited her requirements. This was to be her home for the rest of her life. She painted many of her best pictures here and entertained her large circle of friends with celebrated parties and gatherings. Maurice Kidd, an advocate friend from the early 1950's, tells of Sunday afternoon tea parties at the flat in London Street, when none of the guests had any idea who they were going to meet. Artist friends might include the MacTaggarts, Willie Wilson, or, from the younger generation, Robin Philipson and David McClure – Bernard Leach and close friends Mary Sturrock and Katie Horsman, all potters, might be there – perhaps a Polish Count or various architects whom Anne had met through Jim. Anne revelled in the company of people of all ages and occupation. Victorine Foot, who had recently married the distinguished sculptor, Eric Schilsky, admitted, however, to being slightly in awe of Anne at these gatherings because she was so in command. Many people, on the other hand, remember Anne's great kindness and generosity. Her son Alastair quotes from a letter he recently received from someone who knew Anne well in which she is recalled as:

". . . not just a painter, but as someone infinitely kind and humorous, and an hilarious raconteur. For a time I lived almost opposite her in London Street, when my first husband and I had just parted company. Alec was about four years old. She was marvellous to me – lent me paintings to hang on my horrid walls, dug out your trains for Alec to play with and, frequently, she had a casserole or something that she 'couldn't possibly eat all of', and generally kept us going: even occasionally found she had an extra theatre ticket and so on and so on. I really loved her. I never, ever heard her complain about anything or be nasty about anyone."

In June 1952 Anne, accompanied by David and Joyce McClure and Hamish Reid, who had both just finished their post-graduate year at Edinburgh College of Art, borrowed the house of a mutual friend in Cupar, Fife. They stayed there for several weeks, travelling by bus to the fishing villages on the coast to paint. Anne produced a whole series of gouaches and watercolours which were later worked up into oils and exhibited at the Scottish Gallery and the RSA. She made what David described as one of her more "dotty" remarks when she observed that "you and Hamish make pictures at the harbours; I just put down everything I see – just like McIntosh Patrick!" This was patently not the case since her works on the spot were highly selective and not concerned with detail. "Pittenweem" (pl 47) is a watercolour painted at this time and is a good example of the confident vigour with which her works on paper were executed. It has a strength of design that is reminiscent of the English watercolourists, Eric Ravilious and Edward Bawden, but executed with a bravura that avoids the neatness, bordering on fussiness, of their paintings.

Anne's reputation grew throughout the 1950's and she became a well recognised figure in Edinburgh to a degree that was unusual in the Scottish art world. She was profiled in numerous newspaper articles, for example as number four in "A Gallery of Famous Scots" in "Picture Post" magazine in 1955. Taxi drivers recognised her and knew exactly where she lived. Whenever she was seen at an exhibition or social gathering she was surrounded by a coterie – the centre of attention.

An incident in 1956 sheds light on Anne's character and charisma. Willie and Fanny MacTaggart hosted a dinner in honour of the great Russian painter Marc Chagall at the headquarters of the Arts Council in Edinburgh's Rothesay Terrace. The dinner was quiet and rather formal until Chagall declared that he thought himself always as an old peasant, to which Anne exclaimed "Yes, that's exactly the way I see myself as well!". They both then talked excitedly in French for the remainder of the dinner. Fanny MacTaggart was a little piqued that Anne had been such a success at the dinner of which she was the hostess. A sad contrast to this story is that the same evening someone had introduced Johnny Maxwell to

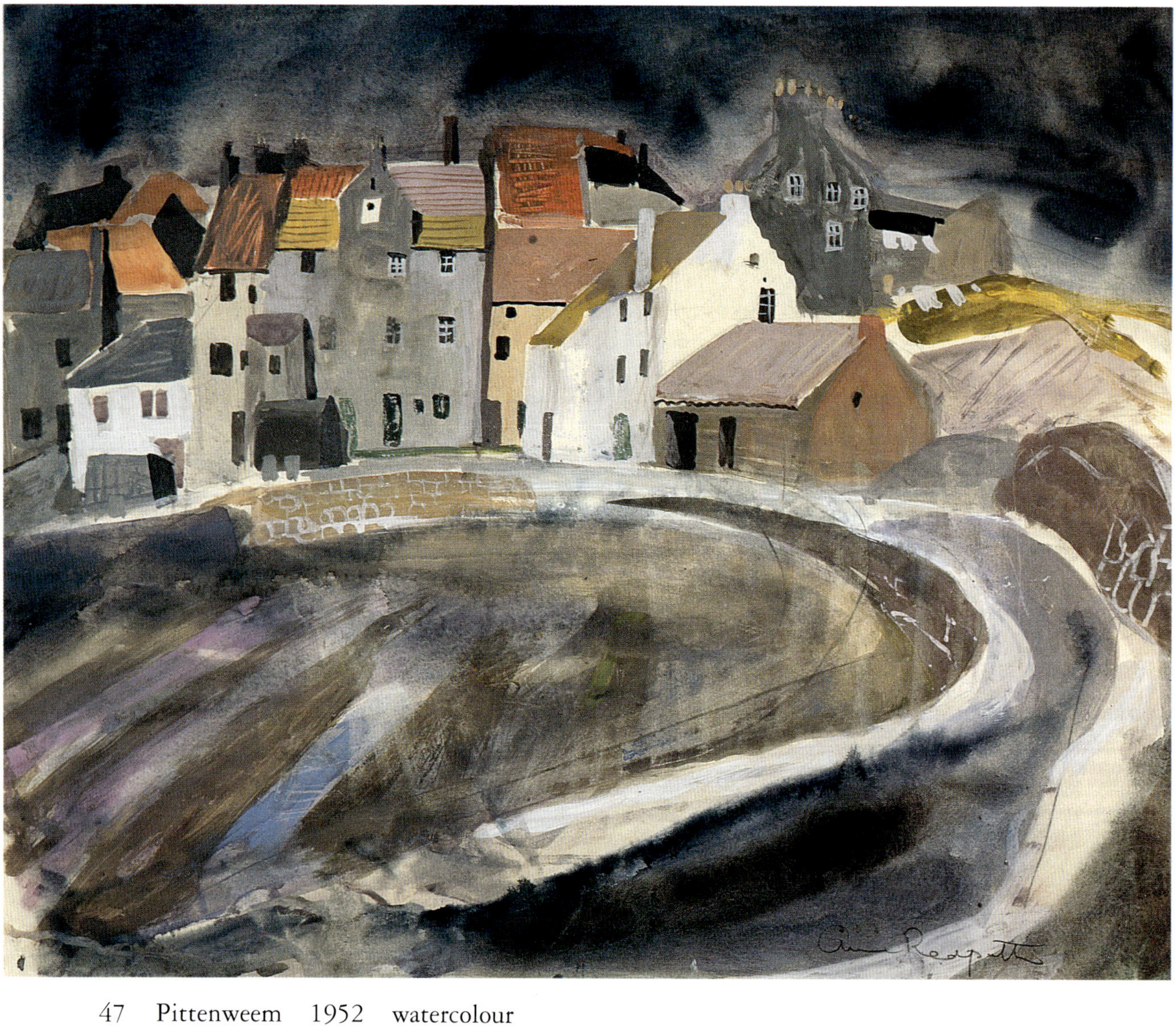

47 Pittenweem 1952 watercolour

Chagall saying only that Maxwell had been a pupil of Leger. "A mathematician" was Chagall's only comment. That was all that passed between the two painters who had so much in common.

Anne's appearance was distinctive. A friend described her affectionately as looking like a teacosy. She often dressed in black with, perhaps, a pair of colourful gloves as a counterpoint. She loved to wear fashionable hats and David McClure remembers her saying excitedly "I have just sold a painting for £80 – now I can buy a Dior hat". After a near sell-out exhibition at the Lefevre Gallery, she rushed out and bought a Dior coat and, for weeks afterwards, was riven with guilt over this extravagance.

Her flat became as idiosyncratic as her appearance. Terence Mullaly, the "Daily Telegraph" critic and a frequent visitor, described the staircase as daunting, but "... on entering everything was changed. Colour and exuberance abounded; from the pottery cat to the putto supporting a table, it was gay and bright. I found it hard to know which was the more fascinating room – her studio or her kitchen. The one, its floor splattered with paint, had scattered about it, among the unfinished pictures, those props that recurred in her paintings. It was a veritable kaleidoscope of colour. But so, too, was the kitchen, a room at once joyous and utilitarian."

The walls of her flat were painted with a house paint that became known as "Anne Redpath White" because she insisted that house-painters produced a pure white for her walls, not off-white or any of the diluted white that everyone else accepted. In the drawing room she hung Venetian mirrors rather than paintings. When asked by a journalist why she hadn't surrounded herself with paintings, she replied "artist's homes are like cobbler's bairns".

In 1952 Anne was elected to full Membership of the RSA. She was the first woman painter to receive this distinction – Phyllis Bone, the sculptress, was made an RSA in 1944. A number of women artists have since been elected to full membership – Joan Eardley, Mary Armour and Elizabeth Blackadder amongst them – but Anne's appointment, at that time, was an achievement of which she was justly proud.

There existed a special relationship between the Scottish Gallery in Edinburgh and the Lefevre Gallery in London; Cadell and Peploe had each been given one man shows in both. It was a natural step for Anne to follow her Edinburgh exhibition with one in the London gallery in 1952. However, she faced the private view with trepidation, since it was bound to be a much less cosy affair than any she had experienced in Scotland. She had the feeling she was being "thrown to the wolves", in an environment where she was not surrounded by friends and admirers.

The Lefevre Gallery produced an illustrated catalogue and the paintings sold well. The exhibition gained favourable publicity in the press when the Government bought "The Red Dish" for the Embassy in Bonn.

In early summer of the following year Anne, accompanied by Lindsay on leave from his job with G.E.C. in Kuwait, spent ten days in Brittany. They made Treboul their base and most of Anne's work was done there and in the fishing port of Concarneau. Many of Anne's contemporaries, including D. M. Sutherland, Willie Wilson and Donald Moodie had spent productive summers in this corner of France. Christopher Wood, too, had rented a cottage in Treboul in the summers of 1929 and 1930 and had painted many of his most admired paintings there shortly before his premature death.

Anne favoured a restrained palette at this time. The harmony she achieves in "Houses at Concarneau" derives from her use of those same colours that she so admired in the work of Braque (the artist she considered to be the most influential of any European this century) –

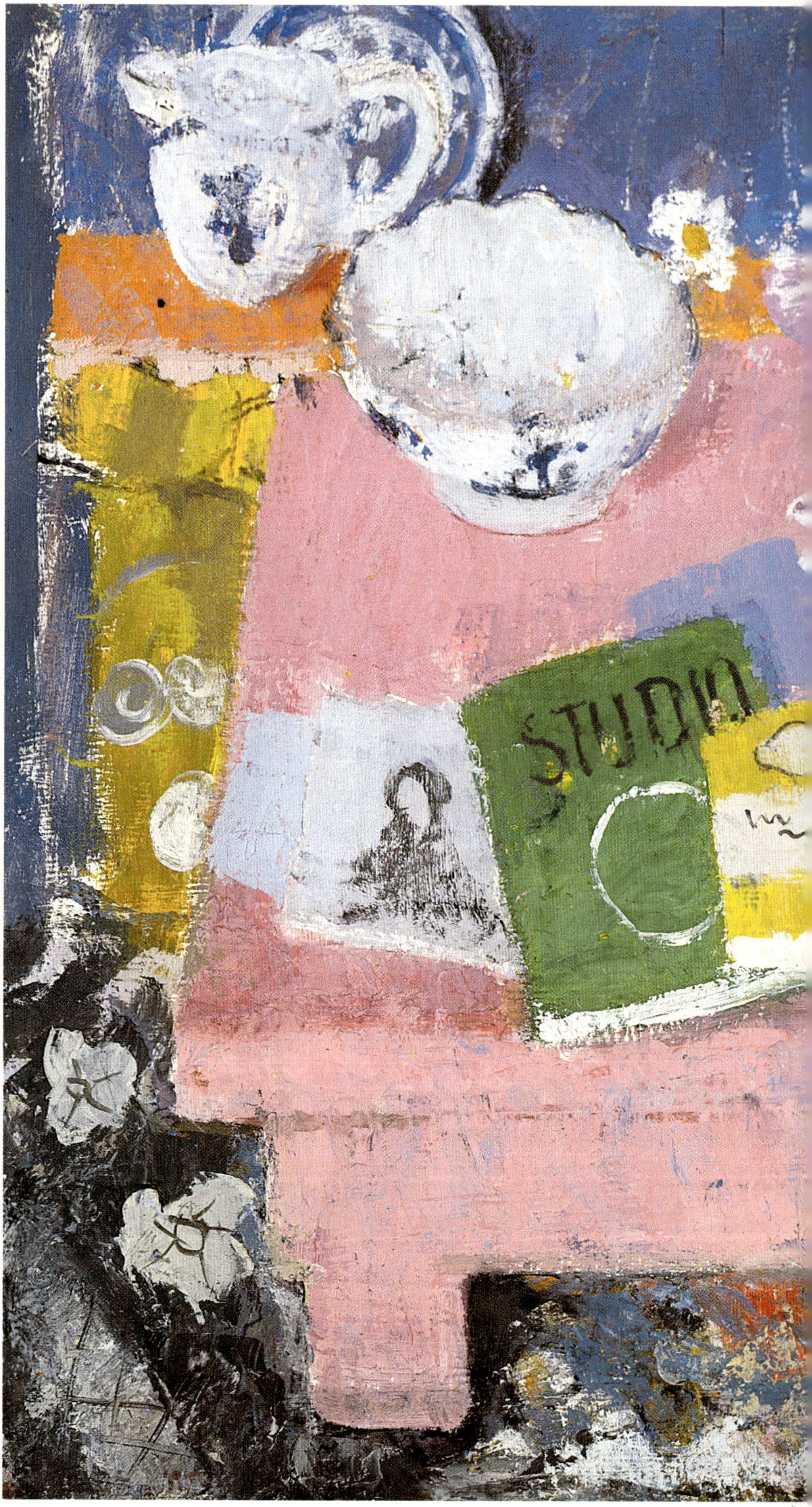

48 The Pink Table c1944 oil

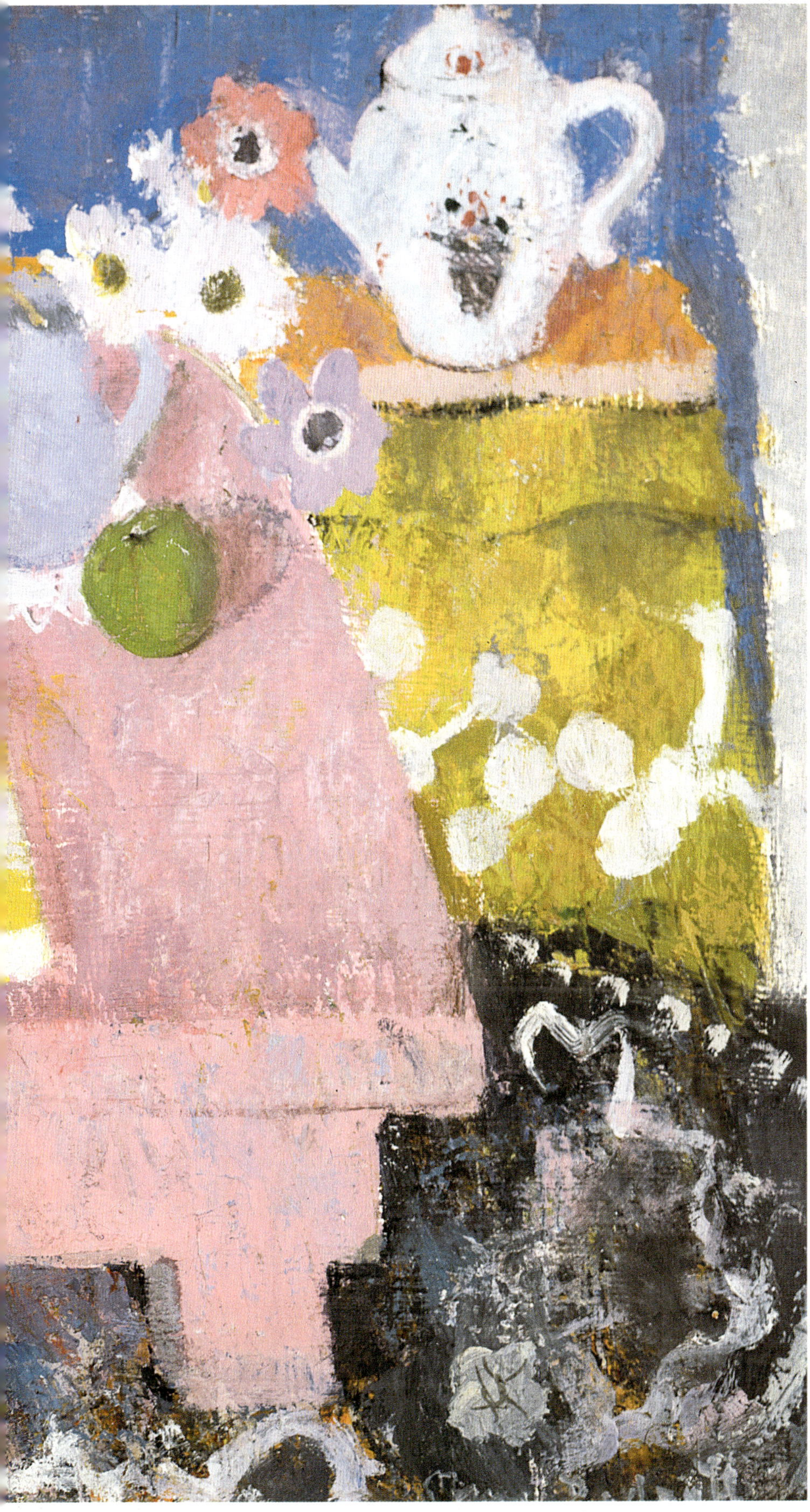

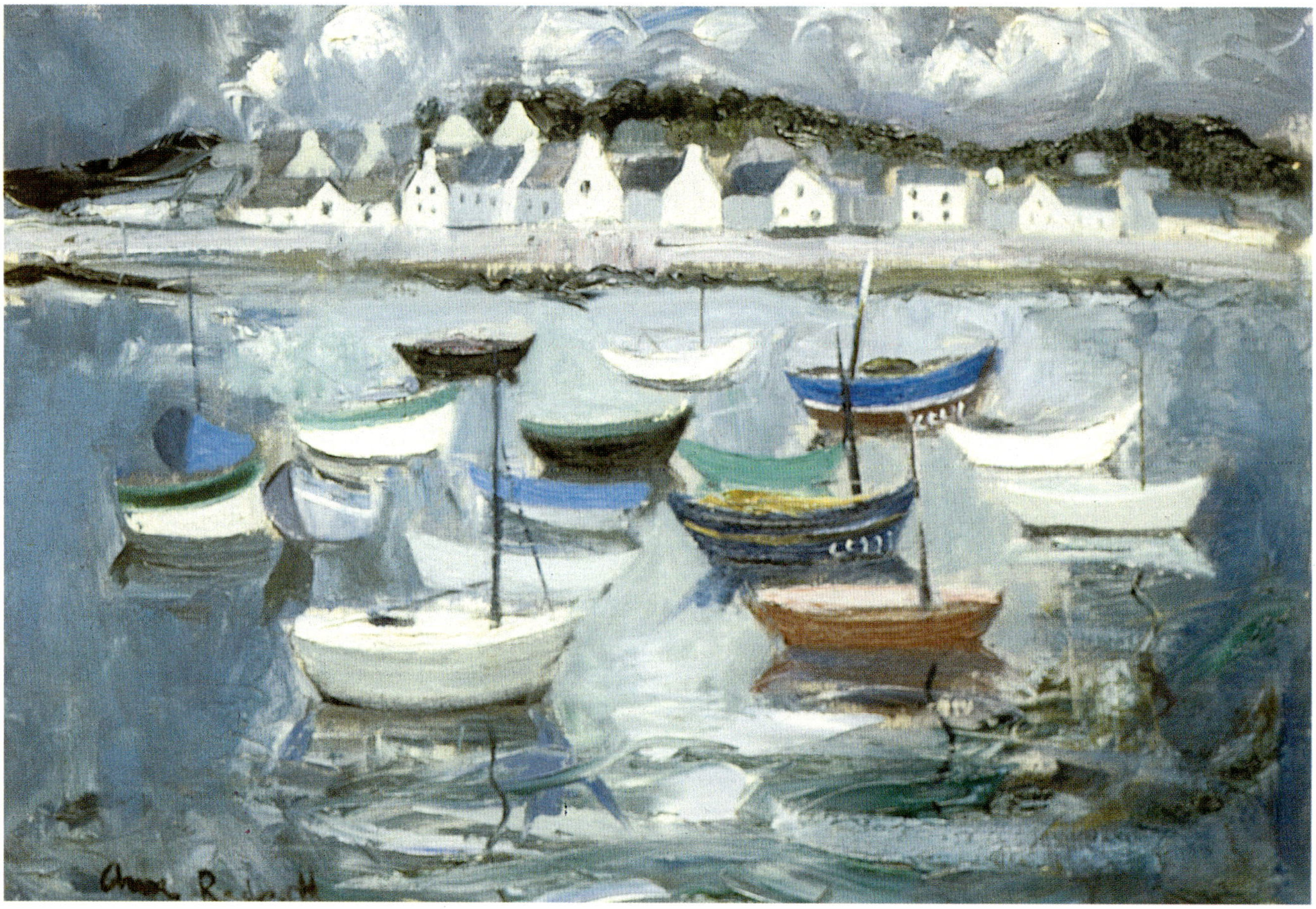

49 Boats at Concarneau c1952 oil

"mouse grey, soft green, and black, both profound yet muted – the colour discreet and restrained in a narrow range". This painting was executed in Edinburgh from a gouache (pl 50) which had been painted on the spot. As with "Sospel, Alpes-Maritime" (pl 38) the gouache and the subsequent oil are very close in terms of composition and detail, but the manipulation of the impasto in the oil creates a satisfyingly trowelled and articulated texture. This, allied to the customary sureness of design, gives the painting its assurance and presence. "Boats at Concarneau" (pl 49), a product of the same trip, has a richer colour scheme and aims at movement, whereas "Houses at Concarneau" emphasises mass.

Although Anne returned from her Continental expeditions brimming with ideas for landscapes, street scenes and church interiors, as many as half the paintings which she exhibited throughout the 1950's were still lifes, featuring objects on a table, plants and flowers. "Spanish Candlestick" (pl 52), which was shown at her Scottish Gallery exhibition of 1953, is a typical example – a still life, designed with confidence and painted with complete assurance. It contains all the staple ingredients of her still lifes of the period – a selection of the objects she had gathered around her, an instinctive control of tone and hue, and her customary flattening of perspective. Typically, she flirts with the commonplace, but what

50 Houses at Concarneau 1953 gouache

51 Houses at Concarneau 1954 oil

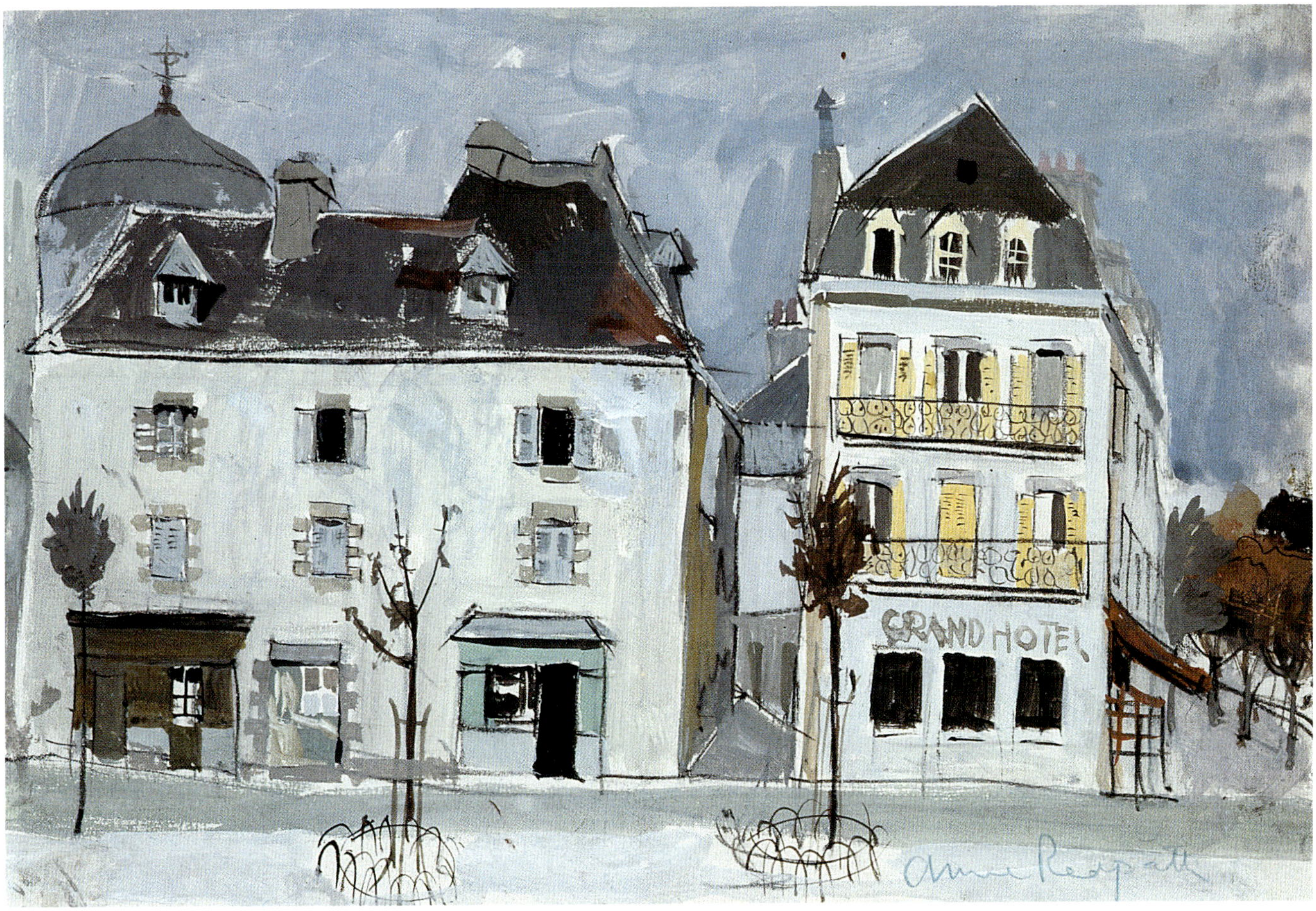
GRAND HOTEL

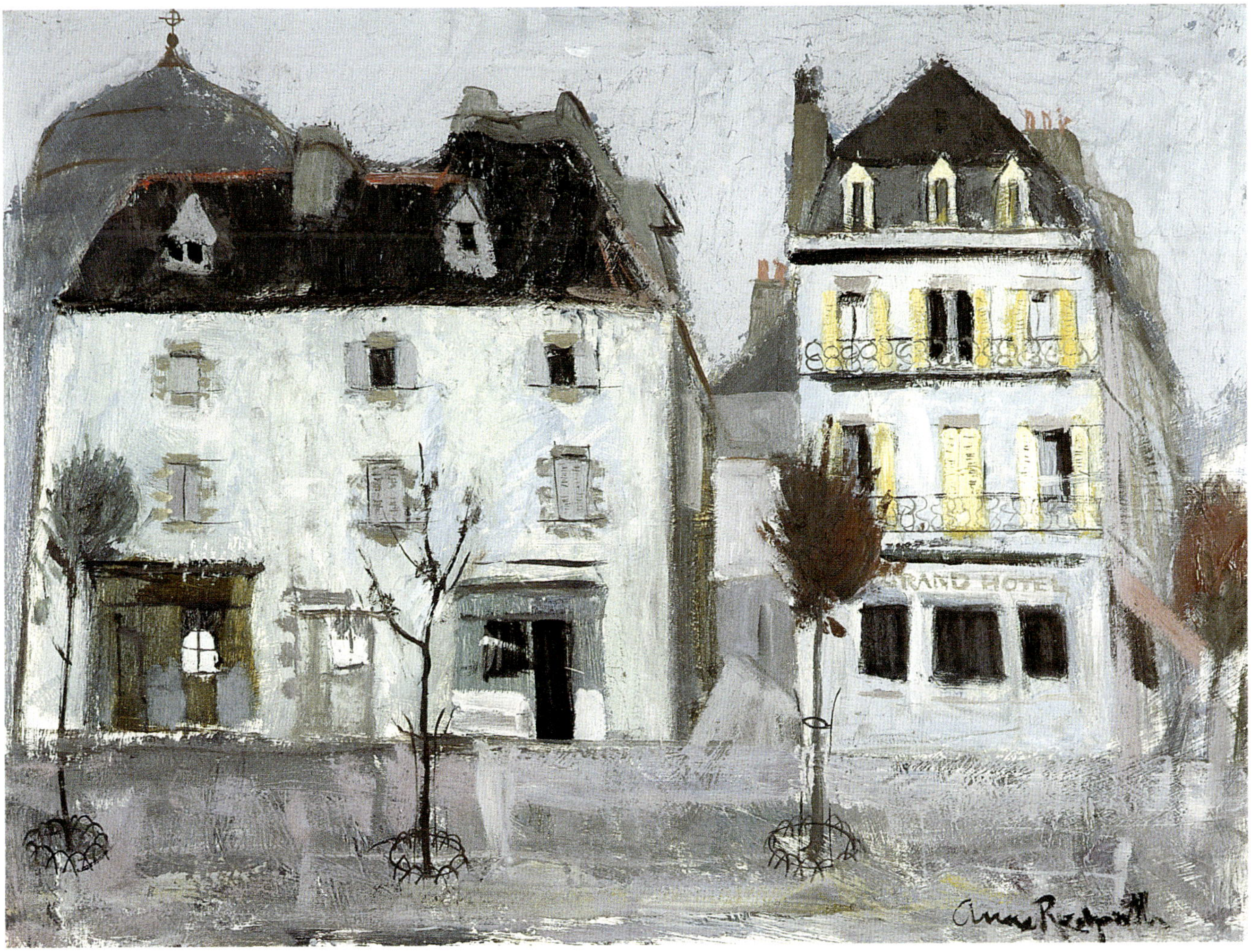
GRAND HOTEL

emerges is distinctly off-beat. The placing of the striped jug, the dramatic verticals of the rug, the angle of the comport and the single, off-centre lemon conspire to create a dramatic tension. When Anne sold the painting to Maurice Kidd, she joked "Be careful the objects don't fall off when you get it home!". Anne sometimes achieved this effect by arranging her still lifes on the floor. This makes the viewer more aware of the form of the objects – a vase or a tea-cup appear much rounder when viewed from above – instead of ellipses, one sees circles. This is an exploration of form and not merely a mannerism. Anne was able to paint a perfectly modelled object with no trace of highlights or exaggerated shadows.

Her exploration of form is also seen in "Eileen in a White Chair" (pl 54), exhibited at the RSA in 1953 . The modelled form of the figure is set against a flattened background with a conscious affinity to Gauguin's work. It displays the stillness and low-key atmosphere that usually characterises her figure studies and portraits.

Anne bought many of the objects which appear in her still lifes from Gordon Small's shop in Princes Street. When she had an exhibition in London, she went to Casa Pupo and a shop selling Mexican crafts. The same items appear again and again – Worcester and Newhall teapots, Portobello figures, pieces of Belleek and a papier-mache cow on wheels. The cow came from the New-Zealand born painter, Frances Hodgkins, in whose landscapes it appears more than once. Anne restricted its use to her still lifes.

As a member of the hanging committee of the RSA, Anne was given responsibility for selecting loan works by non-members for the 1954 summer exhibition. She soon discovered that her interest in progressive and challenging painting was not universally shared. The "Glasgow Herald" published a lengthy article under the heading "The Return of the

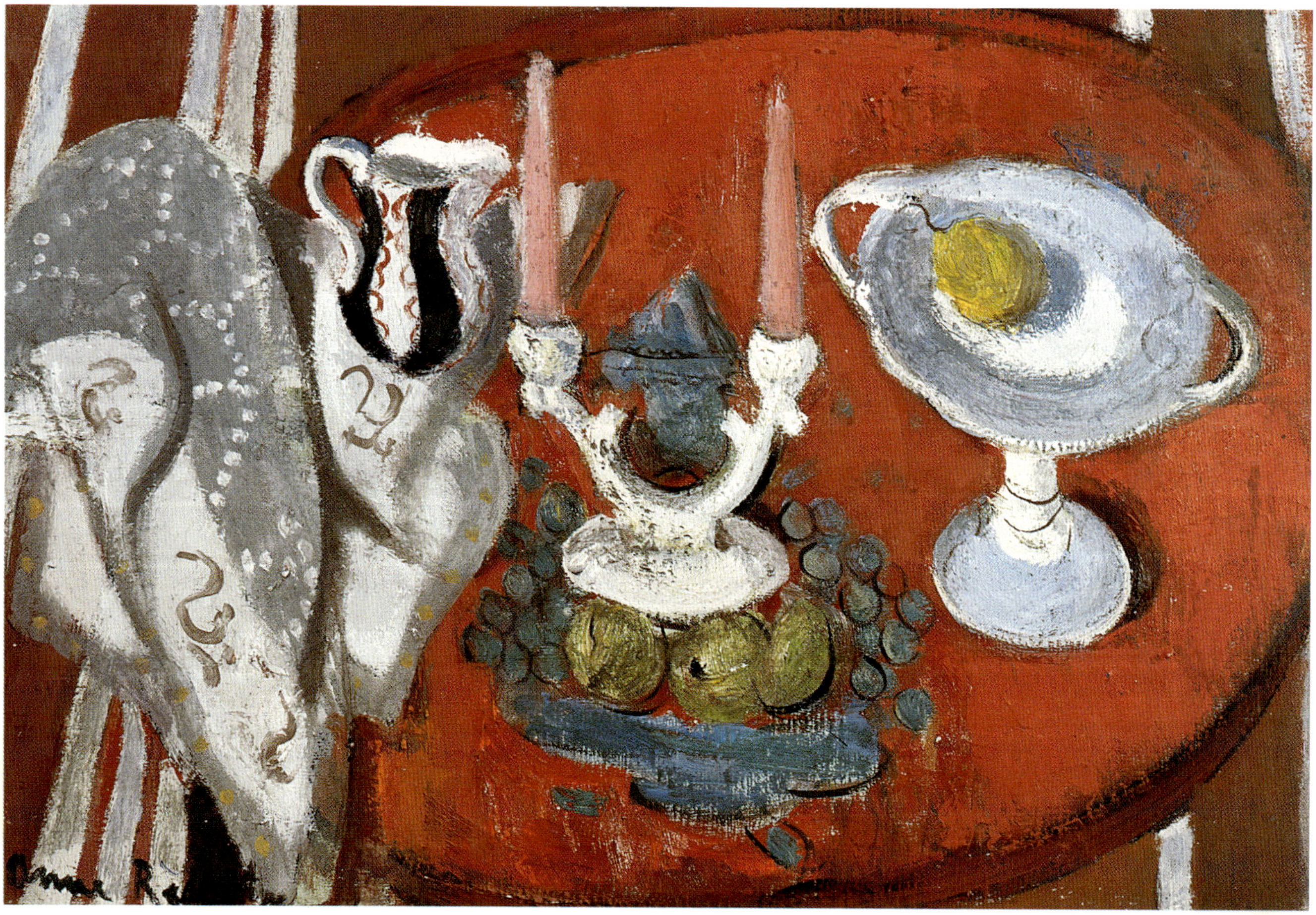

52 Spanish Candlestick 1953 oil

Problem Picture". There were complaints that the RSA had "... surrendered to modernity and the Arts Council". Artists represented included Henry Moore, Jankel Adler, Oskar Kokoschka and Francis Bacon, whose large oil "Cardinal" was at the centre of the most heated debate.

In another year Anne secured paintings for the RSA by her Italian contemporaries Giorgio Morandi, Massimo Campigli and Mario Sironi. They were artists with whom she felt a close affinity since they shared her interest in creating a sense of form against a flattened background.

In June 1954 Anne travelled to Europe again. She went first to Paris for a few days with David and Eileen. David recalls a chance visit to an exhibition of the paintings of Antonio Tapies, the Catalan abstract artist, which impressed them all. Although Anne insisted on the primacy of subject in her own paintings, she happily accepted total abstraction in the work of others. Tapies was a distinctly avant garde artist in the mid 1950's. He was a controversial figure in his native Barcelona, exceptional for having had no formal art training. His heavily textured paintings and constructions, using ground glass and earth, contained no drawing; indeed, sometimes the gestures were so minimal as to be merely a couple of scratches. Given Anne's pride in her own hard won technical mastery, it must have required considerable objectivity for her to accept a theoretician such as Tapies as an equal.

Anne left Paris and continued on to Corsica unaccompanied. She flew to Bastia where she stayed with Donald Duff, a friend from Edinburgh who was teaching there. In Spain Anne had found "dark grey skies and white villages", but in Corsica she discovered "violets and scarlets on the hillsides". Corsica enriched her palette and invigorated her painting. "Roofs at Calvi" (pl 57), painted from her hotel bedroom, has Soutine-like twisting architectural angles, and forms described with primary red lines. The effect is powerful and totally committed.

In her paintings of Corsica she creates the impression that the houses really are as old as the hills – she gives them a "buttress-like" presence. She suggests, simultaneously, erosion, decay and permanence. For Anne Corsica had the same harsh, infertile aspect as inland Spain, but also heat and blue skies. Whereas her Spanish paintings depict village life with black figures and white churches, Corsica is shown unpopulated and unadorned. The cross in "Wayside Crucifix" (pl 56) is painted as something as primitive and natural as the plant growing next to it. Her interest in surface decoration has evaporated – the subject is pared to the essentials.

In the Corsican oil paintings Anne began to bend the lines of the landscape and architecture. Things have become sculpted and rough-hewn. In "Pink House, Corsica" (pl 62) she has created a rhythm of elliptical lines in which the road echoes the shape of the hill and the tree magnifies the arabesques of the iron-work balcony. A gash of crimson defines the contour of the hill, a streak of yellow ochre creates the end in the road and is taken up by the blue shadow of the tree. In Terence Mullaly's phrase, the handling of the paint is "voluptuous yet controlled".

In comparison, the watercolour study (pl 58) is more naturalistic, prettier and lacking the tautness and muscle of the oil. Anne spoke of using the watercolours to capture the essentials but, in this instance, the outdoor esquisse contains details which have been rejected in the finished oil painting. The wrought iron spiral, deftly defined to the left of the pink house in the watercolour, has become an abstracted echo of the shape of the tree and balcony at the front of the main house in the oil. The paintings that were inspired by the Corsican trip are concerned with strength and elemental forces – prettiness and elegance have been cast aside. Anne had initially responded to a pretty pink house by the roadside,

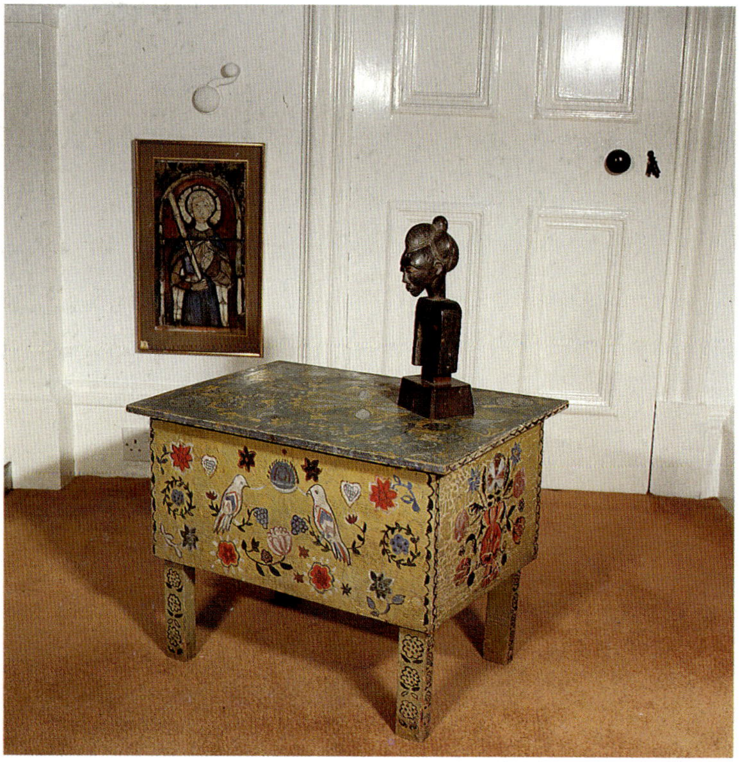

53 A painted chest decorated by Anne c1950

but when she returned to Scotland and painted the oil painting two years later, she created something much more weighty and powerful.

As with her Spanish paintings, many of the Corsican pictures were not completed for exhibition until two or three years after the trip. Other influences shaped her approach in the intervening months and a Corsican landscape painted in 1956 represents more than the subject matter implies.

In 1955 Anne suffered a coronary thrombosis and temporarily lost the use of her right arm. She was never again to enjoy complete good health. It was not until 1959 that she felt strong enough to travel abroad again. Frequently she would feel forced to take to her bed for a few days' rest. Taking this into account, it is remarkable that she produced so much work during her last years, steadily developing her style and expanding her subject matter throughout. In this respect there is a parallel with the career of her contemporary, Joan Eardley. Whilst Anne had heart trouble, Joan suffered from cancer. They both produced their most powerful work in their final years when their health was failing, painting with a vigour and robustness that refuted their infirmity.

Anne was warned by her doctor that she could no longer "burn the candle at both ends", painting by day and going to parties at night. She had to choose between the two. Some of the best parties were held at International House on Princes Street, which was a meeting place for foreigners, refugees, painters, au pairs etc. The atmosphere there suited Anne's cosmopolitan outlook. Anne had the knack of being able to amuse people with her slightly caustic wit concerning mutual acquaintances without ever giving offence. Almost invariably she was the centre of attention at social gatherings and this must have made her doctor's advice hard to follow. Her strength of purpose, enabling her to choose painting and forsake to a considerable extent the social side of her life from then on, was perhaps the major factor in her transformation from a good painter into a great one.

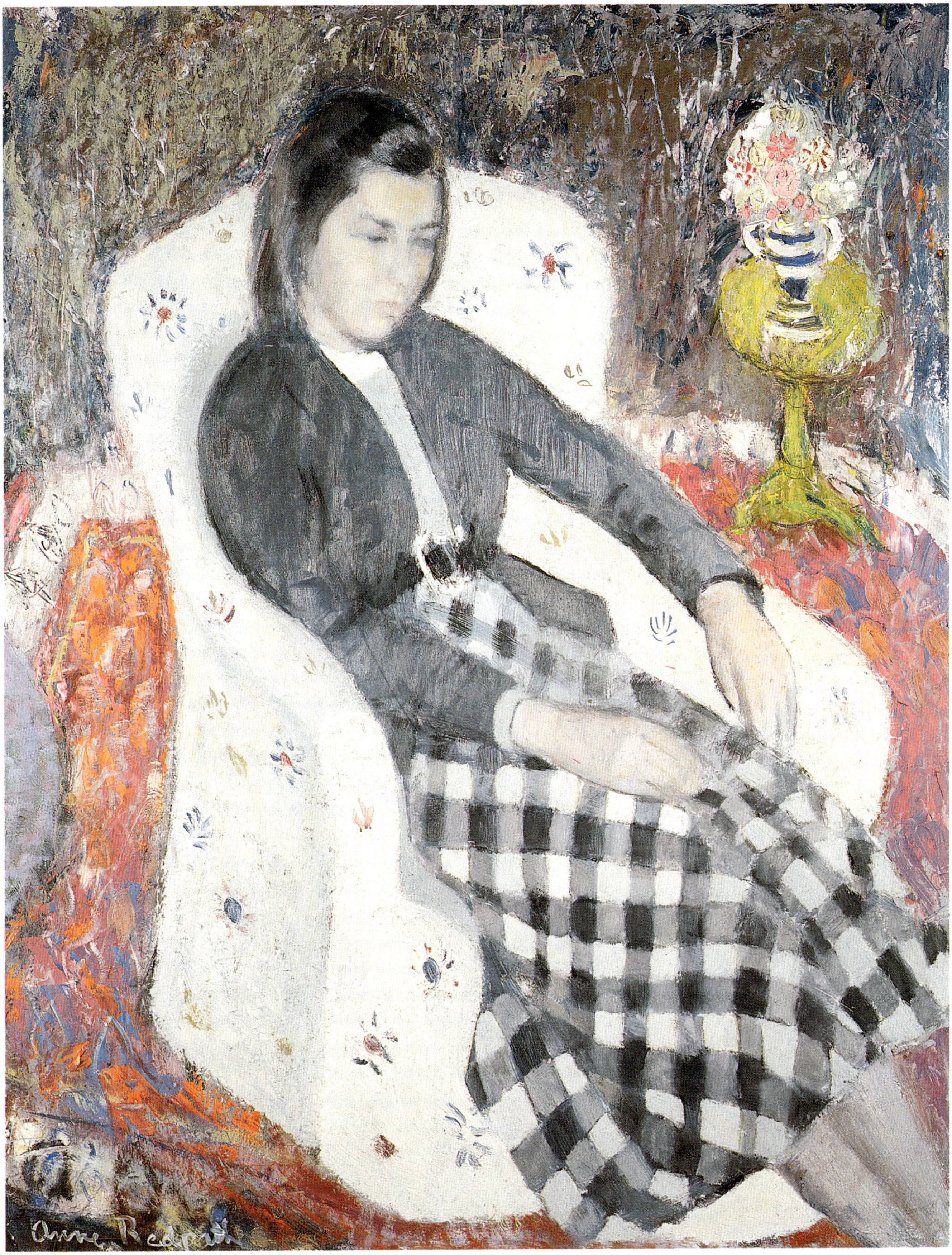

54 Eileen in a White Chair 1953 oil

As a result of her illness Anne did not travel abroad again until 1959, when she went to the Canary Islands. She continued to exhibit Corsican, French, Italian and even Spanish subjects (she had not been back to Spain since her 1951 trip), but still life, and especially flowers, began to play a more important role as subject matter. Out of the forty four paintings she exhibited throughout 1958 (including an exhibition at the Danish Institute in Edinburgh) thirty were still lifes. In the following year (including an exhibition at Lefevre) the number had increased to twenty six out of thirty three.

When discussing the effect of the Spanish trip on her still lifes, Anne said "They were stronger. They were harsher if you like, too. That has been the result of every trip abroad." These comments demonstrate the level of objectivity that Anne could employ when painting, say, a jug of flowers. The object in front of her did not necessarily dictate the mood; she could draw on all her experience for this. Consequently she could paint the watercolour "Flowers in a Teapot" (pl 55) with a delicate lyricism, whilst another watercolour "Poppy-heads in a Newhall Teapot" (pl 75) is painted with an almost aggressive dynamism. The painting of still lifes was not in the least restricting and it is possible that Anne was completely satisfied painting table tops and still lifes throughout these years. The decision to travel again in 1959 was based on her realisation that her Festival Exhibition at the Scottish Gallery would have more appeal if it contained fresh subjects and a new theme.

In the summer of 1955 Edinburgh University bestowed on Anne the degree of Doctor of

55 Flowers in a Teapot c1955 watercolour

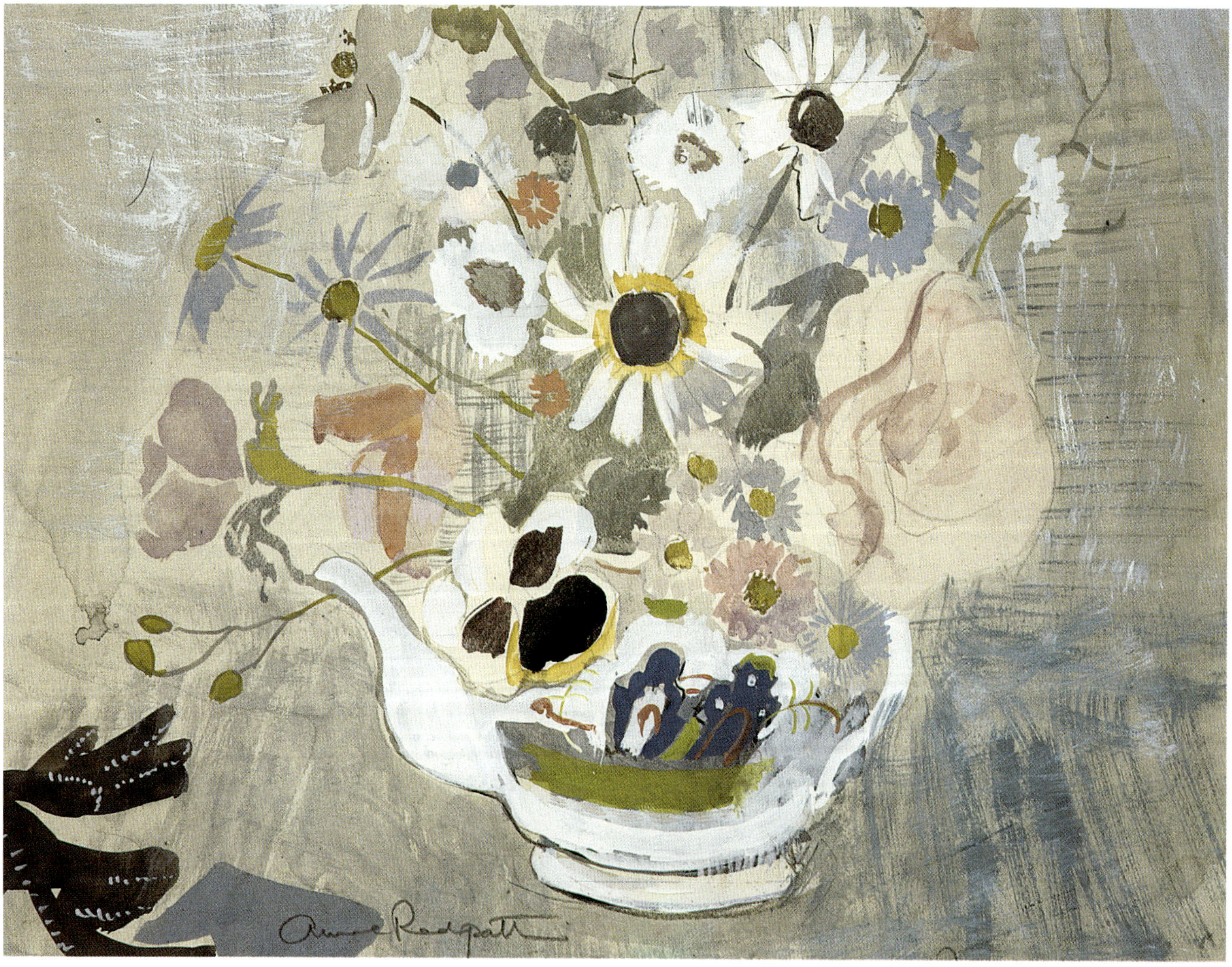

Laws. In a ceremony that gained wide press coverage, Sir Edward Appleton, the Chancellor of the University, said:

"Miss Redpath's father wanted her to go to university but she chose art college instead. Today she has fulfilled her father's wish. In her triumph as an artist she has made the doors of the university open before her."

56 Wayside Cross, Corsica c1957 oil

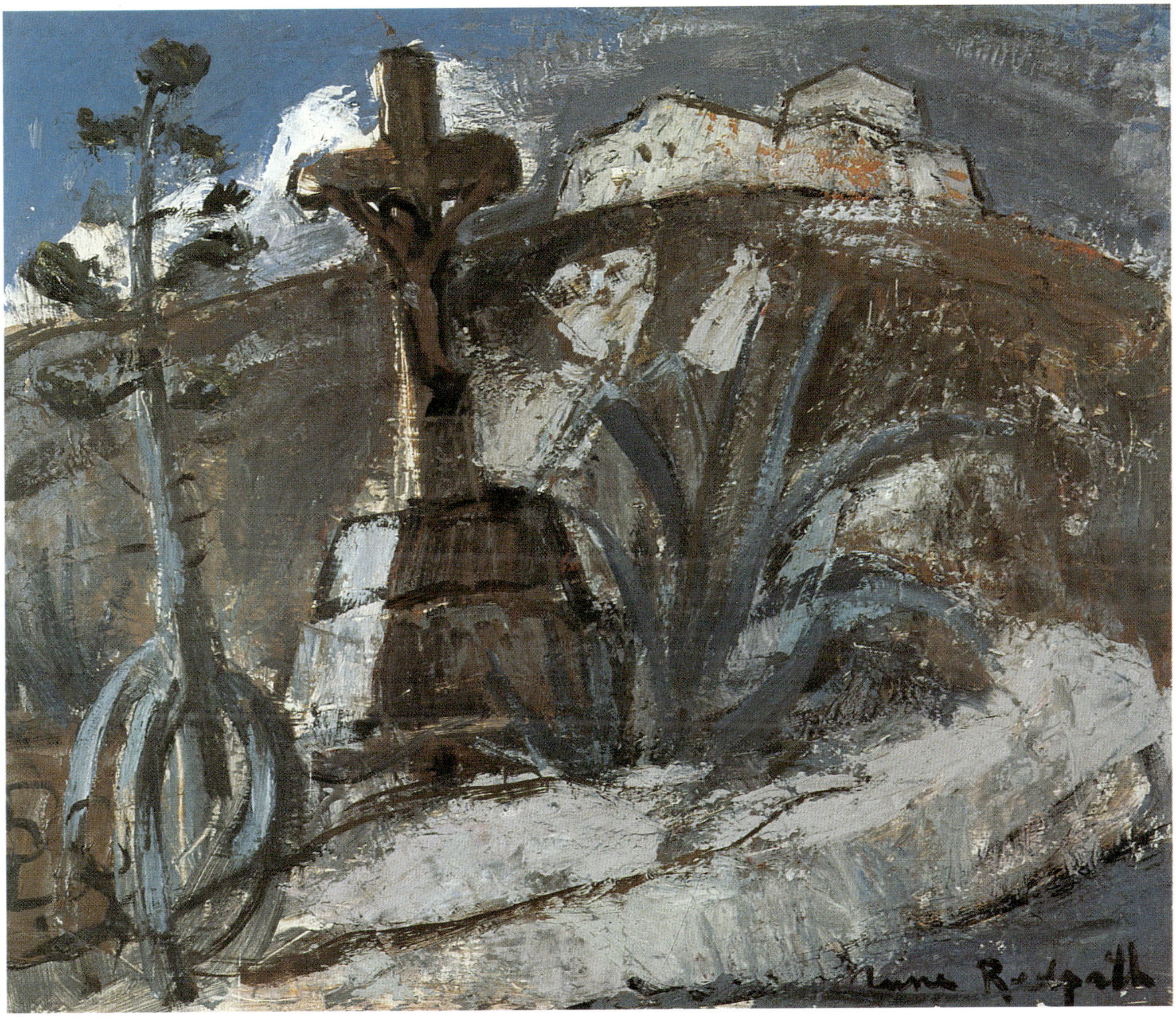

Within a few months of this honour she was awarded an OBE. Anne enjoyed this recognition without either false modesty or any feeling of self-importance. In 1960, when she was elected an Associate of the Royal Academy in London, she told "The Scotsman" journalist who interviewed her that she was the first woman to receive the honour for fifteen years and the first "family" woman ever. Such acknowledgements served to spur her on, giving her the confidence and courage she needed for continual development and never tempting her to play safe. Throughout her career she worried, before important exhibitions, about the reception of new paintings, but it was not in her nature to give the public what they wanted or what they expected.That fundamental weakness has been the debilitating and stunting malaise of Scottish painting from the time of the Nasmyth family, with some of the most glaring examples amongst the later careers of the Glasgow Boys – E.A. Hornel, George Henry, David Gauld and Stuart Park in particular. Conspicuous exceptions are the elder McTaggart, Eardley and Redpath.

Although Redpath paintings were always amongst the first to sell at group exhibitions, and her one-woman shows, whether in London, Edinburgh or the provinces, were without exception successful, Anne never quite lost her inherent anxiety over money and security. Two stories, a decade apart, demonstrate this. In 1953 she invited Michael Weir to her studio in London Street so that he could choose a painting as a wedding present. He picked a Spanish scene which she had only recently finished. When he returned to collect the picture some weeks later, Anne admitted that it had since been sold to pay a grocery bill – so he went away with a still life instead. She was always an exceptionally generous person, as many people still testify. However, throughout her career her paintings remained her only source of income. Unlike the majority of RSA painters, she did not have an income from

57 Roofs at Calvi c1957 oil

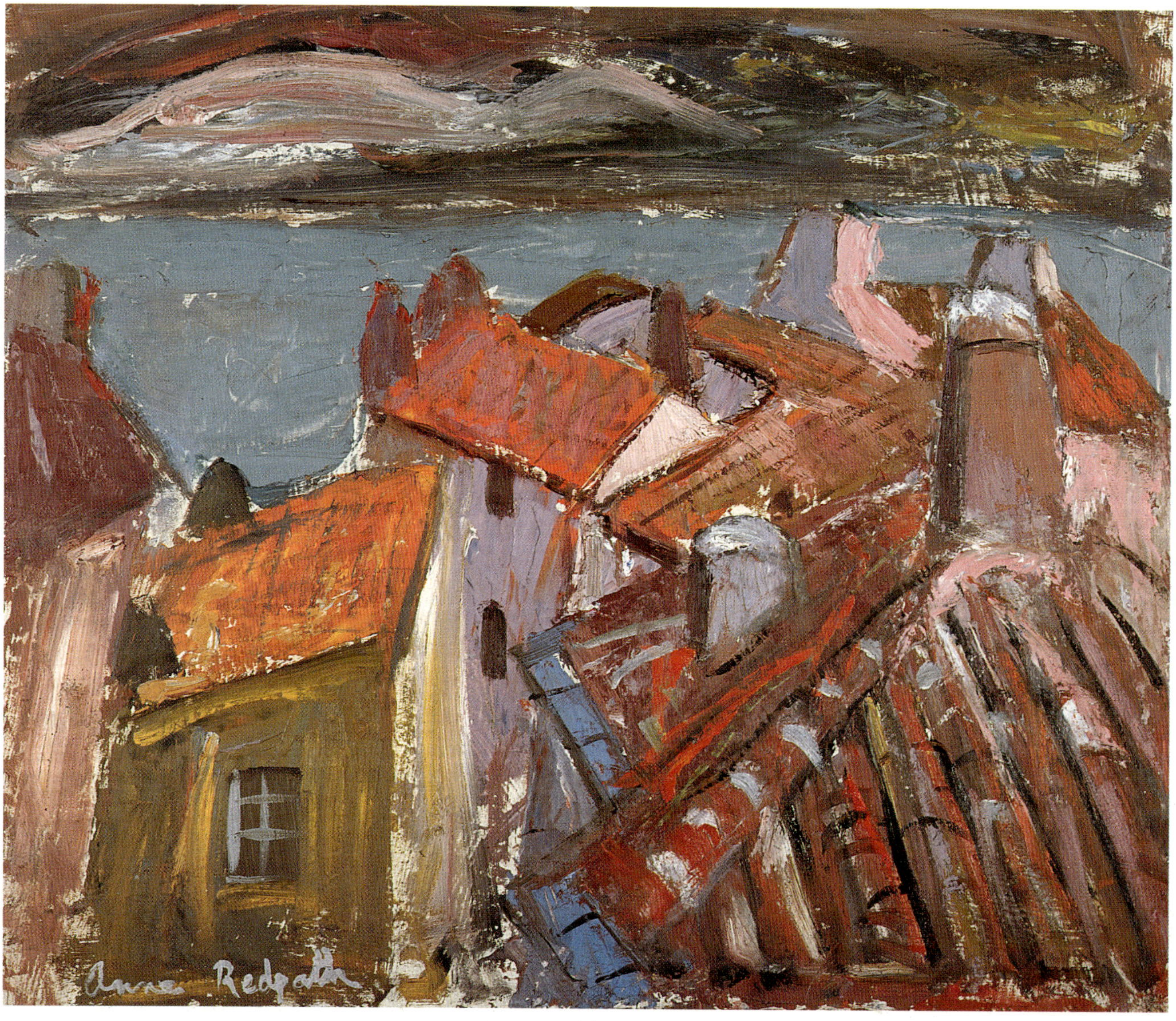

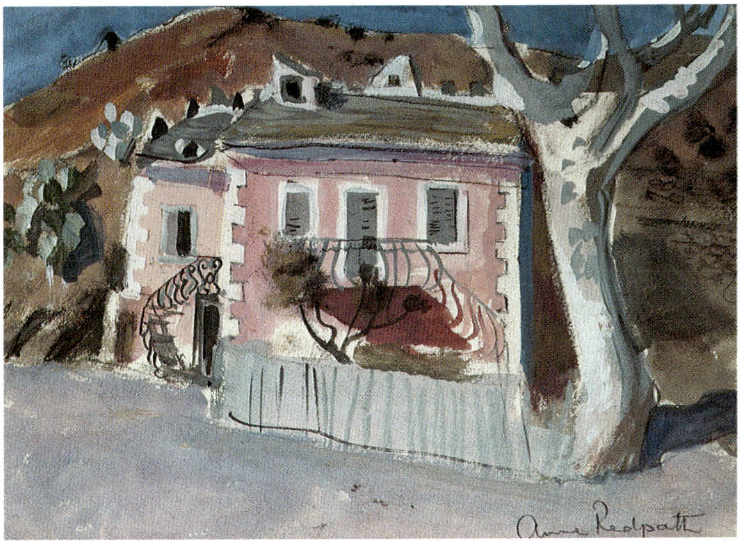

58 Pink Cottage in Corsica 1954 gouache & watercolour

59 In the Chapel of St Jean, Treboul c1954 oil

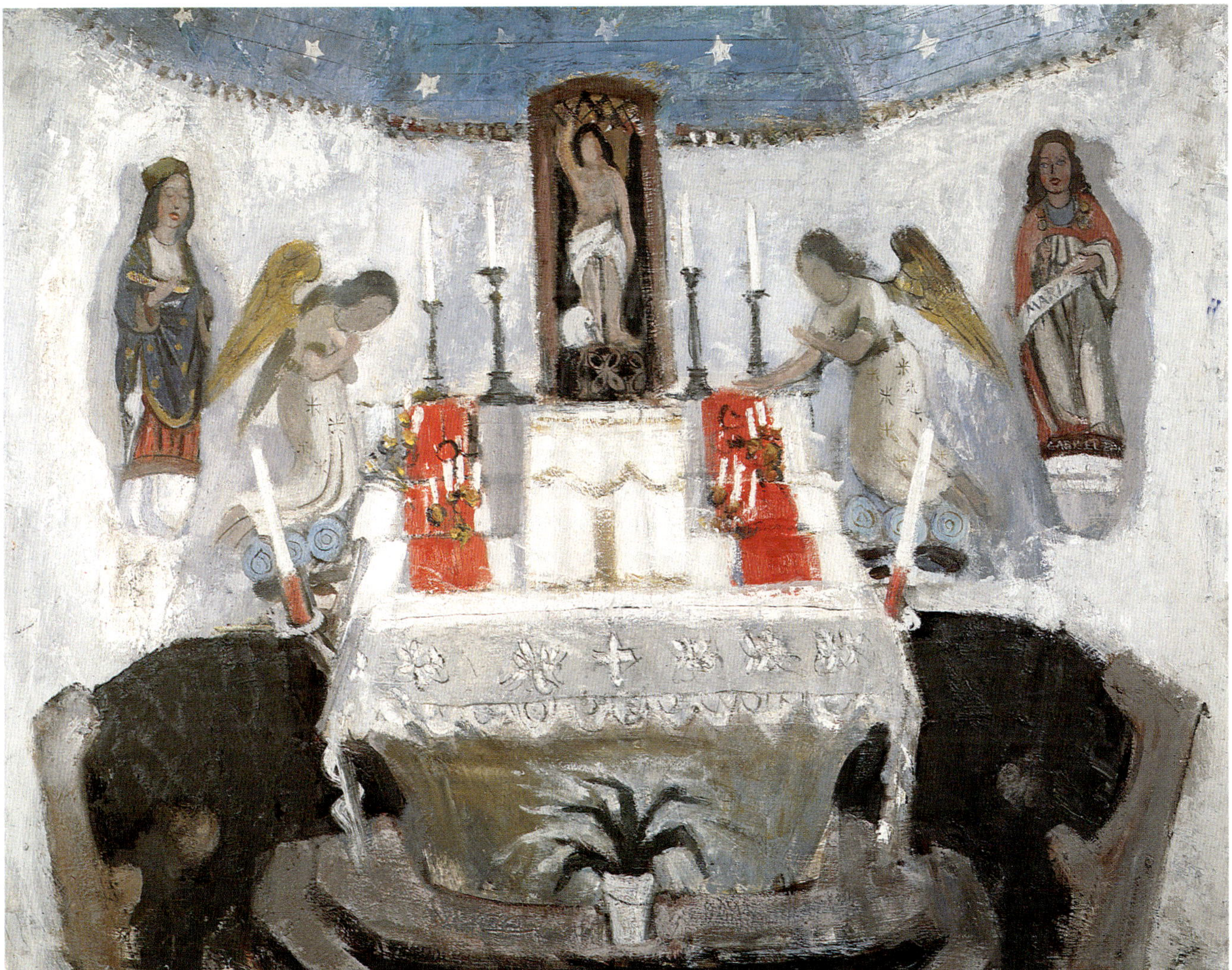

teaching and, in 1960, when she became eligible for a pension from the RSA, it only averaged forty pounds a year.

When Yonty Solomon visited the London Street studio in 1963 to buy one of her paintings, the one he set his heart on was "Window in Menton", but Anne very firmly explained that it was not for sale. A week later she had changed her mind and she sold it to him for £650 – the most she had ever asked for a painting. In no time at all she regretted this; she had been forced to make the decision by her concern that given her constant poor health, she might become too ill to paint and earn her living.

Although there was an eager public waiting to buy her paintings as she produced them, she did not have any individual patrons. Cadell and Peploe had had the Service family and Ion Harrison respectively. Johnny Maxwell had Dr Fletcher and Bill Gillies had Dr Lillie. Anne's concern was that, with her constant refining of style and the uncompromising shift from charm and delicacy towards strength and robustness, she could never be sure that her latest work would prove popular.

Probably through the influence of Jim, Anne was invited to have a solo exhibition at the Royal West of England Academy in Bristol in May 1956. This was part of the Academy's new policy to raise money and it was the first in a series that included Duncan Grant, Vanessa Bell and Terry Frost. According to the Academy's records, the exhibition was a commercial success and both parties were happy. There were fifty-eight paintings and watercolours, including several loan pictures (one of which was her recently presented RSA diploma work "In the Chapel of St. Jean, Treboul" (pl 59). In some ways the exhibition was a retrospective of the last six years' work, including work from the Spanish, Corsican and Brittany trips as well as still lifes and interiors. After this show Anne exhibited regularly at the RWA and in 1959 was elected an Academician.

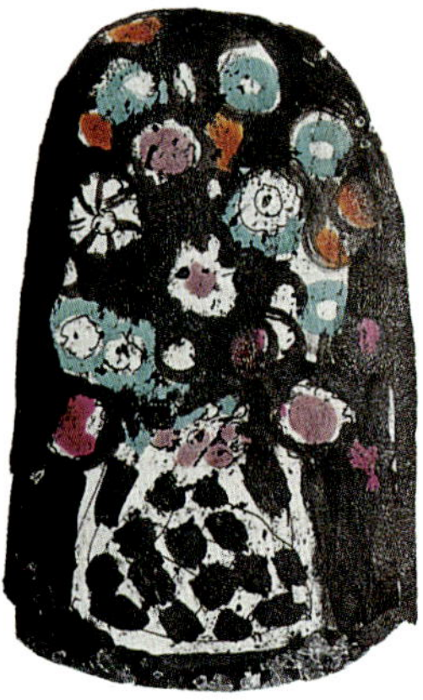

Chapter Seven

While she was in London for the opening of her second exhibition at the Lefevre Gallery in 1959, Anne suffered a second coronary thrombosis. She had never lost the feeling that in London she was showing to strangers, exposing new and untried work to a more demanding audience than she knew at home, and this must have been a contributory factor. She was taken to Nuffield House, the private wing of Guy's Hospital, where she remained for five weeks. Dr. Ralph Kauntze, the consultant physician, remembers her well as "a splendid patient who showed great bravery. She was also most unusual in that she contemplated her future with great detachment." Apart from Alastair and Lindsay she was not allowed any visitors. Doctor's orders forbade painting or even drawing; these she observed without complaint.

Dr. Kauntze privately thought that his patient could not expect to live for more than three years. Despite the fact that she never broached the subject with him, he had the impression that she knew this to be the case. Before she left hospital Anne said that she was going to produce a painting for the doctor. A few months later, to his great delight, Alastair delivered to Dr. Kauntze's London home a painting Anne had completed for him, which, in typically generous manner, was a much more important work than he might have anticipated.

The Scottish Gallery's 1960 Edinburgh Festival Exhibition was "Gran Canaria Paintings by Anne Redpath". The catalogue contained only twenty-one works, all oil paintings of the Canary Islands, which Anne had visited the previous February with Lindsay. Whereas the paintings from the Spanish and Corsican visits had in some cases gestated in Anne's mind for as long as four years, the Canary paintings came to fruition more quickly. It was as though she knew that, following her recent illness, she no longer had the luxury of prolonged reflection. This was her first exhibition on a single theme. It was a considerable success, not least because she had painted the landscape of the islands in different moods, giving the exhibition variety and balance. In "The Scotsman" Sydney Goodsir Smith enthused that "... the best of them are the best Anne Redpaths I have seen". He went on to say that these Canary Island landscapes were so good that Anne should not paint any more table tops because they were not worthy of her talent.

The variety of moods is well illustrated by comparing "Ploughed Fields" (pl 60) and "Houses on a Hill" (pl 66), both of which were in the Gran Canaria exhibition. Both are hillsides with the horizon near the top of the canvas, but there the similarity ends. "Ploughed Fields" is dark and brooding with a slow, lugubrious rhythm in the landscape, whereas "Houses on a Hill" dances and coruscates with dazzling light. In a radio talk in 1956 Anne said she agreed with Braque's dictum that "one should want to feel a painting as well as look at it" and this is just the effect that the Gran Canaria paintings have. The paint is applied in a great multi-layered impasto; the foreground of "Houses on a Hill" in particular has the effect of an old crumbling white plaster wall. Anne was continually adding to her great armoury of techniques for marshalling and manipulating the pigment in her oil paintings. In the late 1950's George Bruce took her to a "happening" on George Street in Edinburgh, where an artist was doing some action painting which included all

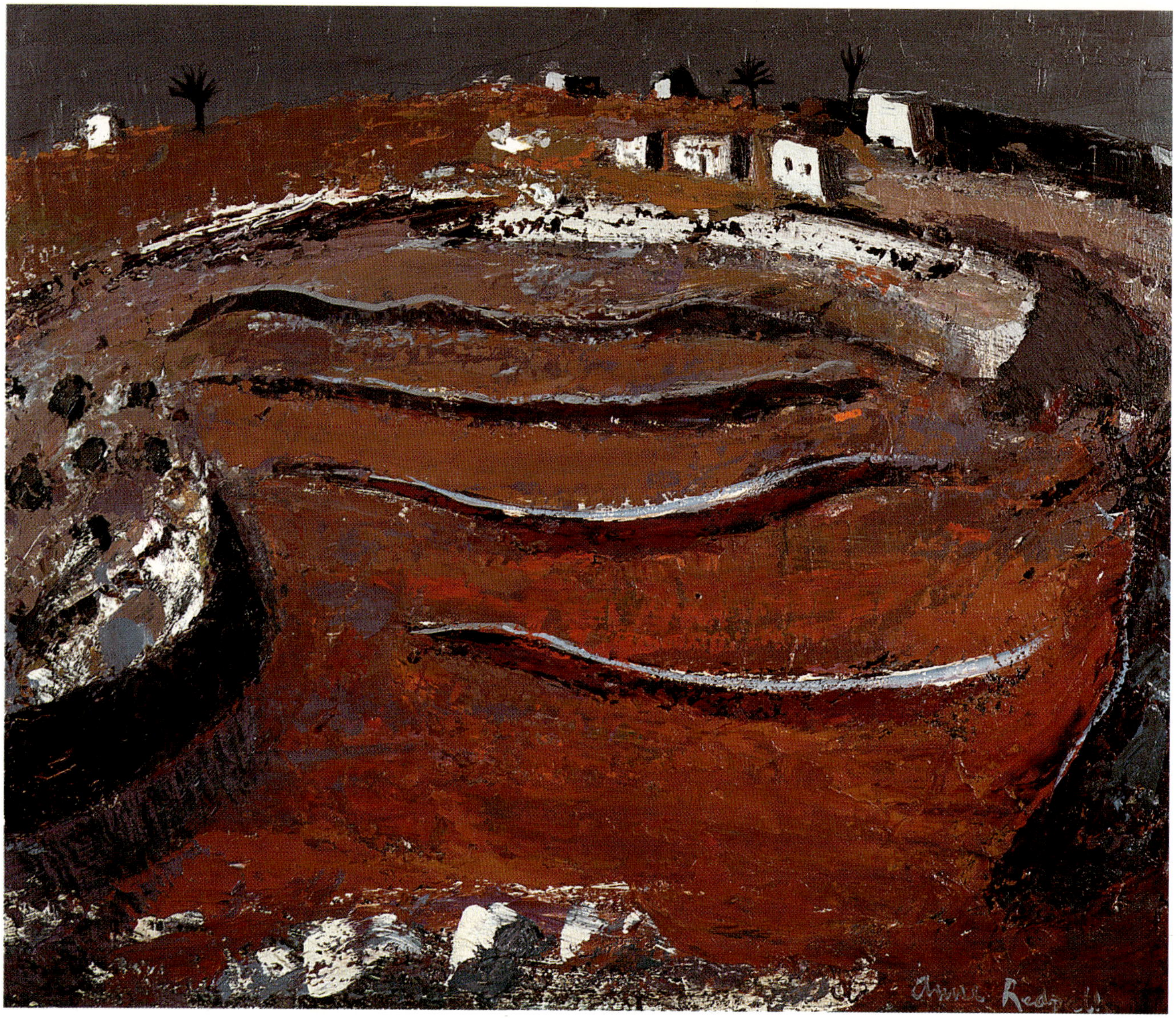

60 Ploughed Fields 1960 oil

sorts of random ways of putting paint on canvas short of riding a bicycle over it. Anne watched this for some minutes in silent concentration, then turned to George Bruce and whispered "I could do that". According to Bruce, the subsequent loosening of Anne's technique was not unconnected with that experience.

In an oil painting like "Houses on a Hill" and, particularly, "Les Tourrettes", Anne has thinned the paint and dripped it onto the canvas in a technique similar to that of Jackson Pollock and in a way that Robin Philipson has done since. In the scrapbook that Anne kept of press cuttings about her own work, there is a carefully cut out article on Jackson Pollock from the "New Statesman" of 1960 (the only other artist in the scrapbook is Modigliani).

In 1959 Anne received news of her husband's death in Bristol at the age of 69. Jim and Anne had lived apart since 1934, but they had never lost touch and he was always intensely proud of his wife's successful career. He was himself a talented painter, as was demonstrated in an exhibition of his tempera paintings staged in Hawick during the Second World War, and can be seen in the commissioned murals which he executed in the South of France and

Norwich. However, their careers were in stark contrast. While Jim was a dreamer and romantic, Anne was practical and realistic. He had an ideal of an artist's life, based on his knowledge of the Italian Renaissance and the Mediterranean way of life, which he only enjoyed for a brief period in the Cap Ferrat years and never recaptured. Despite the long separation, he is fondly remembered by his family and also by the architects who were his students in Bristol.

Around this time Anne started to worry that she was becoming old fashioned. David McClure remembers her saying to him "I must try to be more modern". Her concern with keeping up to date with the latest techniques did not mean, however, that she was prepared to compromise on sound and correct methods. She was very concerned when, after using some paints that had been made for her by a new manufacturer in Edinburgh, her paintings started to "bleed" and after a few weeks white pigment began to turn pink. The thought that her paintings might not be stable unsettled her. She had used the method of "degreasing" since her days in Hawick. This involved putting the paint on blotting paper to drain out the poppy oil and give it a dry, chalky appearance. The whites in "Houses on a Hill" have probably had this treatment, but it is also particularly effective on dark pigments which contain more oil. She hardly ever varnished her oil paintings, preferring, like Peploe and Cadell, to see them "in the raw". For this reason the exhibition oils were always under glass. Another of her methods for getting texture and rough surface was to scour the paint with what her son David describes as a small piece of chain-mail.

In 1962 her accountant explained that the reason she was not making a better living from her painting was the inordinate amount of money she spent on paints. Anne explained that the problem with her method was that she scraped off more paint than she left on the

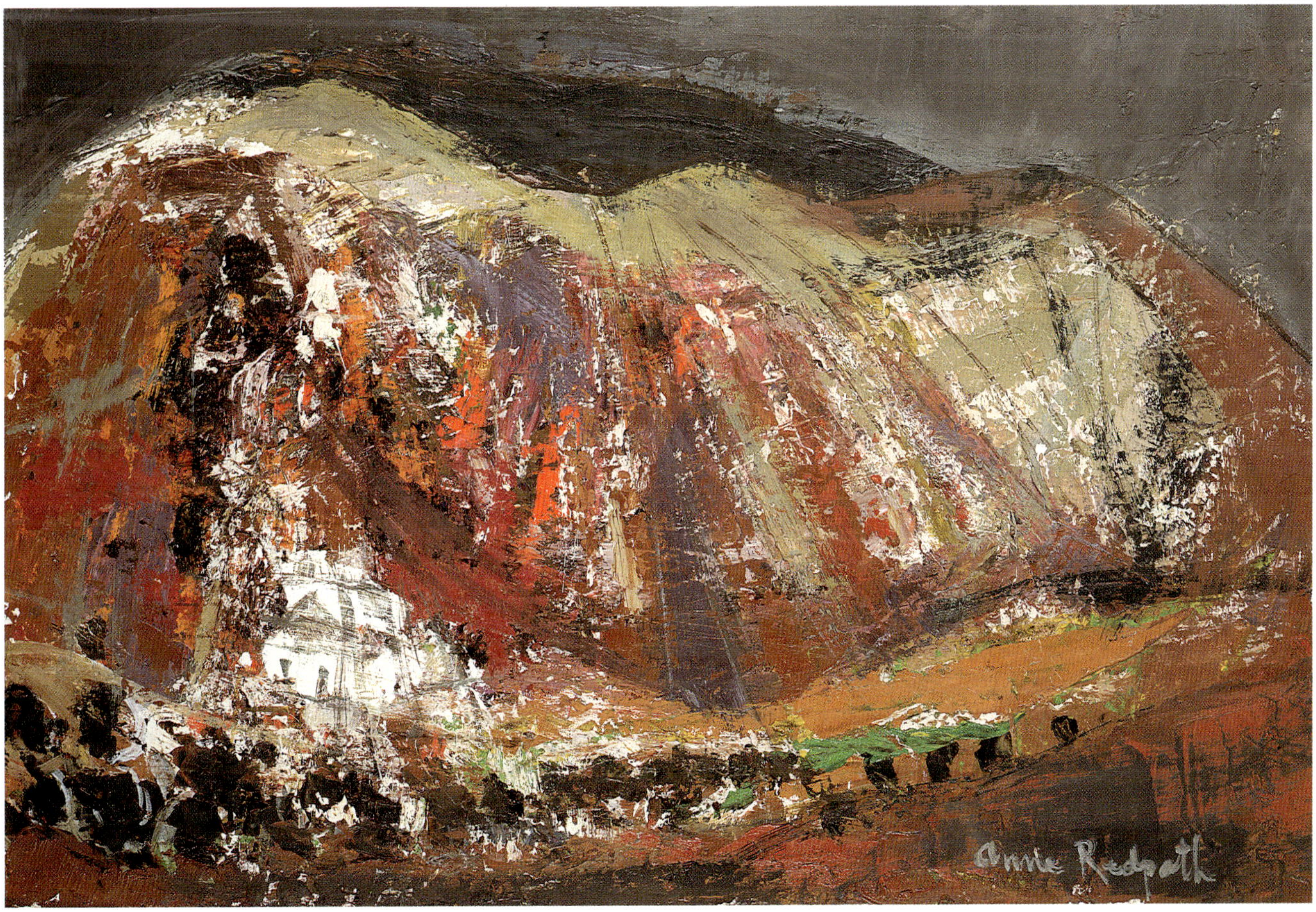

61 Red Hill, Corsica c1955 oil

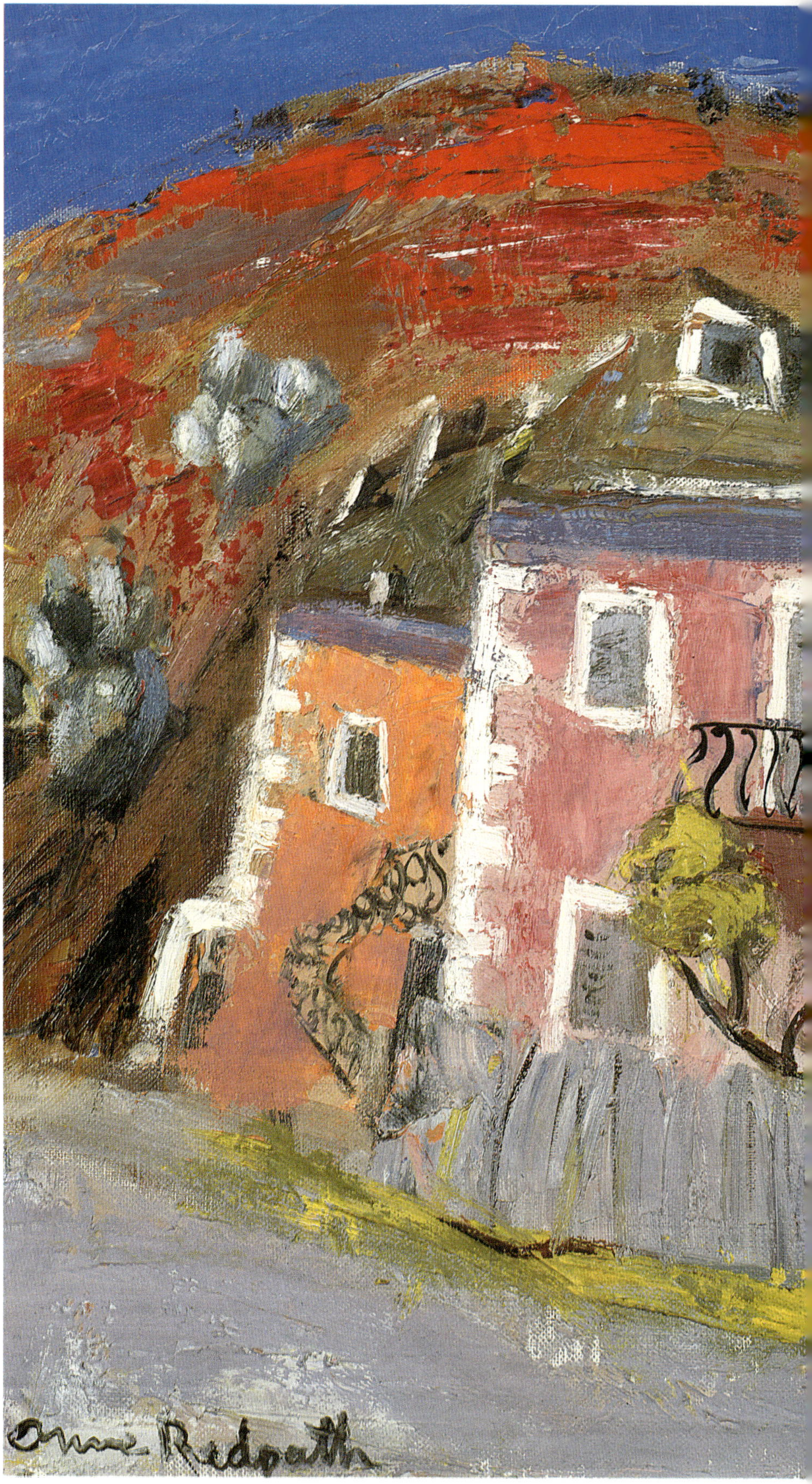

62 Pink House in Corsica c1955 oil

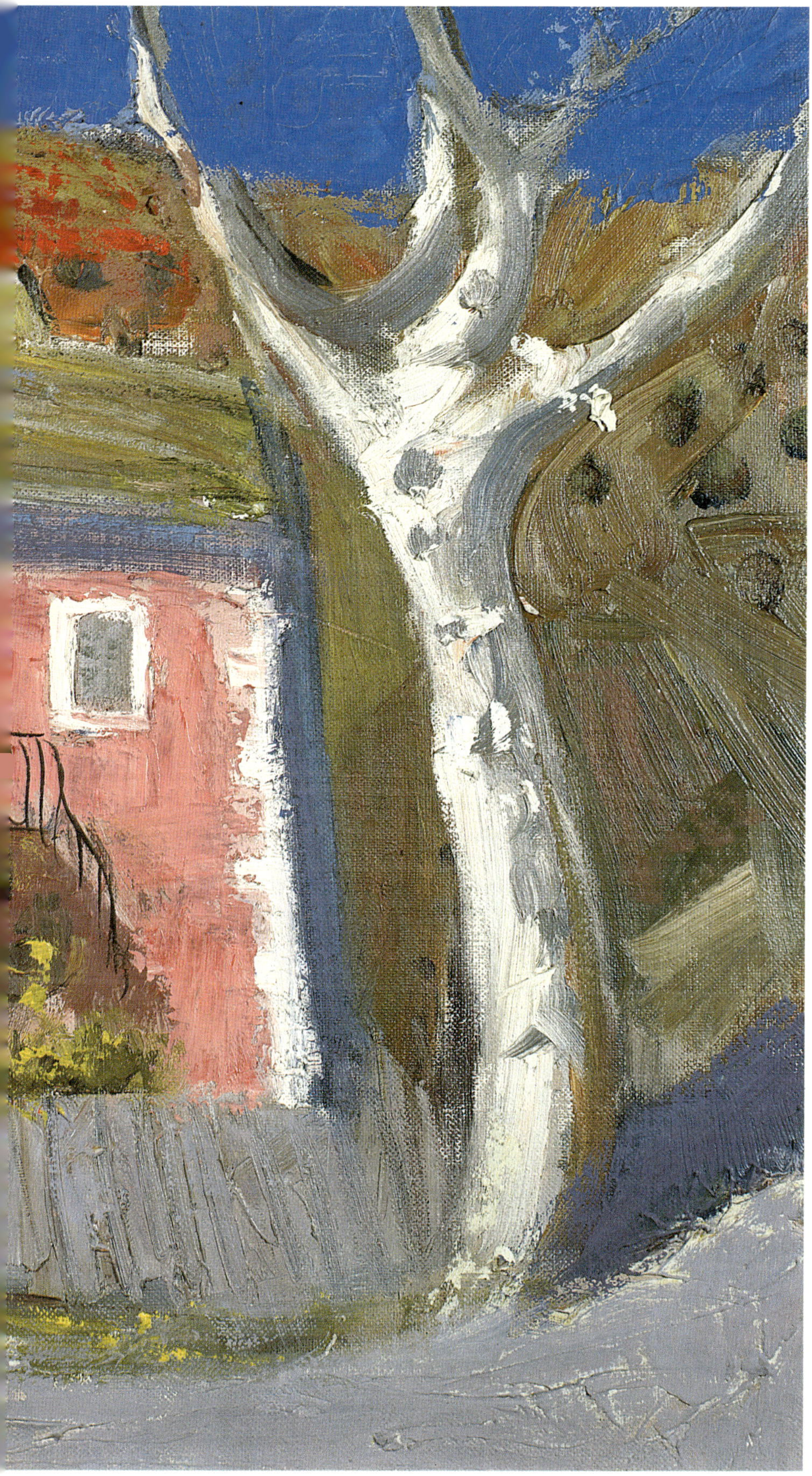

canvas. Her accountant's suggestion that perhaps she might re-use the discarded paint was not put into practice!

In 1961 Anne went to Portugal with David, who was by then President of the SSA and an Associate of the RSA. While he painted street and harbour scenes, Anne did the greater part of her work inside the churches. She had fallen in love with the Manueline style of Portugese Baroque architecture when she had been in the Canary Islands two years earlier. When David and she first discovered the church of San Roque in Lisbon, David said she was "staggered" by it. In Lisbon, in her own words, she "went mad" – scribbling down details of architecture and ornament in the glowing golden interiors of San Roque and Madre Dios. She would draw on the spot with a soft pencil or black chalk. Later in her hotel room she added watercolour or coloured chalks. The result would be a spirited colour sketch like pl . Although these esquisses have an immediacy and excitement of their own, they were only intended as notes for the oil paintings that would be painted back in Edinburgh. One wonders what her father, a strict Congregationalist, would have thought about Anne's love affair with Catholic churches and ornament. Anne delighted in the apparent contradiction she found working on these church interiors – that places which filled her with such excitement should themselves be so cool, tranquil and quiet. When painting out of doors she often attracted inquisitive groups of children and, being an outgoing person, she found them difficult to ignore. The vigour and energy evident in the paintings of this period make it easy to forget that in 1961 she was 65 years old and not in good health. She became short of breath at the slightest exertion. The series of paintings of altars and crypts were justified on physical as well as aesthetic grounds. In 1958 she had remarked to Margaret Moodie "I have now passed the stage of sitting on a hillside in a cold east wind".

In November 1961 the Stone Gallery in Newcastle upon Tyne staged an Anne Redpath exhibition. Willie MacTaggart, a friend of the Marshalls, who owned the gallery, had made the introduction. The Marshalls had built up a small but discerning clientele from amongst the traditionally conservative north east collectors. Their most recent MacTaggart exhibition in 1959 had been a sell out and this proved to be the same for Anne. She attended the private view and came back the following day to meet Terence Mullaly, the "Daily Telegraph" critic. Mullaly was a most enthusiastic supporter and, when writing about the Royal Academy exhibition that year, had given Anne one of the best reviews she ever received:

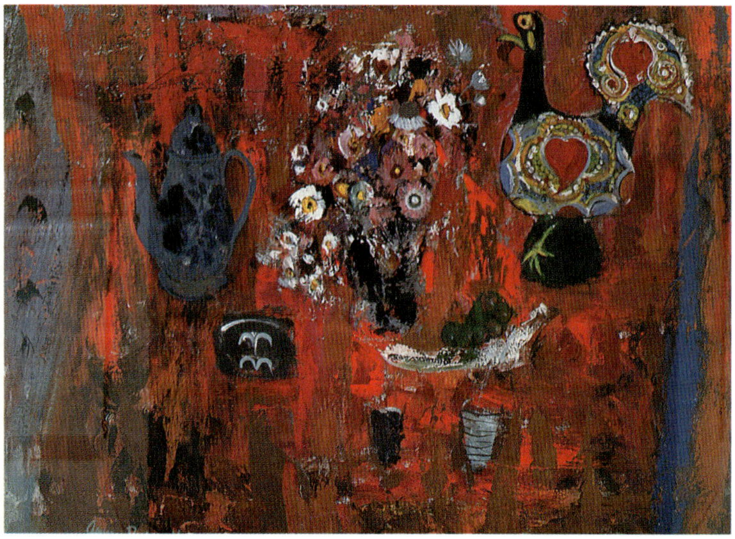

63
The Portuguese Cockerel 1962 oil

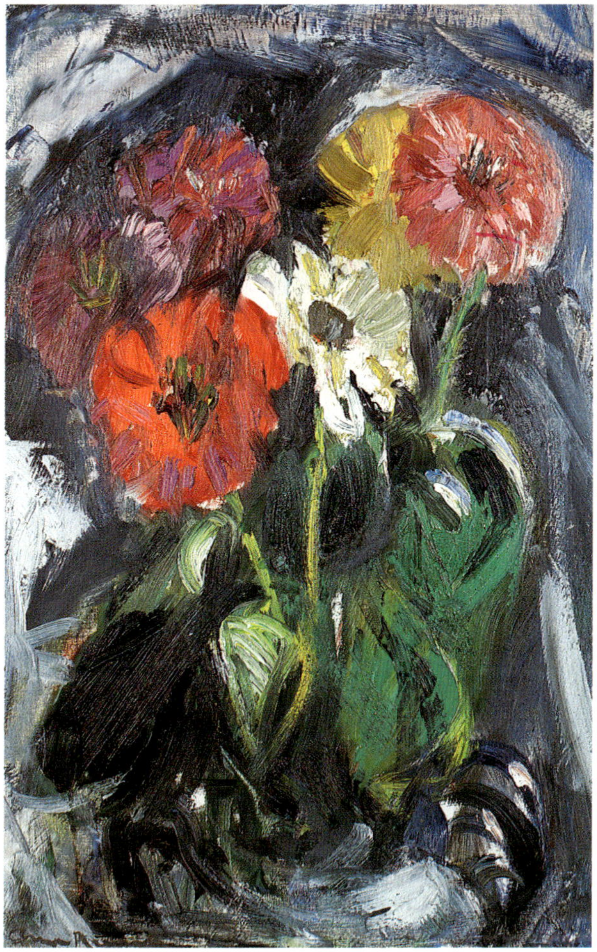

64 Zinnias 1957 oil

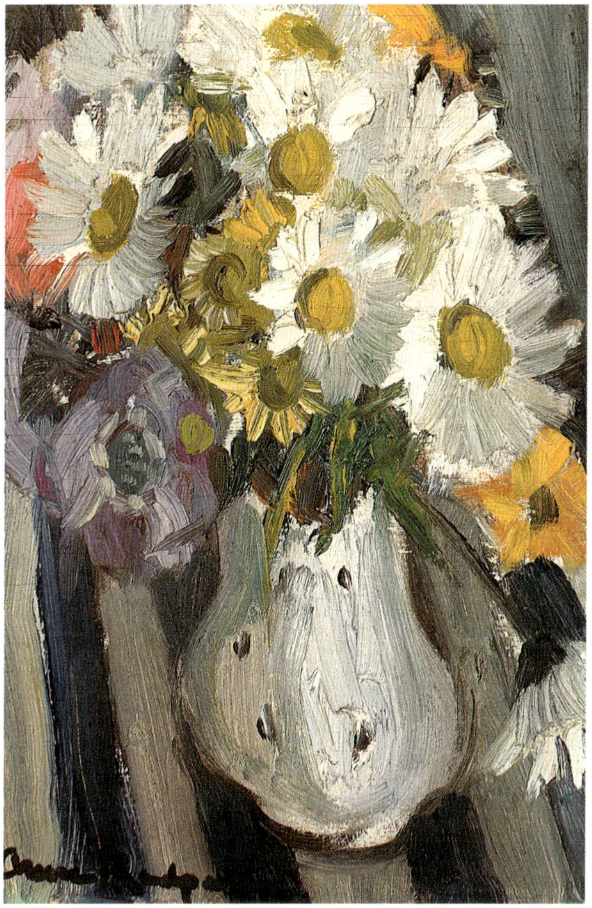

65 Marigolds and Marguerites 1953 oil

"There are many possible justifications for the RA's vast and unwieldy anthology. One of the most cogent is satisfied if it represents even one really exceptional work. This year there are eight of them, two by William MacTaggart and six by Anne Redpath."

The "Manchester Guardian" printed a laudatory half page article on the Stone Gallery exhibition, to which the Marshalls attributed the appearance at the gallery soon afterwards of L. S. Lowry. It was around this time that he and Anne became friends (they were brought together by Bill Macaulay of the Scottish Gallery when Lowry expressed his admiration of her work at a Redpath exhibition). Lowry always seemed to feel rather competitive about Anne. They both had Lefevre as their London agent and perhaps he felt that Anne threatened his position as the most popular painter from the North. However, following Anne's success in Newcastle, Lowry started to exhibit at the Stone Gallery.

In 1962 Anne received a commission from the Scottish Widows' Fund and Life Assurance Society for a tapestry to decorate their refurbished boardroom at their head office in Edinburgh. She made several designs in gouache and finally decided on a composition comprised of a massive urn of flowers, two doves and fruit trees, designed to create a two dimensional effect, standing out from an orange background. The composition is contained

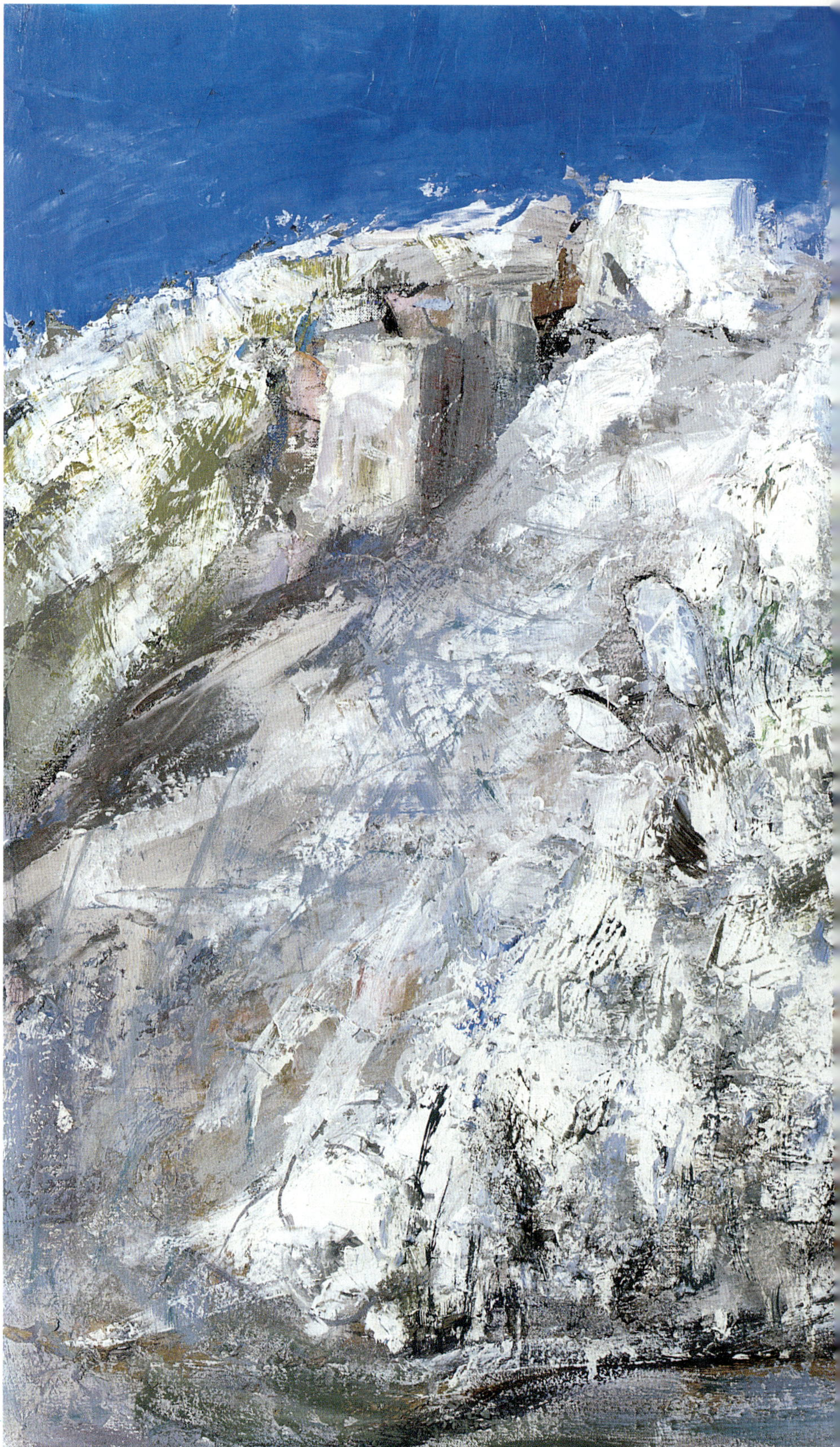

66 Houses on a Hill 1960 oil

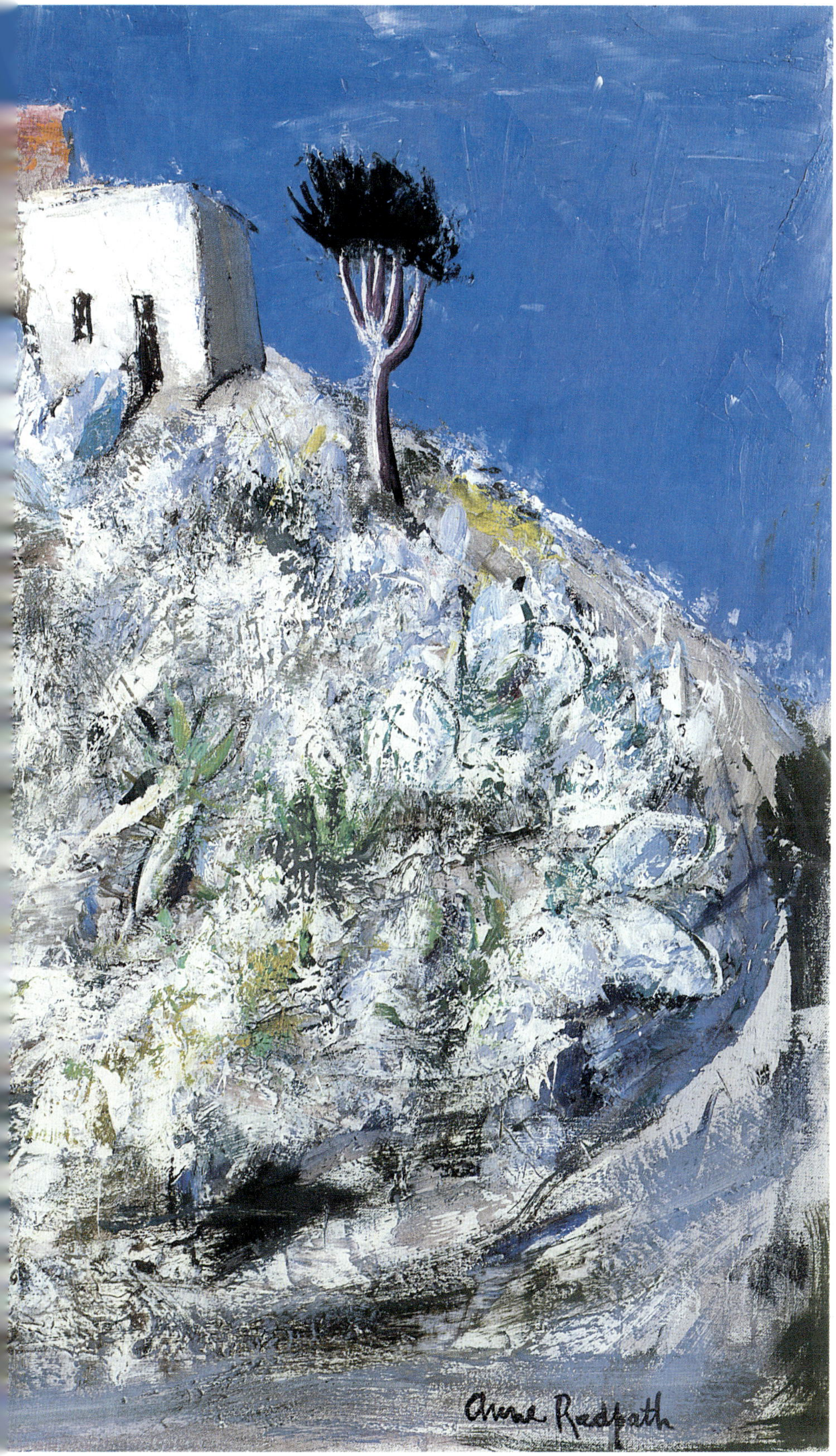
Anne Redpath

within a substantial grey border, the whole creating the effect of an Indian rug. She had successfully translated her skills to a different medium, using motifs from folk art similar to those used in her furniture decorations, rather than merely attempting to adapt her painting style. The piece was woven by Pinton Freres, Aubusson which, in view of Edinburgh's tradition for weaving, is surprising. It is curious that Anne received no other tapestry commission.

"The Portuguese Cockerel" (pl 63) of the same year has elements in common with the tapestry. The flattened objects are also set against a textured background of orange and red, the huge bouquet of flowers reappears, and the Portugese Cockerel is a dominating folk art symbol. The painting is as gaudy and gorgeous as a tapestry.

In the same year a row which blew up over the purchase of one of Anne's paintings gained a great deal of press coverage. It concerned Manchester City Art Gallery's decision to buy "Table Top" (pl 67) for the City's collection. The Gallery's Curator had gone to the Lefevre exhibition in March to choose a painting, but had been disappointed to find everything

67 Table Top 1958 oil

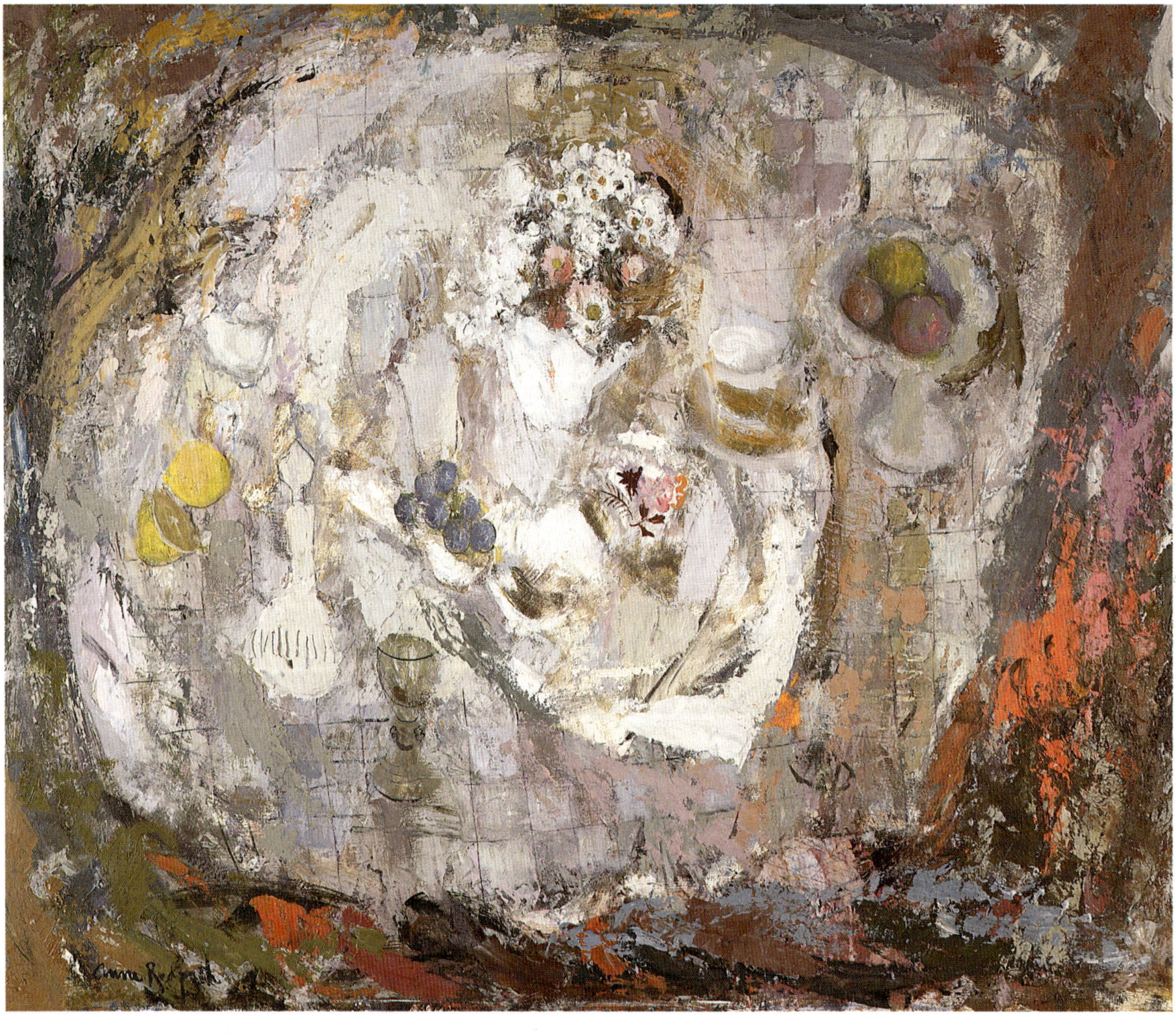

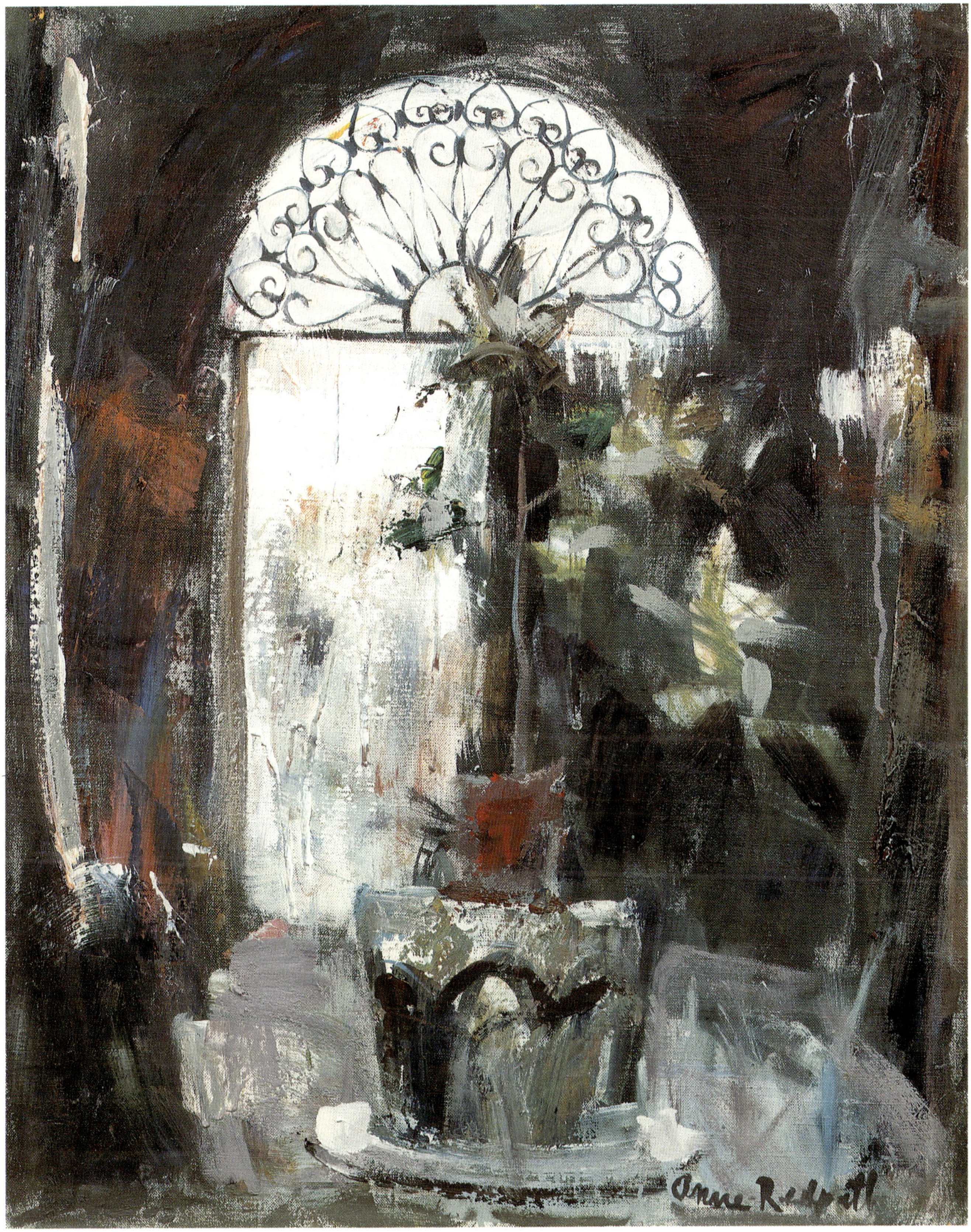

68 Courtyard in Venice 1964 oil

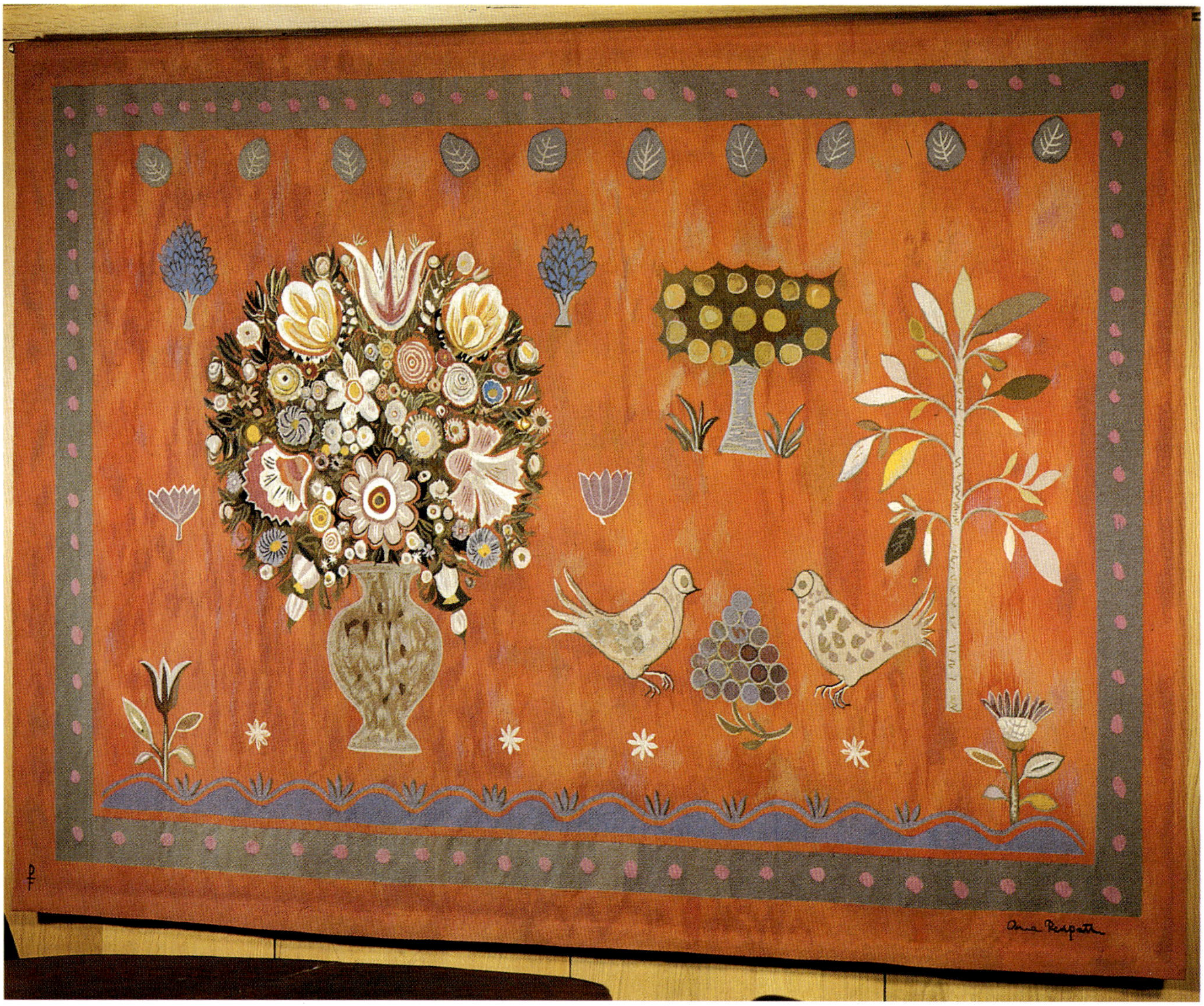

69 Design for Tapestry by Pinton Freres 1962 gouache

sold. When he wrote to Anne to ask if she had anything available in her studio, she sent down to Manchester a selection including "Table Top", which was one of her favourites. It had been hanging in London Street since she had painted it four years before. Eric Newton had described it on BBC's "Arts Review" as having "a resonance that can be matched in France but hardly ever in England". When the Curator chose "Table Top" he was pleased to discover that Anne asked only 230 guineas for it – about half the price Lefevre would have wanted. However, some of the councillors tried to block the purchase when they saw what the money was to be spent on. Finally, the full Council met to take a vote on whether the City should buy the picture or not. Despite a vociferous opposition, which described the painting as "monstrous" and "resembling a boxer's black eye", the purchase was approved by 57 votes to 46.

Anne's reaction to all this fuss and controversy was to declare that while she thought it was a good thing that there should be all this frank discussion about paintings, she really would have something to worry about if a hundred town councillors all agreed that they liked her pictures.

The apparent casualness that the councillors objected to in the painting is an artifice. The nonchalance is strictly calculated. Their reaction is similar to Ruskin's when he accused Whistler of throwing a pot of paint in the public's face. This complex picture, with its panoply of strong and subtle colour, was the result of a lifetime's experience of painting still lifes. The composition is confined by the geometric shape of the table top on which the weightless objects float. The local colour dissolves, yet the control of hue and tone is absolute.

In October 1963 Alastair and Anne spent a fortnight in Venice. Her only previous visit had been almost forty years earlier, when she was living at Cap Ferrat, and it seems likely that she had not painted whilst there. In later years she had developed a certain reluctance to paint a city which had already served as an inspiration to so many artists. The advantage of places such as Corsica and the Canary Islands had been that the landscapes there had no close association with the vision of other artists, so her objectivity was not compromised by a history of received responses. Moreover she could not imagine herself painting pictures of canals and gondolas.

Despite all this, when they arrived in Venice Anne was immediately bewitched by the dimly lit splendour of St. Mark's and S. Nicola dei Mendicoli, even though she thought she had "painted churches out of her system" in Portugal three years earlier. She admitted "I don't voluntarily choose subjects, rather they choose me." The heavily encrusted, jewel-like impasto that these churches inspired stands in contrast in terms of handling and technique to a painting like "A Courtyard in Venice" (pl 68), where the handling is spirited and free, similar to that of many of her late still lifes (for example, pl 78). There is an element of relaxed enjoyment in such paintings.

They stayed at the Grand Hotel on the Grand Canal, living well and travelling extensively by gondola and moto-scaffi. They explored the Lagoon, were impressed by the Byzantine church at Torcello and watched the glassblowers at Murano. Alastair was furious with a gondolier who quoted a price for a boat-trip and then asked for a multiple of the agreed amount at the end of the journey. His mother's reaction was that it was nothing to get annoyed about because, after all, it was "only paper money". However, Alastair remembers the holiday as a marvellous time for both of them. He did not paint but spent the time when his mother was working taking photographs for her to use as an aide memoire on her return to Scotland.

An exhibition of Anne's Venetian paintings was scheduled for the following April at the Lefevre Gallery. She had worked extremely hard and in seclusion in the intervening months.

70 Church at Las Palmas
1959 watercolour

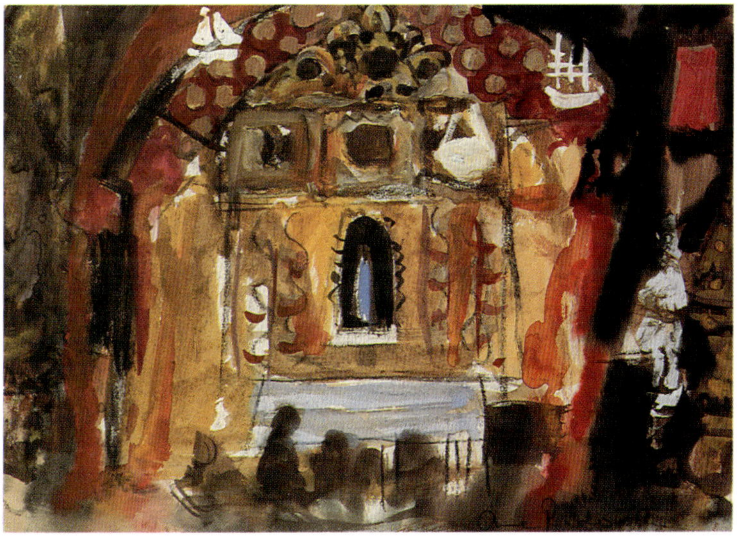

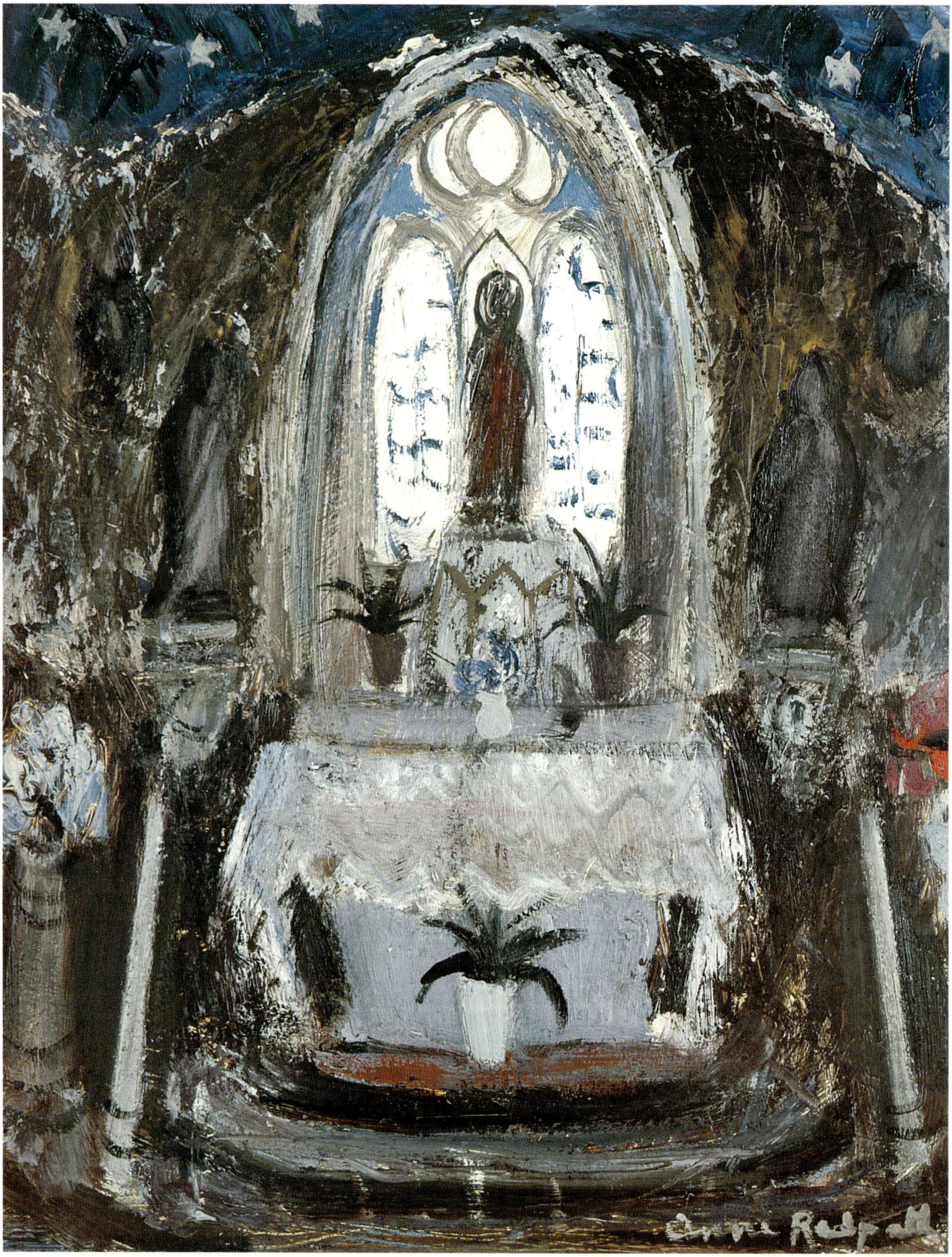

71 Church Interior, Portugal 1962 oil

When the time came for the carriers to pick up the paintings and ship them to London, she postponed the move till the following day. She asked George Bruce, who had directed a BBC film about her the previous year, to come round to London Street and look at the paintings. After Bruce arrived he was bemused to be kept chatting for two hours about everything but painting, with no sign of the pictures ever being produced. As he made to leave, Anne finally asked him "aren't you going to take a look at my paintings?". She had them lined up facing the wall and now she turned them round one by one for Bruce to see. He admired them and asked why she had been so reluctant to show them. "I was worried that people would think I was a foolish old woman" was the disarming reply.

The exhibition was a monumental success. The twenty four oils, all of Venice, sold within the first two days. For the first time all three of Anne's sons, with their wives, were able to attend her private view together – fortunately, since this was to be her last exhibition.

On December 20th 1964 Anne tripped over the carpet in the drawing room in her London Street flat and broke her arm. For some time her health had not been good and she had been taking a variety of medications. Complications set in. Soon her condition had become so critical that she was moved to the Drumsheugh Nursing Home and only her closest relatives were allowed to visit. All her friends waited anxiously for news, finding it impossible, according to Katie Horsman, to concentrate on their work. On January 7th, 1965, her death was announced.

The funeral took place at Warriston Crematorium on January 9th, 1965. A staff reporter on the "Evening News" wrote:

"In eloquent silence and sombre dignity, Scotland and Edinburgh have taken leave of Anne Redpath, but what will linger long in the mind is not the ceremony or, more precisely, the impressive lack of it; nor the presence of the elite of town and gown, of the arts, the law, and the church, though they were there in suffocating number. Rather is it the compulsion which drew to dreich Warriston less prestigious, but no less worthy folk.

One expected her fellow Academicians, but not her waiters; a law lord or two but not her cabbies; a councillor maybe but not her dustman – or that group of young artists and student painters who shattered an age barrier which she detested and largely ignored.

Few had come to mourn the passing of a painter, and why should they? Anne Redpath's art is still with us and well able to look after itself. But all were united in sorrow, and a sort of wonder at the extinction of a warm, indomitable, unique personality, and by their diversity they confounded that possibility."

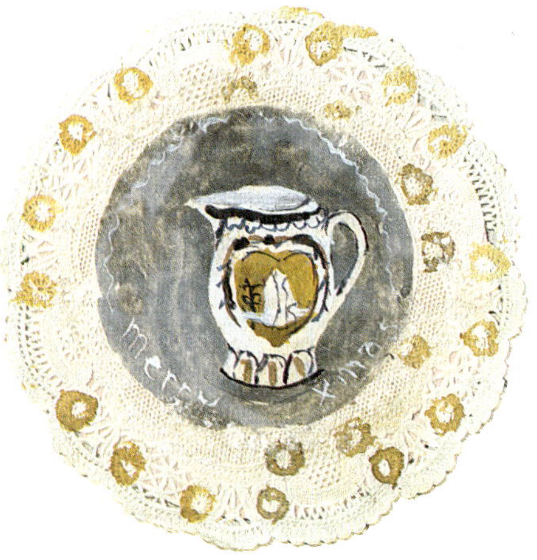

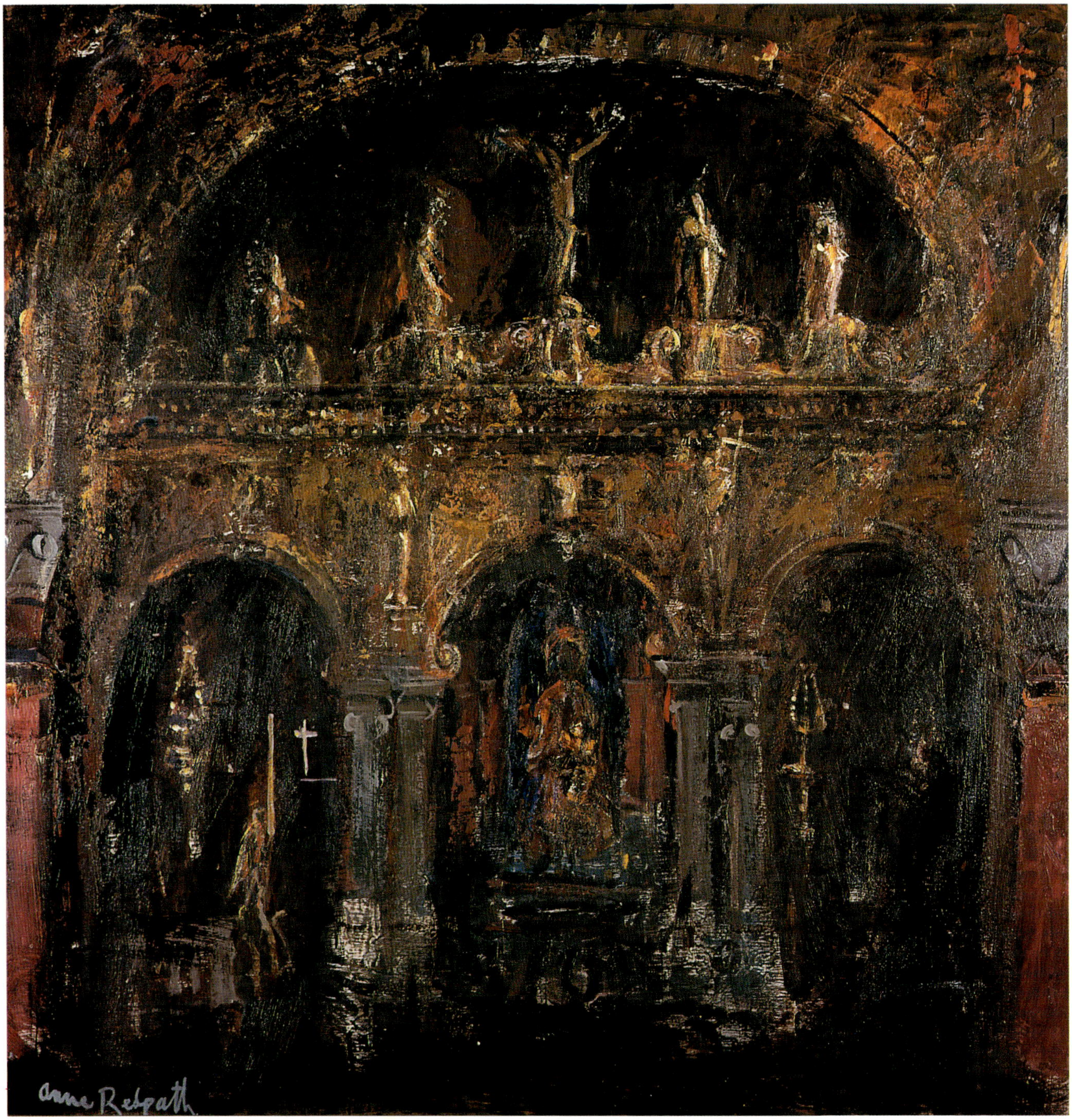

72 Rood Screen, Torcello c1964 oil

EPILOGUE

The lack of ceremony in the funeral service meant that some of Anne's friends felt that it was an anti-climax with no catharsis. It must have been a surprise that, despite her fascination with Catholic iconography and decoration, Anne had rejected so completely religious observance for her own funeral.

The major Memorial Exhibition organised by the Arts Council, which opened in Edinburgh in the winter of 1965, proved to be a more eloquent tribute. The eighty oil paintings, watercolours and drawings gave a complete survey of her achievement from childhood and student works to the final splendour of the Venetian church interiors. The exhibition lasted almost a year and toured throughout Scotland and the north of England. It was seen by four thousand people in Edinburgh and five thousand in Glasgow and was judged by the Arts Council to have been a "considerable success". There was no showing in London, which seems surprising since she had been highly regarded there by both critics and public since the 1940's. An exhibition organised by Eastbourne and Worthing Art Galleries in 1969 went some way towards rectifying this omission.

The full extent of Anne's achievement displayed by the Arts Council exhibition was a revelation for many people. The development from the spareness and economy of the early Provencal and Borders landscapes to the complexity and involvement of the later oils revealed an artist of impressive technical range. This was allied to a consistency of vision. Although she was inspired by Persian and Indian arts, she painted only in Europe – almost exclusively old Europe. One is never aware of new buildings or new industry in her paintings. She depicts the changes wrought by time and weather in her landscapes, but not by twentieth century man. When she returned to Cap Ferrat in 1963, thirty years after she had lived there, she could not have avoided noticing the effects of the growth of the tourist industry; yet she excluded it from her vision.

Needless to say, this was not from any wish for her paintings to be quaint or idyllic. Rather her conception of the spirit and essence of a country or culture lay beyond appearances. She sought the inscape under topographical fact. For much of her life she lived and painted in a city noted for its mediaeval and Georgian architecture, yet she never used it as a subject ("I'll paint Edinburgh when I'm old" she said in the 1950's). This suggests that she had to be distant from her subject to capture its essence. In this she was the antithesis of the other two major figures in post-war painting in Scotland, Gillies and Eardley. They both had to live with, and be immersed in, their subject matter.

Like all truly original artists in this century Anne shows us aspects of her subject matter that we ourselves have seen but not acknowledged; she also reveals aspects that we would never have seen. She manages to communicate her experience of life, both the familiar and the exotic, with an exceptional degree of individuality. No mature Redpath painting could ever be mistaken for that of any other artist.

What most impresses about Anne Redpath's work is its consistently inspired quality. Right until the end she allied the sense of excitement and enquiry of the youthful painter with the sureness and mastery of the mature painter, which is a powerful combination. It is one that is as unusual in European painting as it is in British.

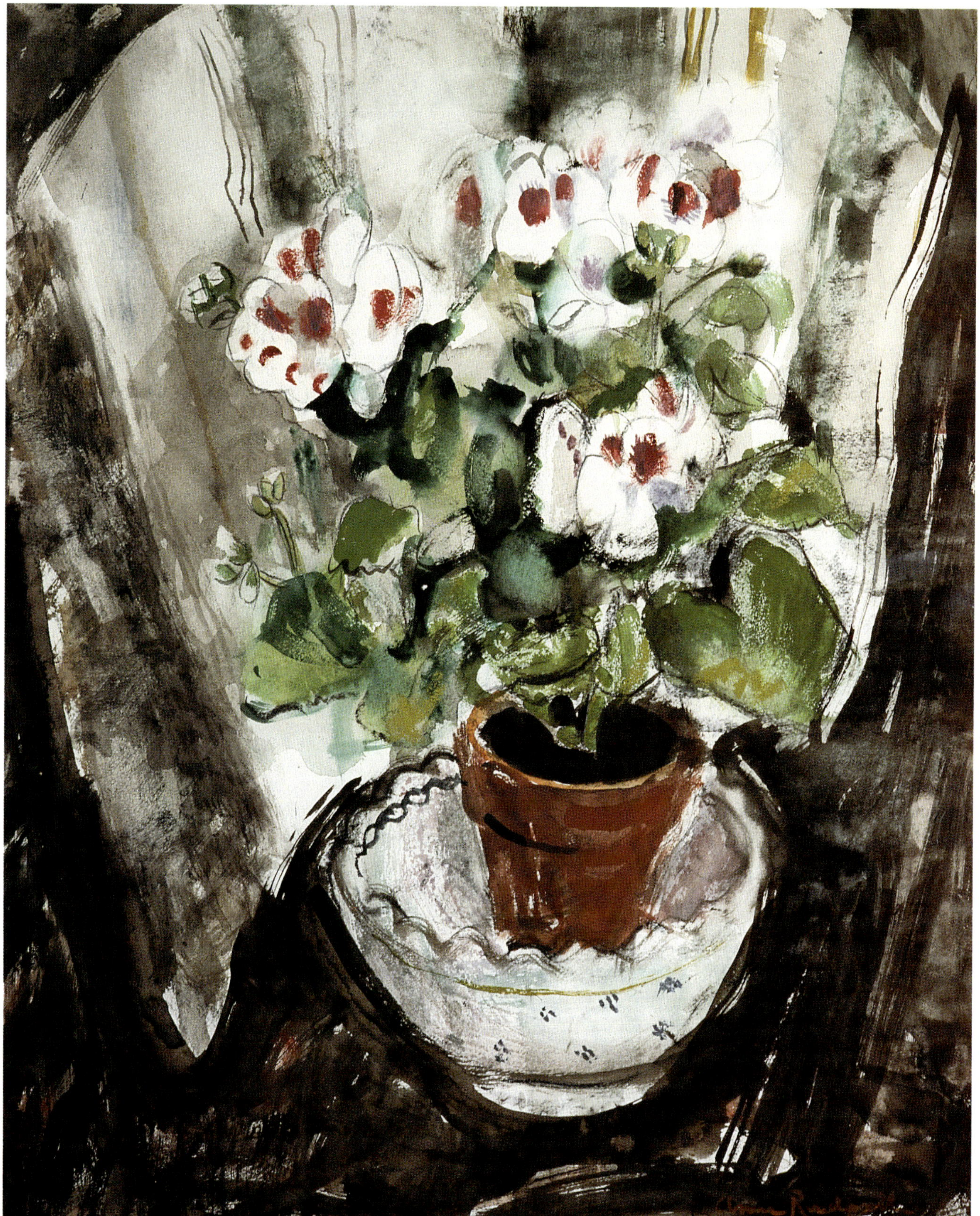

73 Pelargonium 1957 watercolour

APPENDIX

Transcript of Anne Redpath talking about her paintings during a ten minute BBC film directed by George Bruce at her London Street flat. It was first shown in 'Counterpoint' on 31 January 1961.

When I was at college, you know, I was very fond of still life, and people said there, you know, that I wasn't actually painting what was in front of me, that it was a vision of a still life. They were more impressionistic than I have ever done since, because I was terribly keen on light, high pitched light, and shadow, and used more of an accidental quality than I have ever done since. But all the same, they weren't ever what you would call photographic or realistic paintings, even still lifes done in a college, in a still life room. My friends used to say 'Of course that's not really what is in front of Anne, she's just made a vision of something that she has seen', which meant that even then it wasn't actually a completely realistic translation of what was in front of me, it was still just a kind of vision, a translation of the vision that I had seen from these white dishes and some flowers on the table. I would arrange a group of dishes, flowers, on a table, and I didn't depart all *that* far from the thing in front of me. Lots of other people thought I *did* depart quite a distance, you know, and they didn't like my idea of things that seemed quite real, and yet looked as if there was no law of gravity, and I have always had to explain that I wasn't interested, and nor was a painter interested, in the laws of gravity. But now that I have no tables at all, that my objects are really just in thin air, people don't mind that at all. They really minded much more when the thing was much more like the object. Sometimes it begins with something actually seen. Something that has suggested a picture. You know, perhaps even just a dish of flowers or a cup, you know, or a jug, or something like that which, therefore, makes the point of departure. But then other times, you see, I just simply see the picture without having anything actual in front of me. I see it as a completed picture, and that means that half the picture is done for me. I see it in colour and in shape. I feel really not responsible for it, and therefore don't deserve any credit for it. It . . . it paints itself after that. That is my easiest kind of picture, but not necessarily my worst. You see, I paint some of these things over and over again, and sometimes, you know, for months, you are not really aware of them, except in a very subconscious way, then suddenly a light changes, or you feel different, and you suddenly see those things as you would in a picture. I think really I am an artist that likes contrasts, both in my life, the things I live amongst, and therefore while I am someone who is very interested in colour, and by that I mean bright colour, gay colour. but at the same time, if you are a colourist, you like quiet colour as well, and I think this love of gay colour contrasted in my mind with this love of whites, and greys, and as far back as I can remember I have loved painting white, and black is the obvious way to use white, you use black because it makes the white more intensified, or gives it more quality. I have always liked white. I have always liked white walls in a room. In all the houses I have ever lived in, I have had a white wall in my sitting room. And I don't know when I began to like a white wall, unless it was when I was a student in Italy, when I had a wall in a room in a pensione, you know, in the Lungarno in Florence, and the walls were white, rough white

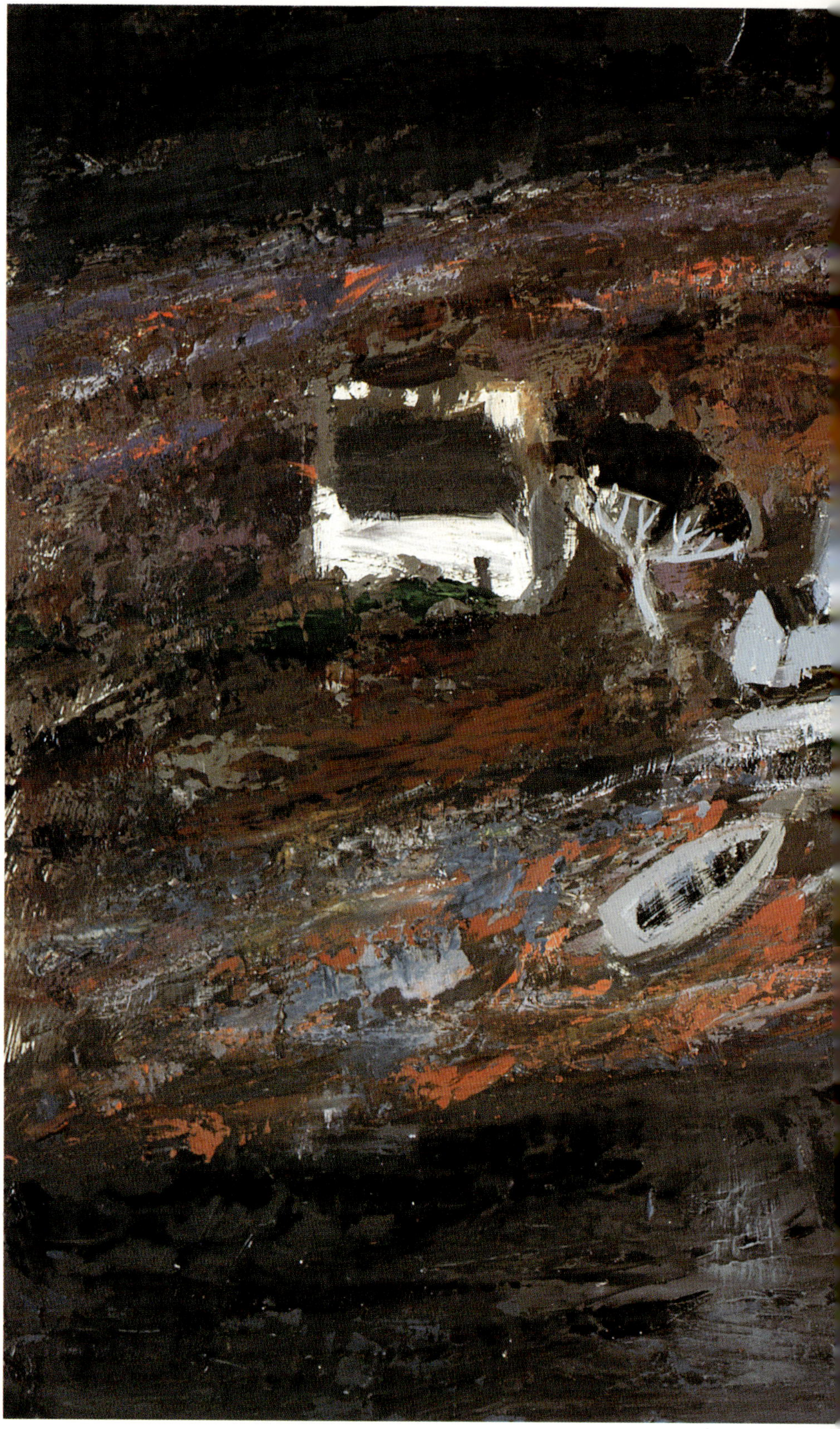

74 Landscape, Kyleakin 1958 oil

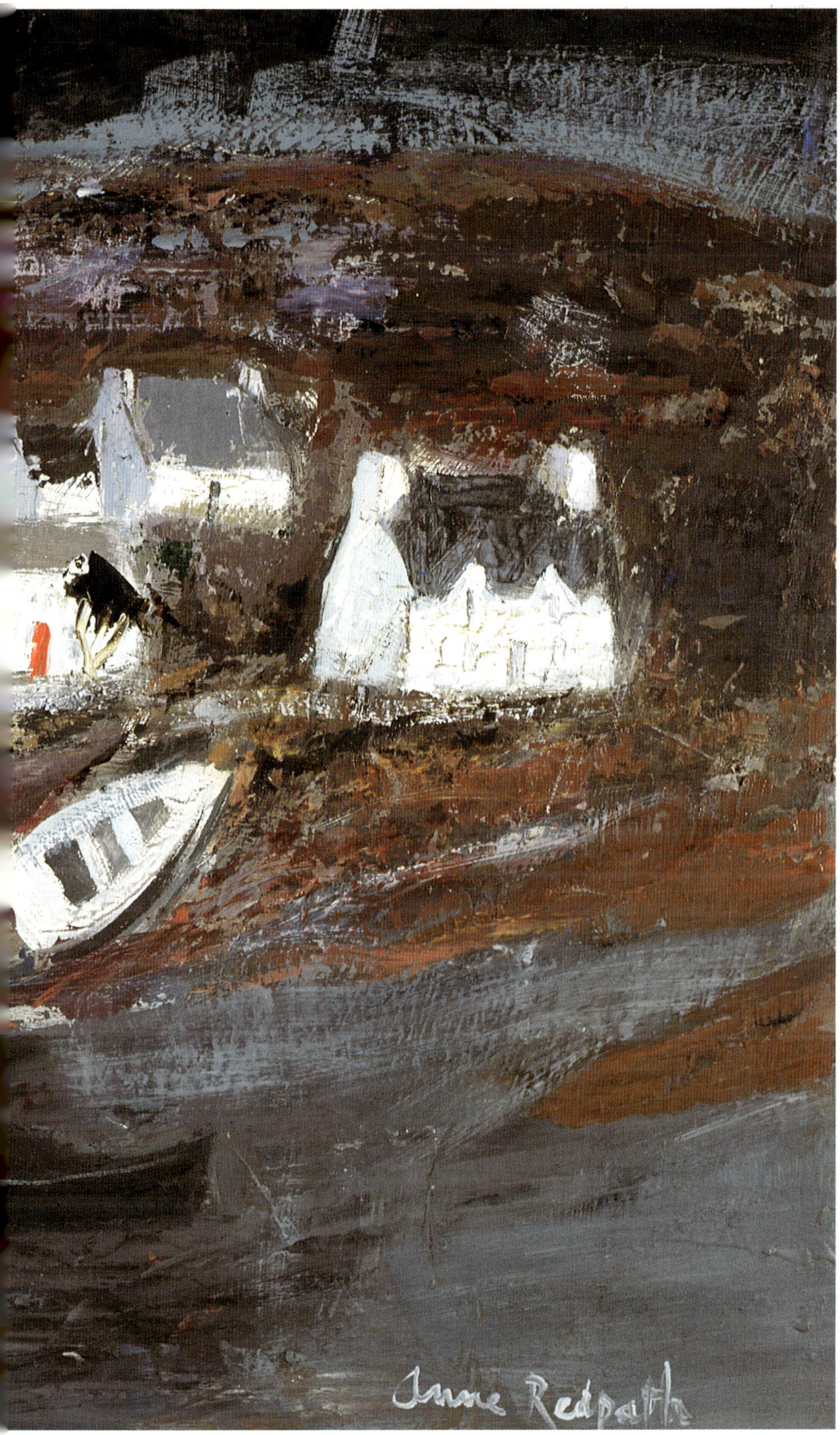
Anne Redpath

plaster. There was a gay orange and red rug hung on a wall. There were cool white tiles on the floor. I had never seen a rug on a wall and not on a floor, but for the heat it was a necessary thing to do, and coming in from the heat of Florence, you know, in the summer, to this cool room, where the shutters, you know, keep it out, the heat, and the lovely bit of colour which had far more intensity because it was against white. I think that really was the beginning of my love of a white wall. And then in the palaces in Florence you get again the rough white plaster walls, with dark medieval furniture against them, giving such verve, and everywhere I have gone, in all the houses I have ever been in, I have had a pure white wall, you know, in my house. You see, I have travelled abroad quite a lot. I have gone to Spain. Well, I couldn't paint Spain the way I painted France. It was a much harsher, starker country. White – it was very bad weather when I was there, and therefore it wasn't the blue skied Spain, it was a dark grey sky, and the white buildings, you know, looked sinister sometimes, you know, in little villages, you know, and little black figures. Most of the paintings I did there were black and white and grey and really quite sinister. One or two funerals, religious processions, which inevitably were more black and white. Well, they had to be painted with a kind of strength of manner, which I didn't have before, when I was painting the gentleness, you know, of even the south of France with its blue skies and palm trees. And therefore, when I came back and painted still life – well I always go back to still

75 Poppy-heads in a Worcester Teapot c1959 watercolour

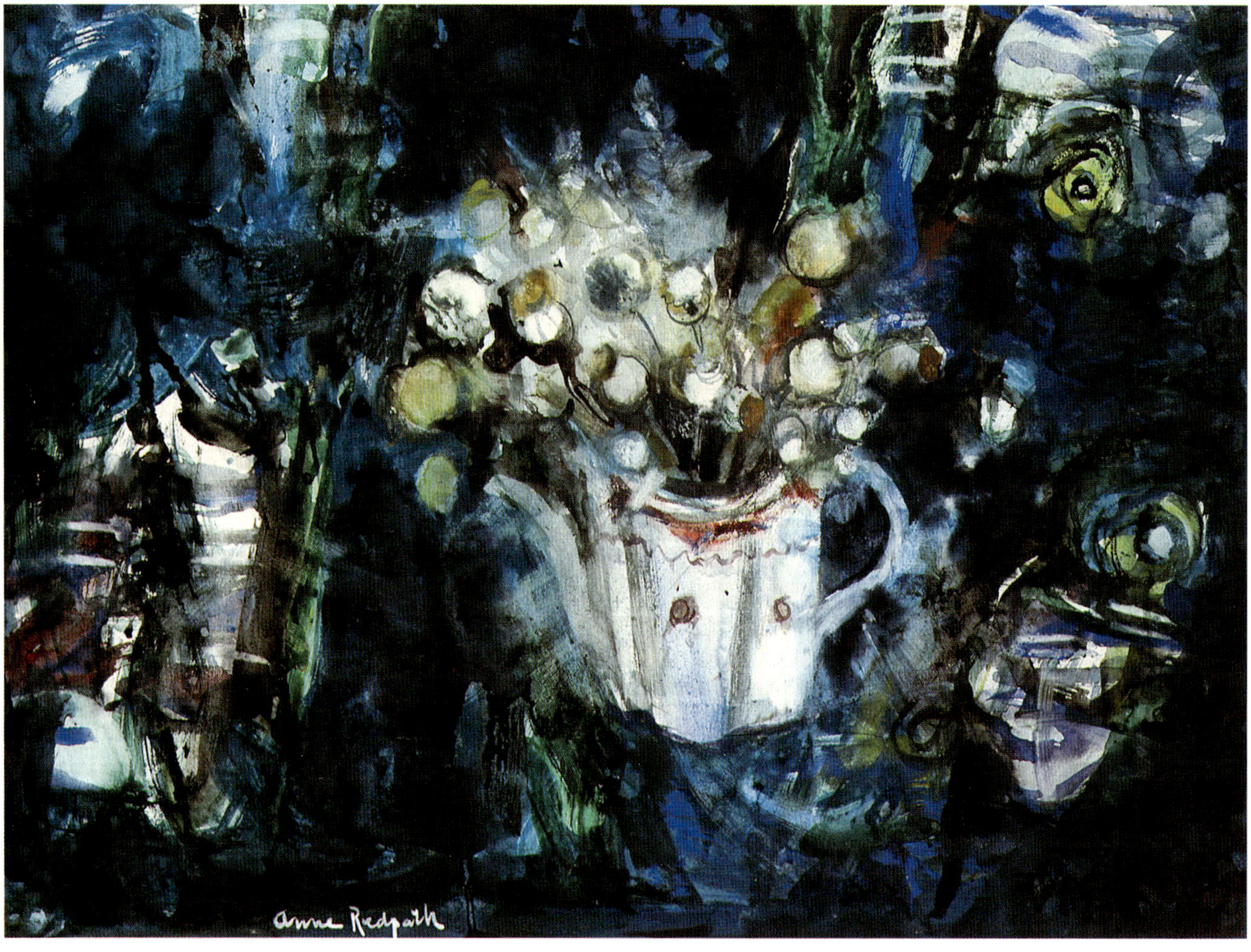

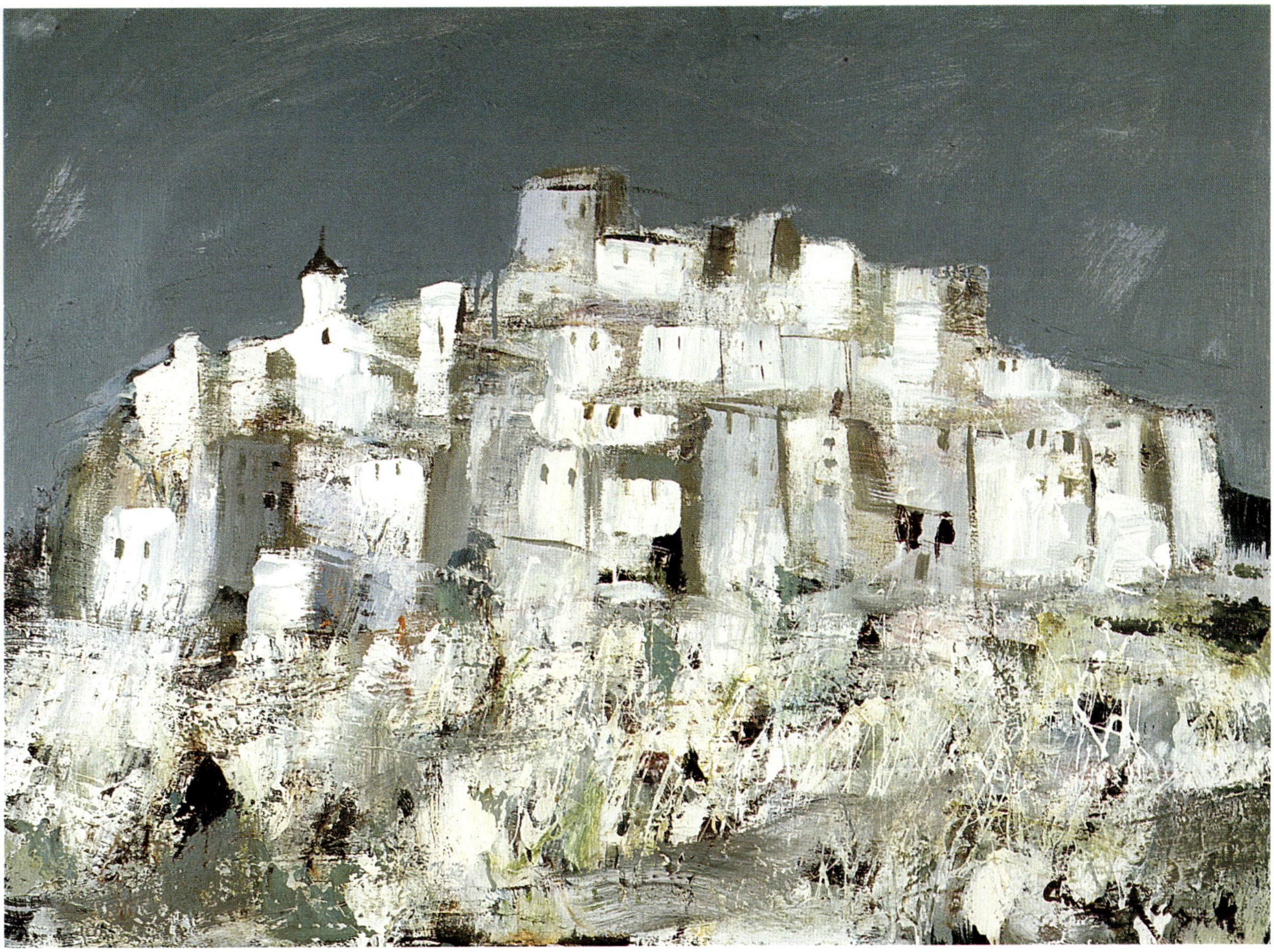

76 Les Tourrettes 1962 oil

life – of course they showed the influence of this kind of painting, and therefore the still lifes that I painted were stronger. They were harsher, if you like, too. That has been the result, you know, of every voyage abroad. Your palette sort of enlarges itself, so that even your very gamut of colour, you know, changes, becomes broader, wider. Then I went to the Canary Islands. The country inland was volcanic and brown. The sands were black, you know, as if they were made of cinders. Purples and browns and black. Well since then, of course, I have painted lots of still lifes that were in schemes of browns and blacks, you know, and dark red and purples, which I didn't do before, and I have just got to get it out of my system for so long. I think that I have always been interested in the textural quality of paint and painting, and I think what I have got out of different countries, like the Canary Islands and Corsica, and Brittany and Portugal is something structural, so you see I haven't gone really away from depicting the object, although it has a kind of abstraction, it is more structural, therefore it is more real in some way. For instance, I can remember painting a crucifix by the wayside in Corsica. It was rough-hewn. Beside it were growing these blue-grey aloes. They were both part of the same thing, you see. They were both primitive. They were both seen against the bare hillside. Well, again I would go to Corsica and paint houses on a hillside, I would exaggerate the buttress quality of the building. I would – instead of having it at right-angles to the earth, I would exaggerate the fact that the broad, the base of it was broader than the top of it, and therefore it looked as if it were growing out of the hill.

So that while I am interested in the structural shapes of the picture, if you like, I am also interested in the structure of the objects themselves, and therefore they are more, they really are more real and convincing than they were before. I think that it is easy to see while in painting these rough-hewn rocks and cactus plants in a strong kind of way, and interested in the texture of these old buildings, and in the rocks, and just in the roughness of the earth, how easy it was to go from there to the kind of encrusted gold of a baroque altar. Then to come back home and paint it as if it were a sort of encrusted jewel. And while in a way they are more abstract, you see, than they were before, yet they are still quite real, and I don't think they ever will be completely lost in abstraction, because I do feel so concerned about the things I paint, whether they are houses, or altars, or just objects in a still life. When I paint cups on a table they are now something more than cups on a table – they are just like houses in a landscape – they have a kind of – well – a strength about them which they didn't used to have. They are not so charming, but they are stronger and better, I think.

An artist's life is, really, by the very nature of the temperament of an artist, I think it is a life of contrasts. They endure heights and depths, and happiness and unhappiness, and I think that the visual awareness of an artist should also want to have that contrast, and I think I was first aware of this kind of life of contrasts in Spain, because you would find in the same church, for instance, which interested me, an altar which was gold and silver and purple, almost vulgar in its extravagance, but very paintable. But not far away from it you would get again a white-washed wall, with a bit of wrought iron and a little black figure, and I found both those things so eminently paintable. And then all Spain, you see, was contrasts, of riches and poverty, and just extravagance, you know, and simplicity, and I think from there, you see, going from there to, say, the Canary Islands, where I found a Spanish Church, an altar in golden baroque, from there to Lisbon, you know, with its golden churches, naturally when I came home I brought a golden table, golden cups, a cockerel that was painted, you know, all those things in my room. They are a mixture, but they have all been chosen by me, and therefore they live together, I think, quite happily and, well, they all have memories, too, you see. Memories of places that I have been, and also of my life. I read once, long ago, that you can't have art without memories, and you can't have memories without experiences, and I feel that all the things that I have, that I lie amongst, have both memories and experiences, and are part of my painting. I think if things are chosen by one person, dominated by one individual taste, they do live together quite well. I could never really live in a one-period house – at least I wouldn't be happy living in a one-period house. Architects' houses, and architect-designed houses – this will annoy the architects, of course – well they want them to be correct, they want them to be in period, and I can imagine my things just wouldn't fit in to this kind of show. But I can't live even in a hotel room for four days without making it my own – I add some flowers to it, a dish, you know, books, you know, and it becomes my own after three or four days. I could never live anonymously in a room.

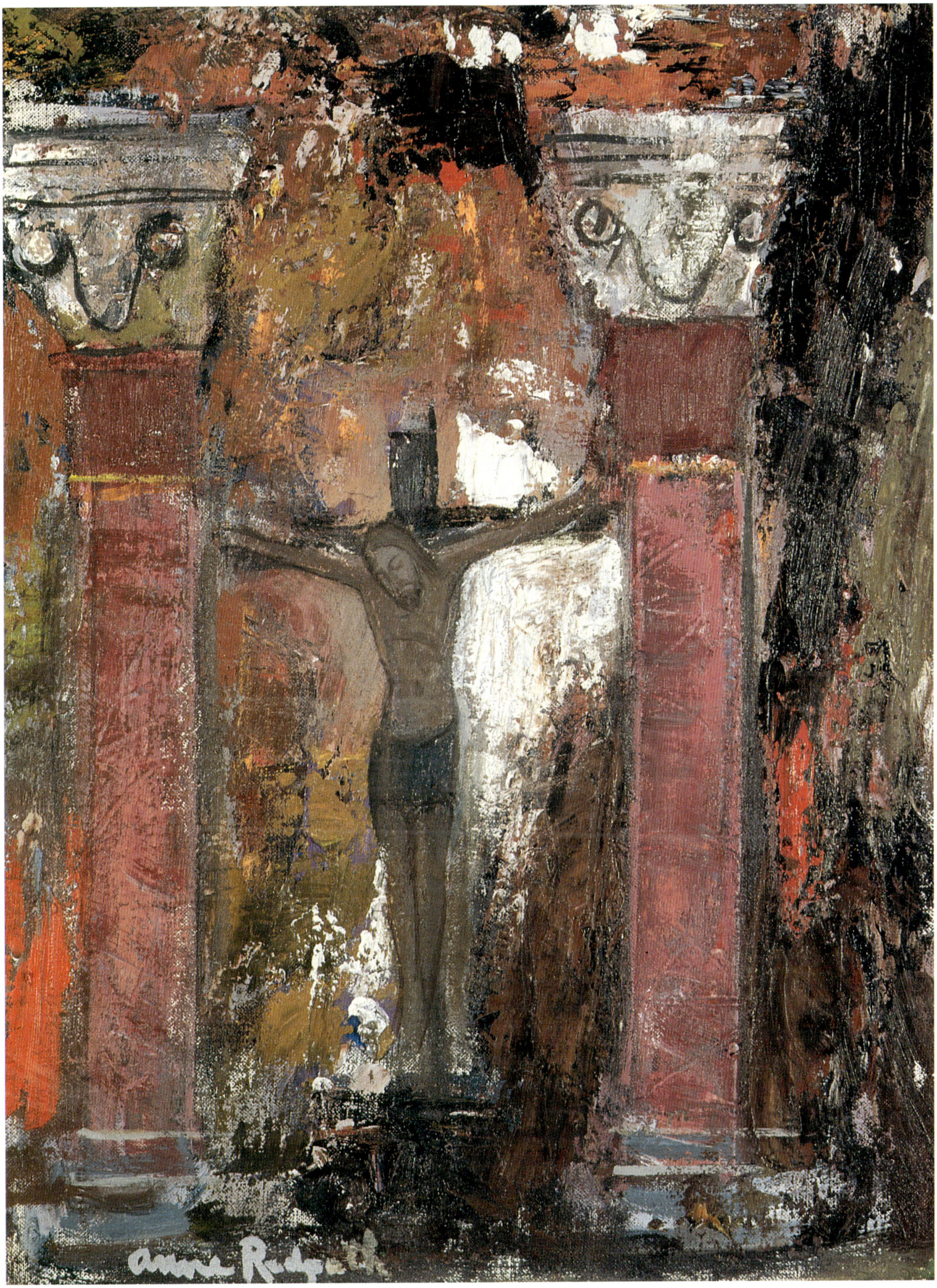

77 S.Nicolo dei Mendicoli c1964

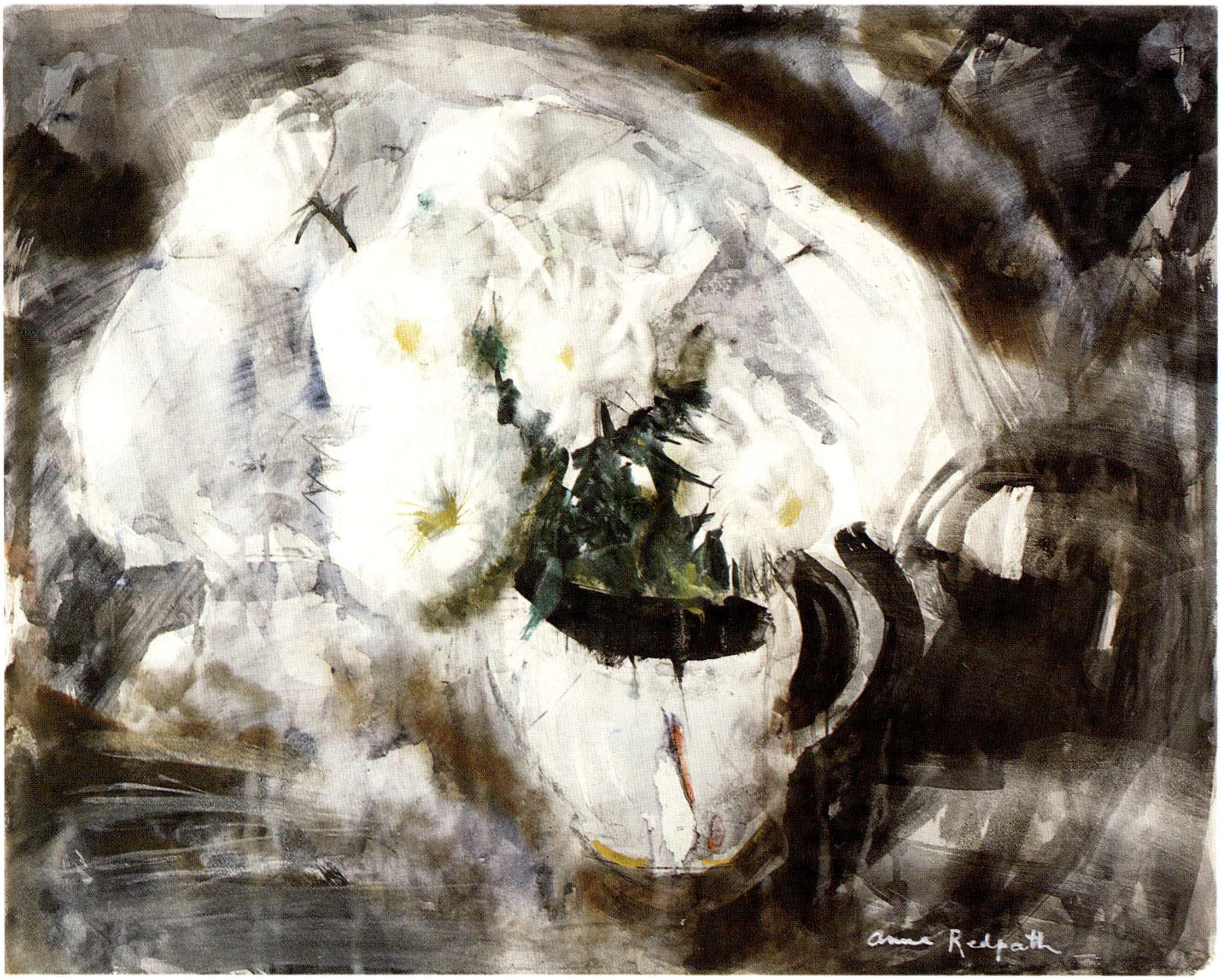

78 White Flowers in a Vase c1962 watercolour

Abbreviations

JM	John Moores Exhibition, Liverpool
MAFA	Manchester Academy of Fine Arts
RA	Royal Academy
RBA	Royal Society of British Artists
RGI	Royal Glasgow Institute of the Fine Arts
ROI	Royal Institute of Oil Painters
RSA	Royal Scottish Academy
RSW	Royal Scottish Society of Painters in Water-colours
RWA	Royal West of England Academy
SSA	Society of Scottish Artists
SSWA	Society of Scottish Women Artists

ONE-WOMAN EXHIBITIONS

1921	St. Omer, France		no catalogue traced
1928	St. Raphael, France	In the Casino	no catalogue traced
1947	Edinburgh	Gordon Small	no catalogue traced
1950	Edinburgh	Scottish Gallery	64 works
1952	London	Lefevre Gallery	34 works
1953	Edinburgh	Scottish Gallery	42 works
1956	Bristol	R. W. A.	58 works
1957	Edinburgh	Scottish Gallery	41 works
1958	Edinburgh	Danish Institute	30 works
1959	London	Lefevre Gallery	19 works
1960	Edinburgh	Scottish Gallery	32 works
1961	Newcastle upon Tyne	Stone Gallery	23 works
1962	London	Lefevre Gallery	23 works
1963	Edinburgh	Scottish Gallery	19 works
1964	London	Lefevre Gallery	24 works
1965	Edinburgh	Scottish Gallery	90 works
1965	Edinburgh & touring	Arts Council	86 works
1969	Worthing	Art Gallery	49 works
1972	Edinburgh	City Art Centre	99 works
1975	London	Mercury Gallery with Scottish Gallery	28 works
1979	London	Mercury Gallery with Scottish Gallery	20 works
1981	London	Mercury Gallery with Scottish Gallery	30 works
1983	London	Mercury Gallery with Scottish Gallery	23 works
1986	London	Mercury Gallery with Scottish Gallery	32 works
1986	Edinburgh	Scottish Gallery with Mercury Gallery	35 works
1989	Edinburgh	Bourne Fine Art	55 works
1989	London	Portland Gallery	55 works

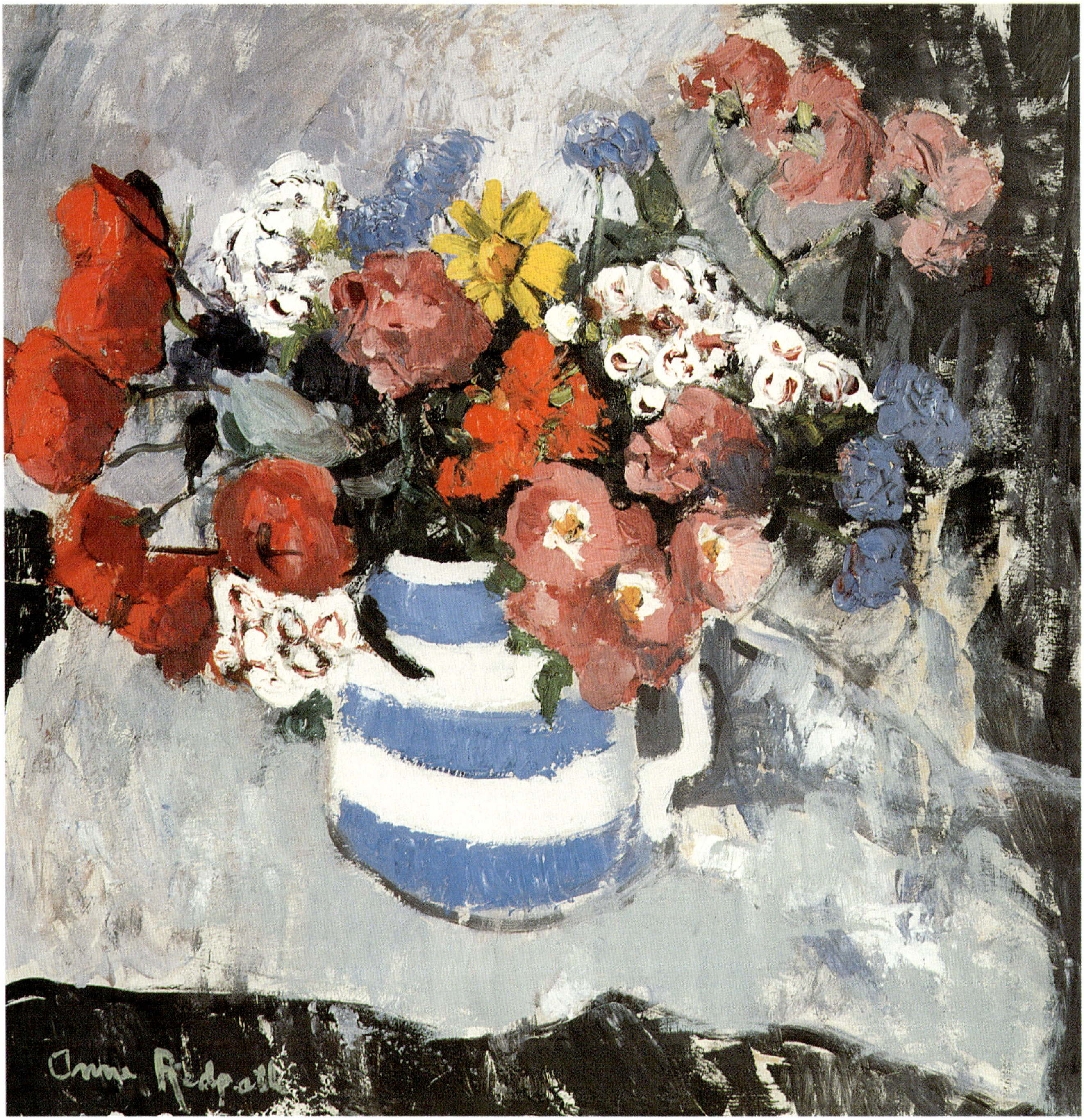

79 Flowers in a Jug c1954 oil

CATALOGUE OF EXHIBITED WORKS

1919	RSA	Still Life
		Sketch
1920	SSA	Head of a Girl
1923	RGI	Decoration
		Paule
1930	SSA	Villefranche wc
		Cagnes-sur-Mer wc
1934	SSA	Boats at St Raphael wc
1935	RSA	Wilton Dean
		The Port Villefranche wc
	RSW	Villefranche wc
		From Cap Ferrat wc
	SSA	Houses at Ashkirk
		Still Life
		Roofs – Wilton Dean
		Cagnes wc
1936	RGI	Wilton Dean
	SSA	Frosty Morning – Trow Mill
		The Mirror
		Portrait
1937	RSA	Interior
		Still Life
	RSW	Roof in Etaples wc
		Houses at Hawick wc
	SSA	Godetias
		The Painted Box
1938	RSA	Still Life
		Lilies
		Cagnes
	RSW	Farm at Smailholm wc
	SSA	Cottages near Ambleside
		Marguerites and Marigolds
		Cottages on the Teviot
		Pattern
		Portrait
		On the Ettrick wc
1939	RGI	Cagnes-sur-Mer
		St Raphael
	RSA	Study in White
		Studio Table
		Border Farm in Spring Sunshine
1940	RGI	On the Teviot wc
	RSA	Study of a Head
		The Blue Tablecloth
	RSW	Still Life wc
		On the Teviot wc
	SSA	Pattern
		Afternoon
		Hydrangea in Pot
		Houses and Haystacks at Eyemouth
	SSWA	Flowers and Green Chair
		Bouquet
		St Abbs
1941	RGI	Still Life
		Still Life
	RSA	Still Life
		Still Life
		Jack Reading
	RSW	Littlecot, Hawick wc
	SSA	Girl from Jamaica
		Pink and Grey – Still Life
		Blue and Yellow – Still Life
		Marguerites and Lemons
		Woman in Red Scarf
	SSWA	Still Life
		Still Life
		Still Life
1942	RGI	Jack Reading
		Pink and Grey – Still Life
	RSA	Still Life
		Boy Reading
		Cups and Saucers
	SSA	Paul Gutmann Esq
		Azalea in Greenhouse
		Red Slippers
		Cornflowers
		Betty
	SSWA	White Peonies
		Summer Flowers
		Still Life
		Still Life
1943	RGI	The French Jug
	RSA	Border Village in Springtime
		Christmas Roses
		The French Jug
	SSA	The Old-fashioned Jug
		Pattern in Grey and White
		Marguerites
		Roses and Sweet William
		Fantasy
	SSWA	Still Life
		Flowers on a White Table
		Michaelmas Daisies
		Primulas
1944	RGI	A Few Jugs
		The Chinese Rug
	RSA	The Lace Cloth
		The Chinese Rug
		A Few Jugs
	RSW	The Yellow Cloth wc
		The Lace Cloth wc
	SSA	East and West
		The Embroidered Horse
		Farm at Spittal on Rule
		Sheila
	SSWA	The Painted Table
		Jack
		David
		A Day in Summer
1945	RGI	David
		East and West
		The Painted Table
	RSA	White Flowers and a Girl
		Prelude to Spring
		Odd Things
	RSW	The Pink Bowl wc
		Cups and Saucers wc

	SSA	The Round Table
		Turquoise and Scarlet
		Interior
		Girl with Blue Ribbon
	SSWA	Two Tables
		Kyleakin, Skye
		The Teapot
		In a Mirror
1946	RA	In a Mirror
		The Chinese Rug
	RBA	Spring Flowers
		A Few Jugs
		Two Tables
		The Round Table
		Cottage at Bernisdale, Skye
		Birch Trees beside the River Atholl
	RGI	Cups and Saucers
		Prelude to Spring
		Black Jug with Flowers
	RSA	The Studio
		David
		Birch Trees above the River Atholl
	SSA	Ebony and Dianthus
		The Worcester Jug
		Spotted Jug with Flowers
		Arnisort, Skye wc
		Village Church in Skye wc
	SSWA	The Pink and White Teapot
		Flowers and a Green Table
		A Day in Summer
		Cottages at Dunvegan, Skye wc
1947	RA	The Worcester Jug
	RBA	The Pink and White Teapot
		Pinks
		Prelude to Spring
		The Candlestick
		The Bouquet
	RSA	A Bouquet
		Lindsay C. Michie
		The Mantelpiece
	SSA	Girl and an Apple
1948	RA	The White Azalea
		The Pink Table
		White Flowers and a Girl
	RBA	Victorian Medley
		Lindsay C. Michie
		Village Church, Skye
		Skye
		Rain in Skye
		Loch Snizort, Skye
	RGI	The Worcester Jug
		The Pink and White Teapot
	ROI	Girl at a Table
		Striped Cloth
	RSA	The Candlestick
		The Fluthers, Cupar
		Cottage in Skye
		Girl at a Table
	SSA	Pinks
		Poppy and Mandragora
		Girl and an Apple
		Spring Bouquet
		K and a Kitten
		Dunlaoghaire Harbour
	SSWA	Eileen
		End of Summer
		Contre-jour
		Bouquet
1949	RA	Dunlaoghaire Harbour
		A Table at a Window
		The Red Dish
	RBA	The Venetian Glass
		Russian Tea
		Kyleakin, Skye
		David
		High Noon at Eze
	RGI	The Venetian Glass
		Eileen
		Dunlaoghaire Harbour
	RSA	Girl in a Check Coat
		Greys
		The Indian Shawl
		The Worcester Jug
	RSW	Girl on Sofa wc
		Young Girl with Posy wc
	SSA	The Pink Decanter
		Sospel, Alpes-Maritimes
		Place de l'Institut, Paris
		The Old Port, Menton
		The Little Hat Shop, Menton
		Venetian Glass and Flowers wc
	SSWA	Spring Bouquet
		The Red Dish
		Boulevard in Paris
		Striped Cloth
1950	RA	Window in Menton
		Place de l'Institut, Paris
		The Pink Decanter
	RSA	Denise
		White Garland
		Paris
		Venetian Vase
	RSW	Bouquet for Isabella wc
		Jane and a China Cat wc
	SSWA	Suggestion for Spring
		David
		Green Jug and Flowers
		Road at Roquebrune wc
1951	RA	Girl in a White Chair
		Victorian Vase
	RGI	Place de l'Institut, Paris
	RSA	White Azaleas
		White Daisies
		Dr Jha
		Ventimiglia
	RSW	Black Lace wc
		Victorian Ornament wc
	SSA	Rain in Spain, Ubeda
		Funeral at Collioure
		Quenca
		Spanish Town, Ubeda
	SSWA	A Few Jugs
		In the Church of Santa Maria, Ubeda
		Requena
		Cottage in Spain
		Rain at Quenca
1952	RA	White Azalea
		Funeral at Collioure
		The Rain in Spain

	RSA	Joyce
		Black and White Check
		Women in Spain
		Spanish Fishing Village
	RSW	Figure and Flowers wc
		Bric-a-Brac wc
	SSA	San Pablo, Ubeda
		Chinchirinches
		Houses Opposite, Ubeda
		Plaza del Santo Domingo El Real Toledo
	SSWA	Girl at a Table
1953	RGI	Summer Bouquet
		St Monance, Fife
		The Black Teapot
	RSA	Window at Night
		The Red Tray
		Pittenweem
		Eileen in a White Chair
	SSA	Boats at Concarneau
		Marguerites and Thistles
		Flowers in a French Jug
		Pink Houses at Treboul
	SSWA	Pale Still Life
		Houses and Sea at Treboul
		Flowers in a French Jug
		Chapelle de la Croix, Concarneau
1954	RA	White Still Life with Mimosa
		Window at Night
	RSA	House at Concarneau
		Grey and White Interior
		Village of St Jean, Treboul
	SSA	Snowdrops on a Check Cloth
		White Still Life and Mimosa
		Houses on a Hill, Brittany
		The Coleus
	SSWA	Corsican Cottage
		A Few Jugs
		Church at Miomo, Corsica
1955	RA	Grey and White Interior
		Something Old and Something New
	RGI	Window at Night
		Island of Elba from Corsica
		La Croix de St Jean, Treboul
	RSA	The Sofa
		Village of Cardo, Corsica
		Old Houses, Corsica
		Cardo, Corsica
		Tulips and a White Dish wc
		Self Portrait
	RSW	Erbalanguna, Corsica wc
		Something Old and Something New wc
		Miomo, Corsica wc
	SSA	The Old Harbour, Bastia wc
		Glass and Old Lace wc
		The Market, Treboul
		The Black Teapot
		Morning Sunlight wc
		The Italian Vase wc
	SSWA	The Old Harbour, Bastia
		Roses wc
		Gladioli wc
1956	RA	The Yellow Sofa
	RGI	Old Houses, Corsica
		Cardo, Corsica
		Mimosa wc
	RSA	Dish of Fruit and Cineraria
		White Tulips
		Victorian Medley
		Anenomes on a Blue Cloth
		Tulips wc
		White Irises wc
		Flowers and Shadows wc
	RSW	The Little Mirror wc
		Winter Bouquet wc
		The Chinese Teapot wc
	SSA	The Blue and White Coffee Pot wc
		Tulips and a Mirror wc
		Autumn Bouquet
		Storm in a Corsican Village
	SSWA	Italian Vase
		The Red Decanter
		Myself in Venetian Mirror
		Michaelmas Daisies
1957	JM	Mainly Grey and White
		The Yellow Sofa
	RA	The Fruit Dish
	RSA	Still Life with Grapes
		Harmony in Red
		Mainly Grey and White
		The Irish Jug
		Self Portrait wc
		The Venetian Vase
	RSW	Corsican Village wc
		White Tulips wc
		Christmas Bouquet wc
	SSA	The Victorian Table
		Shooting Stall at a Fair, Fontainbleau
		Fruit on an Ashet
1958	RA	The Glass Figure
		Flowers and Fruit
		Winter and Spring
	RSA	Table Top
		The Decanter
		Tulips in a French Jug
		Bouquet for Spring
		The Little Posy wc
	RSW	House at Barbizon wc
		Chapelhill wc
		Dish of Fruit wc
	RWA	Tulips in a French Jug
		Bouquet for Spring
		The Decanter
1959	JM	Studio
	RGI	The Yellow Sofa
	RSA	Winter and Spring
		The Glass Figure
		Red and White
		Gourds on an Ashet wc
	RWA	Mediterranean
		The Little Mirror
		Gloxinia
		Table Top
		Tulips in a Coffee Pot wc
		Pansies wc
	SSA	Summer Flowers
		Flowers in a Blue Dish

1960	RGI	Harbour in Ireland
		Corsican Gallery
		The Victorian Table
	RSA	Studio
		Victorian Posy
		Ubeda, Spain
		The Spanish Dish wc
	RSW	Poppy Heads wc
	RWA	The Yellow Sofa
1961	JM	On the Way to Maspalomas
	RA	Studio
		Rocks and Houses and Orange Trees
		Trees at Las Palmas
		Village of Gran Canaria
		Houses near Las Palmas
		Lenten Roses
	RGI	The Pink Decanter
		Table Top
	RSA	Gloxinia
		Dishes on a Dark Blue Cloth
		Hillside in the Canary Islands
		Houses near Maspalomas
	RWA	Gloxinia
		Day in a Dust Storm, Gran Canaria
		Honesty and Eucalyptus wc
		The Pink Goblet
1962	MAFA	Table Top
		The Pink Decanter
	RA	Flower Stall
		The White Cineraria
		The Portuguese Dish
		Cagnes
		Tulips in a Blue Jar
		The Black Teapot
	RGI	Day in a Dust Storm, Gran Canaria
		White Hyacinth wc
	RSA	Palacio de la Fronteira, Lisbon
		The Lily
		Terraced Houses in Lisbon
		Boats at Nazare
	RSW	The Red Cloth wc
		Everlasting Flowers and Fruit wc
	RWA	Amsterdam
		Church of Madre Dios
		Autumn Bouquet
		Sunflowers
		The Portuguese Cockerel
		African Violets wc
	SSA	The White Begonia
	SSWA	White Flowers
		The Mexican Figure
		The Fruit Stand
		Boat Yard, Amsterdam
1963	MAFA	Fruit Stand
		White Flowers
	RA	Villefranche
		Hillside in the Canary Islands
		White Flowers on a Dark Ground
		The White Azalea
		Cineraria
		Town in Spain
	RGI	Two Posies
		Objects on a Table
	RSA	White Tulips
		Dried Flowers
		Village in Fife
		Flowers in a Teapot wc
1964	MAFA	Window in Menton
		Window at Night
	RA	Objects on a Red Cloth
		Dolce Aqua
		Spring
		Kaleidoscope
		The Pink Goblet
		Freesia
	RGI	Chapel in Portugal
	RSA	Gorbio, Alpes-Maritimes
		Magnolia
		The White Gloxinia
		The White Azalea wc
	RWA	White Peonies
		In a Chapel, Torcello
		Gloxinia Pink
		Canary Island Hillside
		Doorway in Valencia
		White Gloxinia wc
	SSA	Mainly Black and White

The following paintings were exhibited posthumously:

1965	MAFA	White Gloxinia
		Two Posies
	RA	The Poppy Field
		Cliffside, Portugal
		Amsterdam Buildings
		Dried Flowers
		White Cyclamen
		Objects on a Brown Cloth
	RSA	Grey Still Life
		Altar at Chartres
		Window at Night

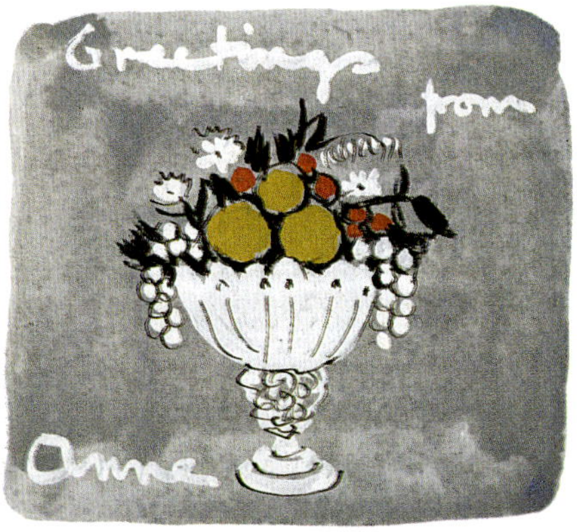

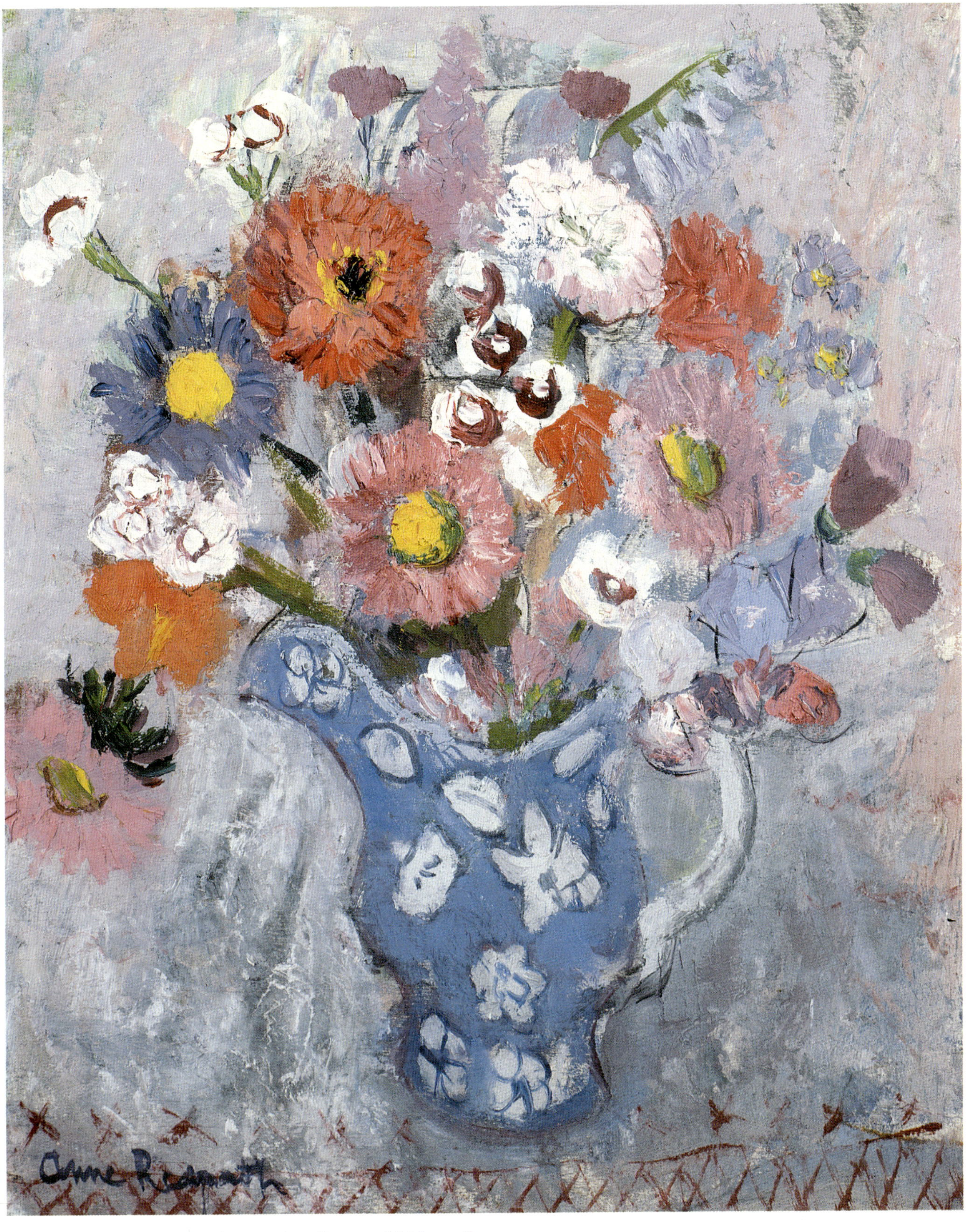

80 Summer Flowers in a Jug c1955 oil

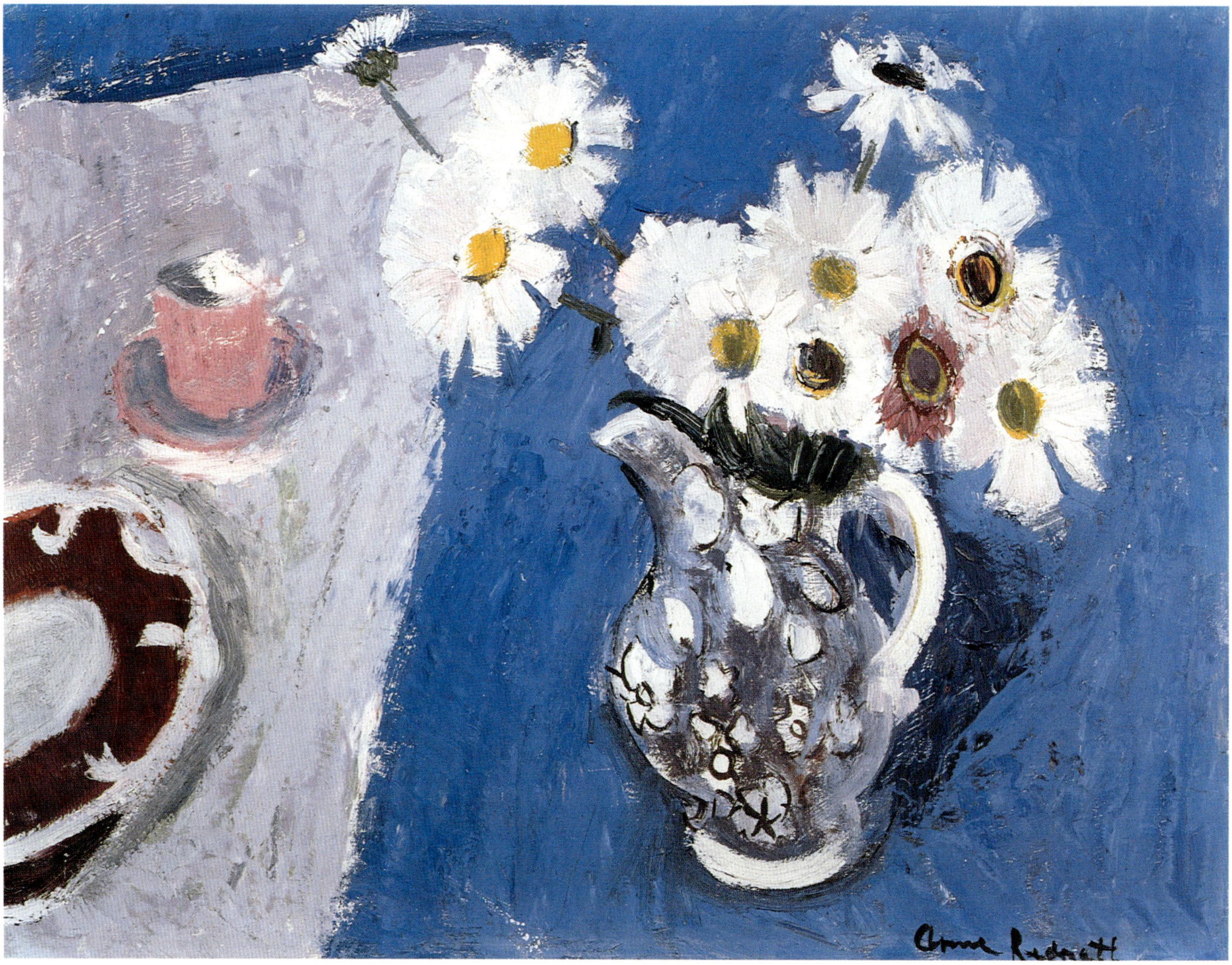

81 Still Life on a Blue and White Tablecloth c1952 oil

BIBLIOGRAPHY

There were many newspaper articles on Anne Redpath and critiques on her work during her lifetime from the mid 1940s onwards, too numerous to mention. Principally these were in *The Scotsman* and *The Glasgow Herald.*

Anne Redpath – Memorial Exhibition, 1965, catalogue introduction by Terence Mullaly, The Scottish Committee of the Arts Council of Great Britain.

Anne Redpath, the first in the series Modern Scottish Painters, George Bruce, 1973, University Press, Edinburgh.

The Studio, June 1945, August 1947, March 1950, August 1952, March 1953, September 1953, August 1956 and March 1960.

Scottish Art Review, vol. V, 3, 1955, and vol. IX, 2, 1963.

Scottish Field, September 1957, article by Dr T. Honeyman.

There have been a number of exhibitions since 1965 with catalogues. These include Worthing Art Gallery, 1969, City of Edinburgh Art Centre, 1972, and joint exhibitions by Scottish Gallery, Edinburgh and Mercury Gallery, London, in 1975, 1979.

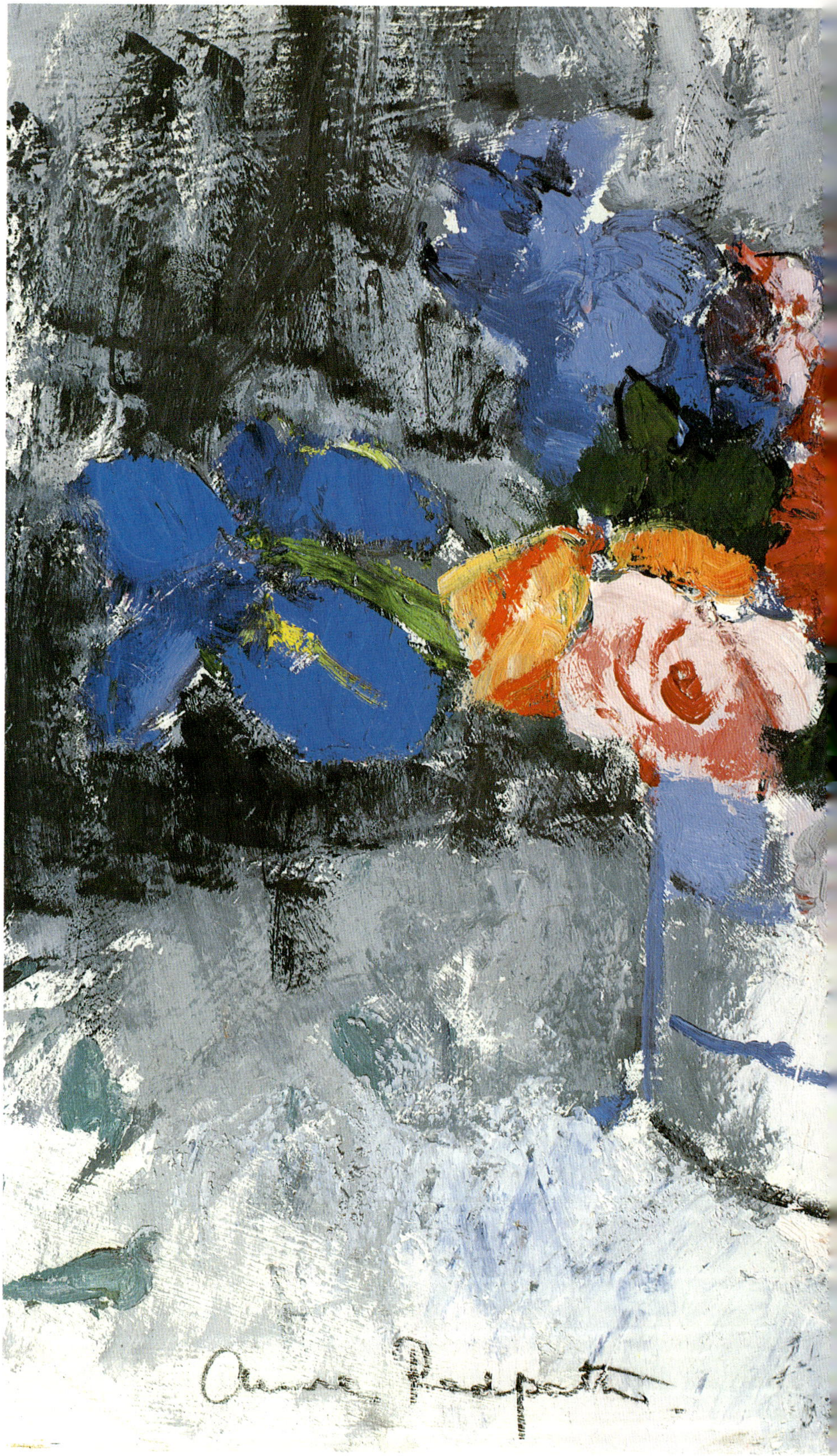

82 Summer Flowers c1952 oil

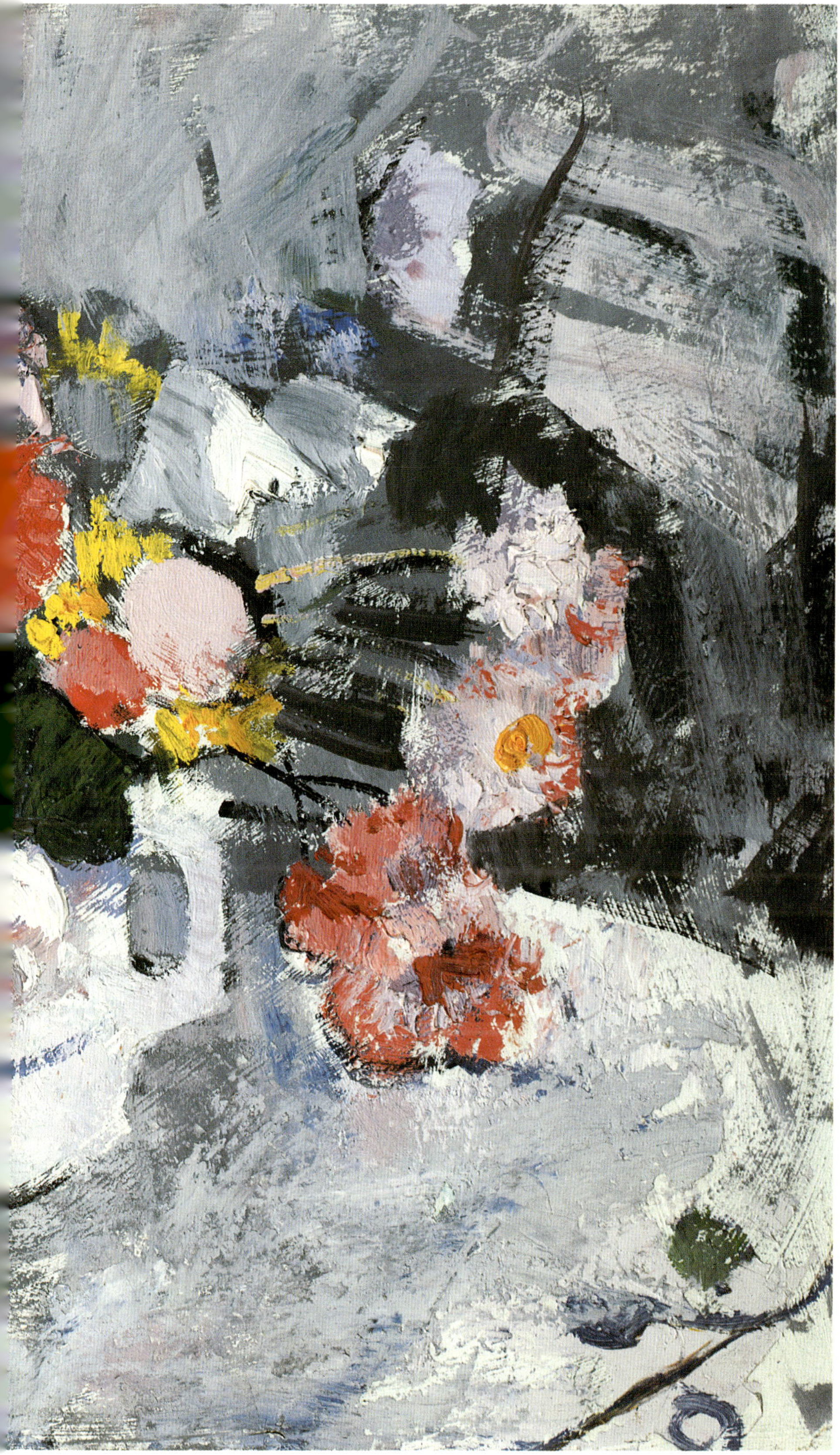

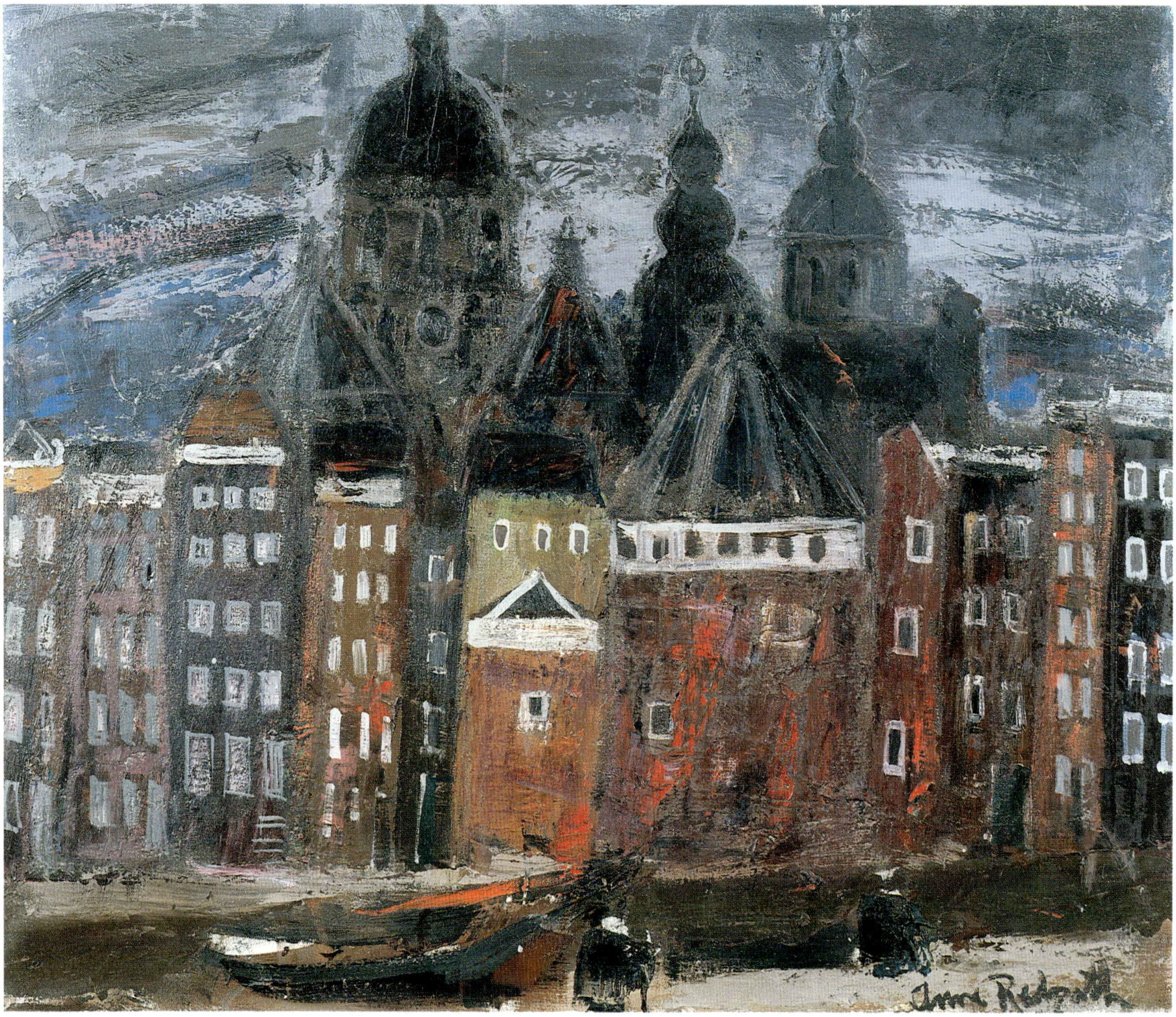

83 Buildings, Amsterdam c1962 oil

INDEX

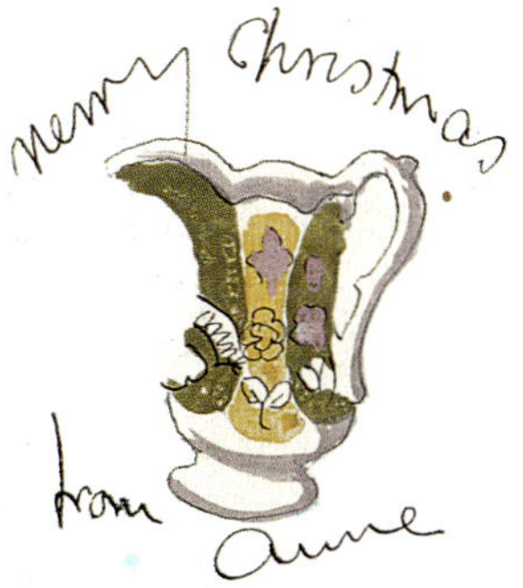
Merry Christmas
from Anne

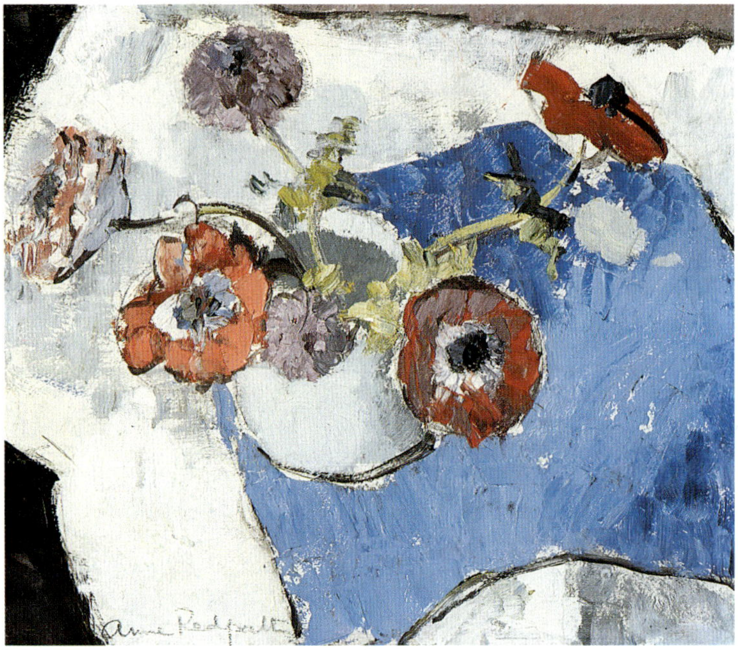

84 Anemones on a Blue Cloth c1953 oil

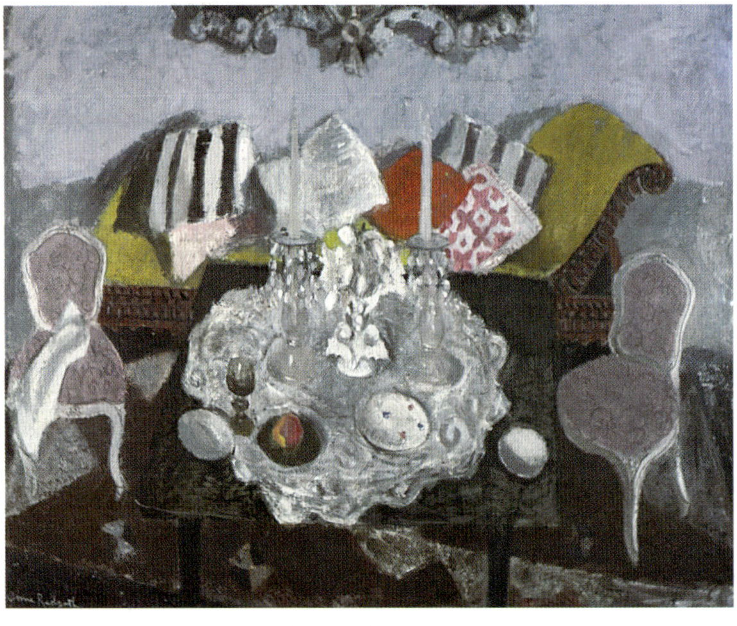

85 The Yellow Sofa c1956 oil

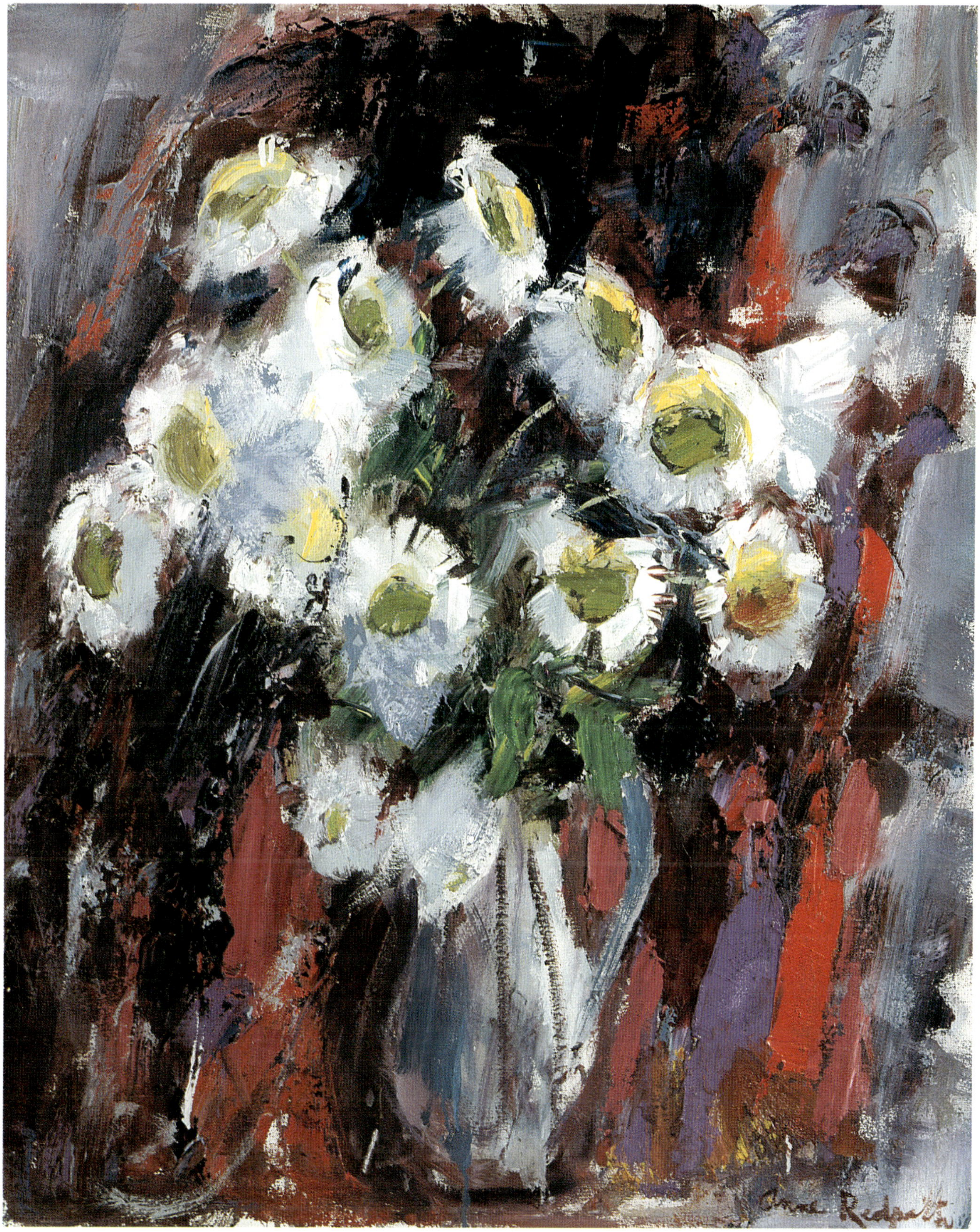

86 Daisies in a Vase 1964 oil

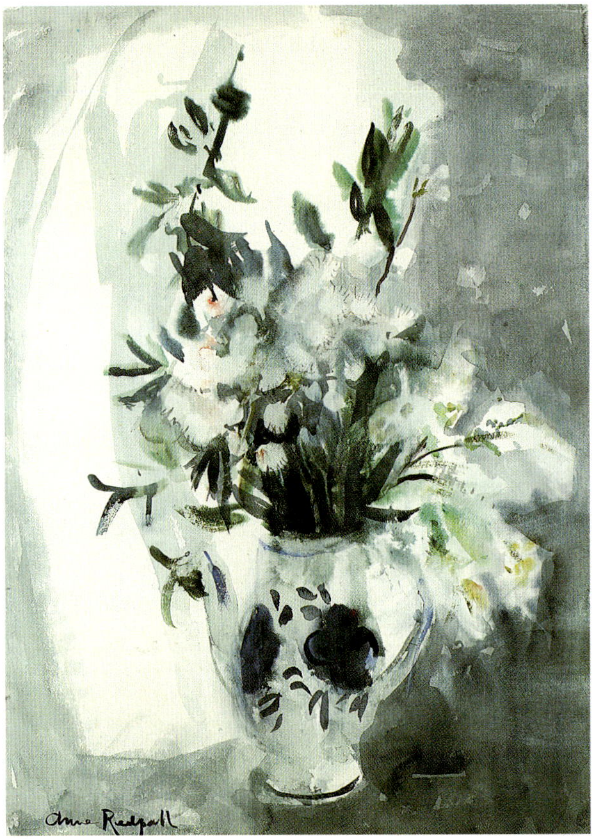

87 Flowers in a Coffee Pot c1960 watercolour

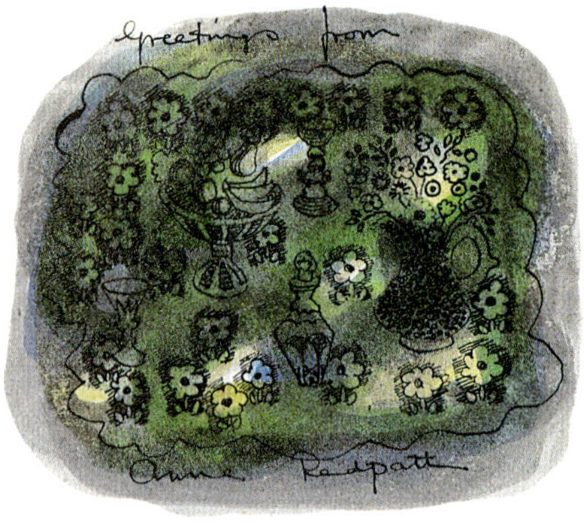

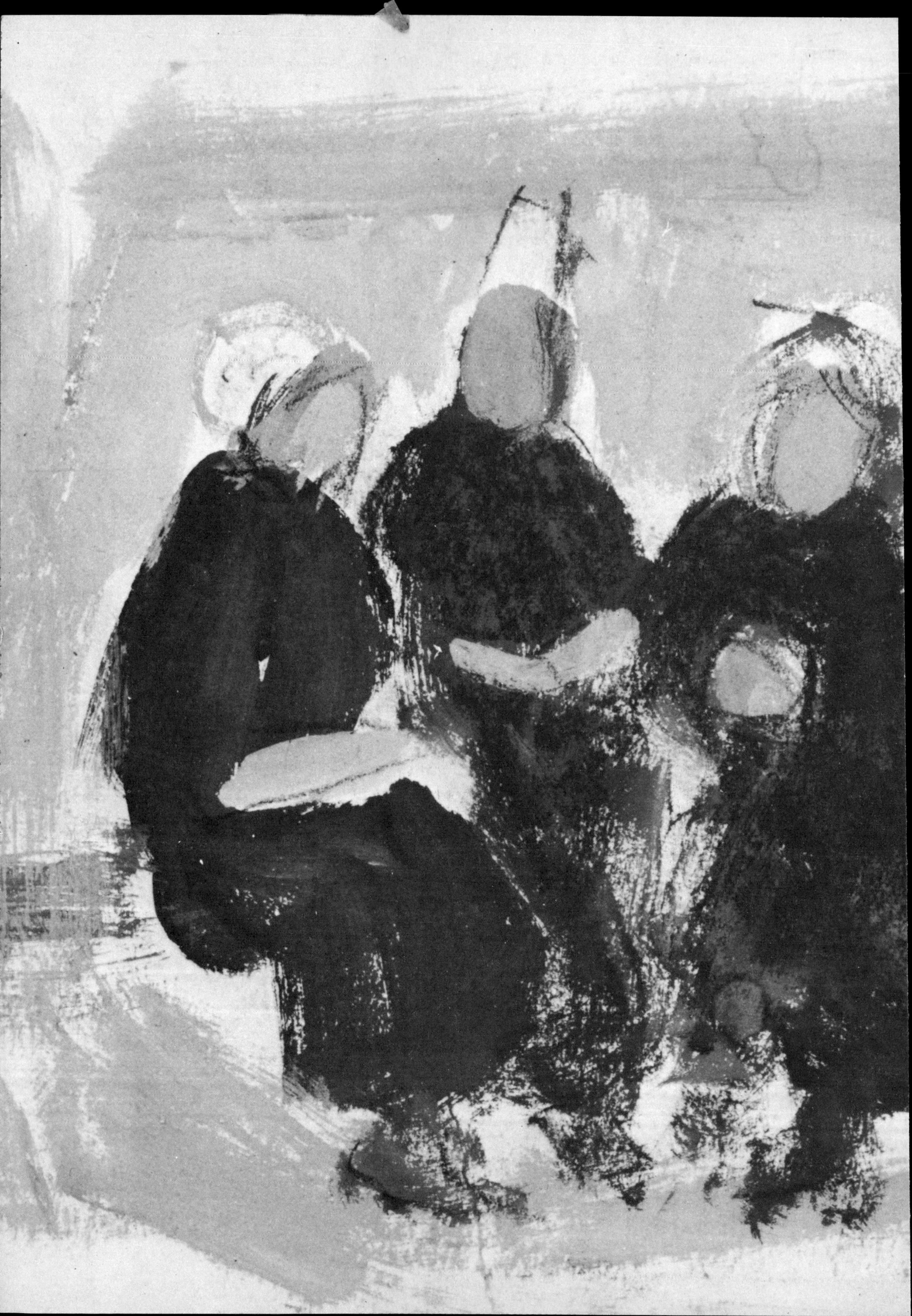